ESCAPE TO
GWRYCH CASTLE

ESCAPE TO GWRYCH CASTLE: A JEWISH REFUGEE STORY

Andrew Hesketh

www.uwp.co.uk

British Library Cataloguing-in-Publication Data
A catalogue record for this book is available from the British Library.

ISBN: 978-1-837600-06-9

The right of Andrew Hesketh to be identified as author of this work has been asserted in accordance with sections 77 and 79 of the Copyright, Designs and Patents Act 1988.

Cover artwork by David Wardle
Author photograph by Megan Hesketh
Typeset by Agnes Graves
Printed by CPI Antony Rowe, Melksham, United Kingdom

The publisher acknowledges the financial support of the Books Council of Wales.

To the memory of all those who lived
at Gwrych Castle between 1939 and 1941

CONTENTS

AUTHOR'S NOTE

Apart from a nominal roll of those who can be identified as being a resident at the Gwrych Castle *Hachshara* (see Appendix I), personal details that would allow for easy identification have not been included in what follows. The exception is those for whom information is already in the public domain or where permission has been granted by the person named or by their descendants. As fascinating as the story of the Gwrych Castle *Hachshara* is, it cannot be – it should not be – separated from the darkness that gave birth to it. Not all of those involved would like to revisit that time, be reminded of it, or be associated with it. I sincerely hope that those concerns have been respected fully in what follows.

Wherever possible, I have used terminology that would have been used by the refugees themselves. Thus, for example, the agricultural training centre established at Gwrych Castle was known as a *Hachshara* (plural, *Hachsharot*). This and similar terms are italicised in the main text, and a glossary for easy reference can be found in Appendix II.

PROLOGUE

'Are you from the castle?'

Even window-shopping could be dangerous for a Jew in Nazi Germany. In October 1939, fifteen-year-old Henry Glanz of Kiel, along with three of his friends, was indulging himself in this harmless activity. He had stopped in front of a confectionery shop and although neither he nor his friends had any money to spend, they eagerly eyed the goods within.

After a short while, one of them noticed a policeman walking in their direction. Henry alerted his friends and a sense of dread rapidly spread through the group. They turned away, scattered and ran. After a short distance, Henry glanced over his shoulder, and was relieved to see that the officer was not pursuing him but one of his friends. Moments later he looked again and was horrified to see that his friend had been caught. For a moment, Henry was torn between continuing his escape or returning to assist his friend. He slowed his pace as he grappled with the decision before finally halting. If he turned back, he knew full well that this could result in serious, if unpredictable, consequences; most certainly an interrogation, maybe a night in a cell, possibly a beating… or something far worse. Henry chose to turn back.

Henry thought carefully about the words to use, and as the officer turned his head towards him, without loosening his grip on his captive's collar, he asked, 'What have we done wrong?'

'Why did you run?' demanded the officer.

Henry replied simply, and with a shrug, 'In Germany, if a police officer approaches Jewish children, that means trouble.'

1

Henry glanced at his terrified friend, who was still desperately attempting to explain himself in a language that the police officer could not comprehend. He offered to translate for his friend as best he could. The officer seemed to spend a moment attempting to make sense of the situation, before asking, 'Are you from the castle?'

'Castle? *Schloss.* Yes,' Henry replied, noticing that the policeman seemed visibly distressed. He thought that he saw tears forming in the officer's eyes.

The officer released his grip on the terrified child, stood back and raised both of his hands to indicate that he meant no harm. Pointing at the boy he had just released, but looking at Henry, he said, 'Tell him he's not in Germany. Here, a policeman is your friend!'

Henry dutifully translated, and for a few seconds the two boys and the policeman stood in silence, glancing awkwardly at each other. Assuming – hoping – that the man in the uniform meant what he said, Henry and his friend then scuttled off.

Policeman Sam Williams, who had been 'on the beat' around Abergele, was shaken by the event. Although few had seen them, rumours were rife of German refugees who had arrived at Gwrych Castle over the previous few weeks. But the look he had seen in the eyes of the boy that he had caught spoke of absolute fear. Why? Who were they, anyway?

A few days later, PC Sam Williams, accompanied by two of his colleagues, knocked on the main entrance door of Gwrych Castle. In one hand, Williams held something covered in a tea towel. The door was opened by a tall, handsome man in his late twenties. In extremely good English, but with a very clear German accent, the man introduced himself as Doctor Julius Handler. He apologised that the leader of the group, his younger brother Arieh Handler, had recently departed for London and was thus unavailable. However, he would be delighted to help the officers if he could.

A little unsure of what to say, Williams, like a magician at the climax of his trick, simply removed the tea towel from the object in his hand and held up a cake. It was a gift, he explained. His wife had baked it.

Julius asked if the officers would like to come inside. Would they like tea? Stepping into the magnificent entrance hall of the castle, with its wood panelling and huge, ornate, crested fireplace, Williams noticed several teenagers gathered around the edges of the room, looking nervously towards their uniformed visitors. The hall quickly filled with a few dozen more, speaking together in hushed tones, as the three policemen became the centre of attention. Amongst them, Williams recognised Henry Glanz and the face of the boy he had momentarily detained the other day, both looking decidedly uneasy. Several minutes of silence passed, during which the three officers smiled and nodded at any teenager who dared to make eye contact. Few attempted this, and those that did quickly looked away again.

Returning with tea, Julius asked the police officers how he could be of assistance. Williams explained the incident with the boys in the town and asked if he could deliver a message to all of the young people at the castle about their new life in Abergele. He wanted them to know that in this country, 'if you are in trouble you look for a policeman, you don't run away from them.'[1]

Julius translated the message for the curious young onlookers, many of whom appeared confused by the sentiment. This was the opposite of what their experience told them to be true. Every one of the youngsters at Gwrych Castle was a Jewish refugee from Nazism. Most were from Germany but a significant number were from Nazi-controlled Austria and Czechoslovakia. They had all arrived in Britain quite recently through various schemes collectively known as Kindertransport, which, by the beginning of September 1939, had provided a safe haven to around 10,000 children. Most of those children had been taken into foster care but a minority had been placed into training centres or *Hachsharot* (known as *Hachshara* in the singular).

PC Williams would have had no idea, but he had walked into the largest and most important *Hachshara* in Europe. He would also have been unaware of why the young people in the hall appeared so fearful and distant; a significant part, if not all, of their entire conscious life experience had been lived as a member of a mercilessly persecuted minority. It was therefore both natural and understandable that they were fearful of the reception they would get from the Abergele community, as they were uncertain of the attitudes local people may have held towards foreigners – especially Jewish foreigners. Why would the Welsh treat them any differently to the way they were used to? On the day that one group of friends had finally summoned up the courage to make their first visit to the town of Abergele, why would they *not* run away from an approaching policeman?

Very cautiously, some of the refugees stepped forward from the shadows and gathered around the three police officers in the entrance hall of Gwrych Castle. As they shared tea and cake with them and listened to some of their welcoming and comforting words, some of the children began to dare to hope that their new life in Wales might just be different after all.

And it would be. For a while.

CHAPTER I

———

'The young generation of a great people'

1933–39
The Jews, the Nazis and Abergele

Abergele is a small town on the North Wales coast, sandwiched between the more famous towns of Colwyn Bay and Rhyl. Its two neighbours grew in the nineteenth century due to holiday tourism brought by the development of the railways but Abergele, the town centre of which is about a mile inland from the coastline, largely missed out on the boom. By the 1930s, there were several campsites in the area for more frugal holidaymakers but, in truth, the place simply did not have the reputation of its more illustrious competitors.

In 1939, Abergele was a Denbighshire town[2] that a visitor might have referred to as 'sleepy'. The urban area was home to a relatively small population of just over 7,000, with another 1,200 people living within the wider rural and farming district. It was the sort of town where the only headline news stories to be registered by anyone other than the local press were things like 'A wasp was responsible for a road accident at Abergele early today ... in trying to ward off the insect, Hawley [the driver] lost control of the steering wheel and his vehicle crashed into a post'.[3]

To improve the town's public image, its Urban District Council established the Abergele Publicity Association and poured as much money into it as they could spare, and probably more than they should have.[4] It made little difference; one Abergele establishment offering holiday accommodation decided to begin adding 'near Rhyl' to its national advertisements. A campsite took time to point out that it was between Rhyl and Colwyn Bay, and even resorted to what can only be described as a lie by including an unattributed quote in its advertising, stating that Abergele was the 'most popular place on the Welsh coast'.

However, in other respects, Abergele was a town in relatively reasonable condition in 1939. The Depression years of the earlier part of the decade had not had the severity of impact felt in many other places. In June 1939, a 'bowls tournament for Abergele's unemployed ... had to be postponed indefinitely' due to the lack of unemployed men available to compete in it.[5]

More importantly, Abergele was the focal point of a thriving local agrarian community. Its weekly horse and cattle markets were very well-attended events of regional importance, where significant sums of money could change hands, and the annual fair in July also attracted buyers from afar.[6] As a result, the town centre, strung along Market Street, boasted a wide range of shops and services, a hotel, several pubs and inns, and even a small cinema.

About a mile to the west on a heavily wooded hillside, Abergele also had a castle. Gwrych Castle is not a 'real' castle in the mould of the huge medieval castles, such as Conwy, Beaumaris and Caernarfon, that North Wales is so famous for. It was built in the early nineteenth century by Lloyd Hesketh Bamford-Hesketh, heir of the Lloyds of Gwrych, as a very impressive home. Boasting a frontage over half a mile long, including the garden terraces, it comprises a main central building of dozens of rooms spread over four storeys, the top three of which are connected internally by a magnificent marble staircase. Accompanied by many outbuildings and boasting eighteen towers, Gwrych Castle has been described as a 'magnificent large scale example of a romantic castellated mansion'.[7] In 1909, the *Rhyl Journal* wrote the following about the castle:

> Among the number of beautiful mansions which adorn the neighbourhood, Gwrych Castle is certainly one of the finest. The principal tower, called Hesketh Tower, is about ninety feet high. This vast and imposing structure will be acknowledged to be picturesque, and certainly may be regarded with admiration. One of the entrance gateways bears several inscriptions, all of which refer to memorable historical events connected with the locality. A short distance beyond the castle is Cefn-yr-Ogof, one of the most magnificent natural caverns in Europe.[8]

Winifred Bamford-Hesketh would be last direct descendant of the family who built the Castle. She married Douglas Mackinnon Baillie Hamilton Cochrane, the son of a noble Scottish family, in 1878, in a union that was most probably arranged. Their relationship was a somewhat cold and rather unaffectionate affair. Winifred was possibly unimpressed by him and, if so, the feeling was probably reciprocated. Douglas was an austere military man. He had been educated at Eton College and was commissioned as an officer into the Life Guards in 1870. He went on to serve in the Nile Expedition and the subsequent Relief of Khartoum in 1885. During that same year, he inherited his title, becoming the 12th Earl of Dundonald and, thus, Winifred became the Countess Dundonald.

The Earl went on to be appointed Commanding Officer of the 2nd Life Guards in 1895 and served in the Second Boer War as Commander of the Mounted Brigade, part of the South Natal Field Force. He had departed for South Africa without even telling his wife; she was informed of her husband's departure by her mother-in-law and later discovered that he had also taken the castle's coachman with him, as well as two of her horses.

Lord Dundonald went on to take part in the Relief of Ladysmith in February 1900 and, as a result, became quite famous, albeit temporarily. His return to his North Wales home in 1901 was greeted by the residents of Abergele as if it were the homecoming of a national hero. The streets were festooned with bunting, large crowds gathered to cheer and wave him to the main castle lodge entrance, and a specially commissioned ceremonial sword was made and presented to him by a local jeweller. The welcome offered by his wife is unrecorded.

Despite this brief period in the headlines, the 12th Earl was, in truth, a rather uninspired and uninspiring officer: largely unimpressed by his limited tactical and leadership skills, his South African troops referred to him as 'Dundoodle'.

There is evidence to suggest that he and Winifred contemplated a divorce in 1901, but in 1902 the 12th Earl was appointed General Officer Commanding the Militia of Canada, and this got him out of the way for a few more years. In that same year, the Countess of Dundonald, as the only surviving child of the Bamford-Heskeths, fully inherited Gwrych Castle, and just before the outbreak of World War One in 1914 she instigated some major redesigns to the castle's fabric without any involvement from her husband.

The Earl went on to serve in the Great War as a Lieutenant General on the General Staff and as Chairman of the Admiralty Committee on Smoke Screens in 1915. He finally retired with the rank of Colonel of the 2nd Life Guards and Honorary Colonel of both the 91st Canadian Highlanders and the Imperial Camel Corps. His career meant that the Dundonalds had been estranged for most of their married life, which possibly suited the pair of them. The 12th Earl was generally away with the army or in Canada and, when he was home, he chose to live in Scotland, whilst the Countess generally divided her time between London and Abergele. There were few times that the couple were in residence together at Gwrych Castle.

When the Countess died in January 1924, she left the castle to King George V in the overly optimistic hope that it might become the royal family's Welsh residence in the same way as Balmoral had become in Scotland. Aside from this hope, the decision was also probably intended as a public and humiliating slap in the face of her Scottish husband. Nevertheless, the Countess was well within her rights: her authority to use and dispose of the estate as she saw fit had been written into their marriage agreement.

The King, however, politely declined Winifred's bequest and ownership was instead transferred to the Most Venerable Order of the Hospital of Saint John of Jerusalem. Known today as the Order of St John, it is most well-known for the work of the St John's Ambulance Brigade, the organisation dedicated to providing free medical care. Perhaps unsurprisingly, the Order also had no real use for Gwrych Castle. Therefore, in 1928, and possibly in a fit of pique, the 12th Earl purchased the castle back for £78,000, though he had to gut the castle and sell most of its contents to help fund the cost. He had absolutely no intention of living there as 'he claimed that she [Winifred] had gone mad and declared that no member of the family shall ever live at the castle again.'[9] When the 12th Earl died in April 1935, the castle passed to his son Thomas Hesketh Douglas Blair Cochrane, the 13th Earl of Dundonald. The 13th Earl also had no intention of living at Gwrych either as, like his father, his home was in Scotland.

So Gwrych Castle was mothballed. Unsold items of furniture were stored in three outbuildings and three rooms within the main building, and only a small skeleton staff was kept on to maintain the estate and keep an eye on the buildings. The Earl's younger brother, who regularly suffered self-imposed financial difficulties, was later given approval to house himself in one of the estate lodges, but otherwise the castle was now largely ignored by the Cochrane family.

Nevertheless, the 13th Earl contributed £4,000 towards the creation of a golf course on the grounds in February 1939 and he also willingly allowed the local community to use the estate for events. In July 1939, somewhere between two and three thousand boy scouts and cubs camped within the grounds, in torrential rain, for a regional jamboree which was 'easily the biggest thing of its kind that has ever been held in North Wales.'[10] In August the grounds also hosted a 'semi-national sheep-dog trials ... [with] nearly 100 entries from England, Wales and Scotland',[11] followed shortly afterwards by a major sports, gymnastics and gymkhana event that attracted competitors from as far away as the Wirral and Stoke-on-Trent, and concluded with an impressive fireworks display.

Following the German invasion of Czechoslovakia in March 1939, the clouds of war had again begun to gather over the whole of Europe. With little use for his property, the 13th Earl offered the castle to the government to be used for military training, a military hospital or whatever purpose they thought fit for the potential conflict that lay ahead. The government did eventually conclude a requisitioning order at a cost to the taxpayer of £200 per year[12] but, like the 12th and 13th Earls, and the Order of St John, they could not think what they would really do with the castle either. By mid-August 1939 the grand castle at Gwrych, with around 500 acres of good agricultural land and forestry, lay uninhabited, unused and apparently undesired.

However, the castle was just about to become very much wanted by a different group of people, as a result of events sparked six years earlier and 700 miles away in Germany.

Following the election of Adolf Hitler as Chancellor in January 1933, Nazi persecution of Jews and other minorities within Germany had grown rapidly. Initial antisemitic demonstrations such as the state-backed boycott of Jewish shops and the subsequent encouragement and emboldening of antisemites to demonstrate their prejudice, developed into the Nuremburg Laws of 1935. These effectively stripped German Jews of their citizenship and thus all the political, legal and social rights and protections that citizenship entailed. There was a brief softening of their stance for propaganda purposes during the 1936 Berlin Olympic Games, but after that the Nazis hounded and persecuted Jews with almost no restriction. Jews were barred from professional careers and their children prohibited from attending state schools. All were given new legal middle names of either Israel or Sarah, depending on their gender, and their passports were stamped with a 'J' for *Jude* (German for 'Jew'). Those passports were important to the Nazis; they were the mechanism to get Jews out of Germany and, following the *Anschluss,*[13] out of Austria as well. To help increase the pace of emigration, Adolf Eichmann established the Office for Jewish Emigration in Vienna.

Although this persecution was designed to encourage – or force – German Jews to leave the country, it was just not that simple and many refused to even consider it. Germany was their home, and many believed that the Nazis were nothing more than a temporary phenomenon. They hoped that life would return to normal if they were willing to ride the storm.

Leaving Germany was also far easier to contemplate than to do. Apart from the trauma of uprooting and breaking family ties, not to mention the sheer cost and difficulties of emigrating, Nazi laws did not allow Jewish emigrants to take any of their money or possessions with them. They would therefore face the prospect of arriving destitute in a foreign land. But which foreign land could they go to, and which foreign people were willing to take them? For Zionists, those who believed in the establishment of a Jewish homeland, by far the most favoured location was Palestine or, as Jews thought of it, *Eretz Yisrael,* the Land of Israel. However, emigrating to Palestine was becoming increasingly difficult, if not impossible.

Following the Great War, many imperial territories formerly belonging to the defeated powers came under the authority of the League of Nations, an international organisation created to provide a mechanism for dispute resolution in the hope of maintaining world peace in the future. The League of Nations assigned mandates to the victorious powers to administer and govern these various territories and the mandate for Palestine had been given to Britain. British imperial interest in the country and the wider region had been long-standing, and British troops had fought against the previous rulers, the Ottoman Turks, in Palestine during the Great War. In 1917, with the war not yet over, the British Foreign Secretary, Arthur Balfour, had declared Britain's intention to assist in establishing a future Jewish homeland in Palestine. The Balfour Declaration was somewhat vague on details, but nevertheless it was the first time that any major power had offered their support towards the long-standing Zionist dream of creating *Eretz Yisrael.*

One of the biggest issues facing the territory's new rulers when British Mandatory Palestine was established in 1923, was the difficulty of balancing the competing desires and claims of the nation's inhabitants. Jews and Christians made up around twenty per cent of the population, whereas around eighty per cent were Muslim. Political and religious tensions in Palestine during the 1920s were exacerbated by the immigration of around 100,000 Jews who had been spurred on by the Balfour Declaration and their Zionist ideals. After Hitler came to power in Germany in 1933, many more Jews began to emigrate to Mandatory Palestine.

The majority indigenous population of Palestine had long sought independence from foreign control and this desire was being further thwarted by what they saw as the apparently limitless Jewish immigration of recent years. Jewish claims on lands they believed to be their own were causing deep anger within the Muslim majority population and this anger spilled over in 1936 when the Arab Revolt broke out. Initially the revolt was largely one of political agitation and workers' strikes but by 1937 it had turned violent. Precise numbers are disputed but by 1939 several thousand agitators had been killed, many in clashes with the British Army and the local police, and over a hundred had been arrested and hanged. The Arab Revolt was quashed. It had failed in its aims but it had far-reaching effects. One of the most serious consequences was felt by potential Jewish immigrants as the British government began putting stricter limits on further immigration into Palestine so as not to fan the flames of revolt any further. By a cruel twist of fate, the doors of Mandatory Palestine were beginning to close to Jews just as their need to get out of central Europe was reaching its peak.

For German Jews wanting to escape Hitler and the Nazis, Austria and Czechoslovakia were early popular choices, too. However, during

1938, the Nazis went on to secure control over the whole of Austria and the Sudetenland of Czechoslovakia. By March 1939, Germany had secured control over the rest of Czechoslovakia. Therefore, moving to either country made little sense as both Austrian and Czech Jews now faced the same kind of persecution from the Nazis as their German counterparts.

Both the USA and Britain were also tightening their immigration policies at this time. Although a recovery was underway, Britain was still suffering severe effects from the Depression. Many Britons feared that refugees would be bad for the economy, either by competing for jobs with British workers or by becoming a burden on overstretched services. There was also resistance to the entry of skilled immigrants; both the British Medical Association and British Dental Association complained about the arrival of qualified colleagues from overseas, partly because of a perceived threat to their jobs but also based on a cynical and incorrect view that they would not be qualified to the same standards as their British counterparts. Consequently, very few people were allowed in, other than 'exceptional' cases which included those with provable and significant independent wealth and those who could find work as a domestic servant, an often poorly paid job that few young British women found alluring by the 1930s. With various countries tightening their borders, there was virtually nowhere for German Jews to easily emigrate to.

There were several Zionist Jewish groups in Germany who shared the same objective as the Nazis regarding emigration, but for entirely different reasons. They too wanted Jews to leave Germany, but they wanted to see them relocate specifically to Palestine. These groups worked under the umbrella of *Hechalutz*, affiliated to *Mizrachi*, the international Zionist movement, and they provided assistance to those trying to depart and achieve *Aliyah*[14] by settling in the promised land.

One of the most important men in Germany in this regard was Arieh Handler who, by 1938, at the age of just twenty-three, had become *Mizrachi*'s Director of Religious *Aliyah*. Although the concept lay in the future, Arieh would go on to be the creator of the Gwrych Castle *Hachshara*.

Arieh was born in May 1915 in Brno, Moravia, within the Austro-Hungarian Empire. Following its defeat and collapse in 1918 at the end of the Great War, that empire was broken up and the infant Handler then found himself living in the newly created and independent Czechoslovakia. Shortly afterwards his family moved to Magdeburg, Germany, where his father had interests in both the metal and textiles industries. As there was no Jewish school in Magdeburg, the young Arieh attended a monastery school where he studied both Latin and Greek. Later, he went to Frankfurt to study at a Jewish *Yeshiva* school and, later, to the Lessing *Gymnasium* (high school). Arieh became active in the Zionist youth movement *Brit Chalutzim Dati'im* (League of Religious Pioneers), more commonly known as *Bachad*, and was soon promoted to a leadership role within it.

Working out of Berlin by the early 1930s, Arieh was involved in *Bachad*'s agricultural training programmes, preparing young Jews for *Aliyah* to Palestine, and partly delivered through its youth wing, *Bnei Akiva*. He also worked with another Zionist youth group, Youth *Aliyah*, who were developing similar schemes. Youth *Aliyah*, for example, offered many Jewish adolescents the chance to spend two years at kibbutzim[15] in British Mandatory Palestine. In these kibbutzim, Zionist-minded parents could ensure that their children would deepen their religious understanding as well as learn the practical skills that their intended future homeland would need. However, for most parents, sending their children to Palestine for two years was a significant financial as well as emotional commitment and thus not always possible. Therefore, in addition to the *kibbutzim* in Palestine, Youth *Aliyah* and *Bachad* set up a number of training and preparation centres inside Germany. Each centre, known as a *Vorbereitungslager* or *Hachshara*, provided short agricultural training courses of several weeks – a much cheaper and easier option for parents hoping to encourage their children towards a future in Palestine.[16] All of the young people who would find themselves at Gwrych Castle in 1939 were members of either Youth *Aliyah* or *Bachad/Bnei Akiva* and many had spent some time in one of these centres.

Part of Arieh Handler's rapid rise to prominence within Zionist circles was due to his immense ability. He was a man of dogged determination who showed great attention to detail and displayed an impressive capacity for hard graft. He saw his work as a mission and he put it before all personal considerations, so much so that he arrived late for his own wedding at Gwrych Castle in December 1940, as will be seen later. His most important attributes lay, however, within his own personality. Although a fully committed Zionist, he was easily tolerant of others, including Gentiles, and 'his charm and beaming smile betrayed a pioneering soul blended with religious and practical Judaism.'[17] He was also happy to work closely with 'rival' youth groups such as Youth *Aliyah* and *Habonim*, which was to prove a crucial factor behind his successful creation of the Gwrych *Hachshara*, where he would ensure that the leadership team contained influences from both of those organisations as well as his own. Arieh had an easy and affable manner and these attributes made him someone that people would happily follow. As an article in *The Jewish Chronicle* stated, 'He knew what it meant to be a leader. He led by example, and he inspired thousands.'[18] He was also a man of great integrity and personal charm, capable of showing enormous empathy with others. The same article went on to state:

> Arieh's absolute sincerity won him the admiration and support (sometimes begrudging) that he sought. When people would occasionally disappoint him, he would brush aside the affront: 'He means well, he has such a good heart.' In any discussion Arieh was always willing to see all sides: 'on the other hand' was one of his bywords.[19]

'On the other hand' is not a phrase that might be associated with senior Nazi officials. However, as Arieh's ambitions tied uneasily with theirs, they were willing to leave him alone to get on with his job of securing emigration for German Jews. He was quite successful in his approach and, working alongside others, his older brother Julius recalled that, 'by a variety of methods of deception and dangerous undercover manoeuvres ... it was possible to bring a number of children to Britain. My brother was a member of this group of "Scarlet Pimpernels".'[20]

Despite taking perilous risks, Arieh benefitted from the Nazis, willingness to turn a blind eye to his activities. He was allowed to travel relatively freely, unlike most Jews, and to ease his path he was exempted from the requirement to have a large 'J' stamped on his passport. Nevertheless, he was watched closely, which resulted in him occasionally crossing paths with the Gestapo and, more specifically, Adolf Eichmann, the senior Nazi in charge of Jewish Affairs and especially focused on their emigration.[21] This relationship was a very difficult one and resulted in a tense encounter shortly after the *Anschluss* between Germany and Austria in March 1938. Austrian Jews had appealed to Arieh for his assistance in helping their children to get on one of his *Aliyah* projects. However, despite his comparative lack of travel restrictions, Austria was one place he was not allowed to journey to. Aware of the potentially serious personal implications if caught, Arieh jumped on a train and went anyway. As he walked along a corridor of the train, he saw Eichmann: 'I froze in terror. Eichmann knew me from Berlin and would realise that I had travelled illegally to Vienna. It was the most dangerous moment of my life. I kept walking, expecting any moment a heavy hand on my shoulders and a shout of "Jude". But nothing happened ... For some reason, Eichmann decided he had not seen me.'[22]

The reason for Eichmann's decision to ignore him can only be guessed at, but it is indicative of the fact that the Nazis' attempts to force Jews out of Germany was not going well and that they were relying to an extent on leaving the likes of Arieh alone to do their job for them. With nothing positive to offer Jews as encouragement to emigrate, there was a significant scaling-up of Nazi antisemitic intimidation during 1938, which reached a crescendo between 9 and 10 November on *Kristallnacht*, the 'Night of the Broken Glass'. Violent assaults on Jewish Germans were carried out across Germany and approximately 30,000 were arrested, some of whom were sent to camps such as the 'model' concentration camp at Dachau. Nearly 300 synagogues and thousands of business premises were damaged or destroyed.

Fortunately for him, Arieh was in Jerusalem arranging *Aliyah* projects when he heard the news of *Kristallnacht*. Believing, with every justification, that it would be unsafe for him to return home, and that at the very least he would not be able to continue to encourage and organise *Aliyah* without interference and obstruction, *Mizrachi* advised him not to return to Berlin and instead to relocate to London. There, he could continue his Zionist mission on behalf of both *Bachad* and Youth *Aliyah*.

Kristallnacht was a hugely significant event. For German Jews who had hoped that the Nazis might be temporary, or that things would never escalate to the level of state-sponsored violence against them, there was now a realisation that they had been horribly wrong. They had to get out, but there seemed to be no easy way to achieve that. Nobody was showing much inclination towards offering them a new home, and so they appeared to be trapped inside Germany, or other Nazi-occupied territories.

In sleepy Abergele in November 1938, oblivious to the horrors unfolding during *Kristallnacht*, the main talking point was the breaking news that the 20th Nottingham Company of the Boys' Brigade, who had camped in the town earlier that year, had enjoyed it so much that eighty of them were intending to return again next year.[23] Nobody could have foreseen that the contemporaneous happenings in Germany had set in motion a series of events that would see more than twice that number of young people from central Europe come to the town ten months later.

Immediately after *Kristallnacht*, the British Jewish Refugee Committee, along with many Christian and Quaker groups, lobbied and appealed to Members of Parliament to provide assistance and support for European Jews caught between maltreatment in their homelands and the world's reluctance to offer them a new place to live. Shortly afterwards, and with increasingly credible stories emerging of persecu-tion across the expanding Third Reich ringing in MPs' ears, a debate was planned for the House of Commons for 21 November 1938. Most could see there was a need for Britain to 'do something' and not just sit idly by. The night before the debate, Samuel Hoare, the British Foreign Minister, met with delegates from a non-denominational organisation called the Movement for the Care of Children from Germany. They convinced Hoare that Britain should offer a refuge to young Jews. They believed that they could organise the necessary homing of refugee children and that they could raise sufficient funding to prevent any immigrants from becoming a burden on the public purse. They also argued persuasively that this would only be a short-term measure. Without the extra difficulties and distractions of their children, their parents might be better able to secure emigration and, having achieved that, the children could then join their families in countries other than Britain. The next day, when Hoare spoke to the House, he summed up the mood of the majority: 'Here is a chance of taking the young generation of a great people, here is a chance of mitigating to some extent the terrible suffering of their parents and their friends.'

A bill was put forward to ease the restrictions on young[24] Jewish people entering Britain, and to provide them with temporary travel documents until such time as they would be able to reunite with their families. To prevent them becoming a burden on the taxpayer, each refugee would have to come with a surety of £50[25] and guarantees from refugee agencies for their ongoing maintenance. The British govern-ment was willing to help, but it was quite clear that it was not going to foot any of the costs that were involved.

In a clear example of the muddled thinking at the heart of govern-ment, at the same time as the Foreign Office and Home Office were working hard to ease access for young Jews to Britain, the Colonial Office turned down over 10,000 applications for Jewish children to enter Mandatory Palestine.

Simultaneously, Youth *Aliyah,* having already realised that sending children to *kibbutzim* in Palestine was a failing programme due to the difficulties of getting there, were looking towards resurrecting the idea by establishing kibbutzim or *Hachsharot* in other countries. Their central aim of preparing their pioneering youth for a life in Palestine would remain unaltered, but that aim would now be achieved by a far slower and more circuitous route. In fact, following *Kristallnacht*, Youth *Aliyah* was also increasingly prioritising a humanitarian approach of seeking places of safety and refuge for its youth members at the expense of Zionist idealism if necessary. Thus, the British government's decision in November 1938 to offer refuge to young Jews now opened up the tantalising possibility of being able to set up *Auslandhachshara*, *Hachshara* training centres outside of Germany or Palestine, within Britain. A significant amount of money would need to be found to enable this, and *Hachsharath Hanoar* (the British Council of the Young Pioneer Movement for Palestine) began exploring various ways of achieving it.

With Britain now actively offering a helping hand, various organisations – Jewish, Christian, humanitarian – seeing the urgent need to help Jews out of central Europe, quickly moved into action. Fundraising was to be a key part of their actions not only in order to cover the stipulated £50 'entry fee', but more significantly the ongoing costs of housing, clothing, educating and caring for the refugees. Movement for the Care of Children from Germany, shortly afterwards renamed as the Refugee Children's Movement, sent representatives to Germany and Austria to begin organising the practicalities of moving thousands of children to Britain.[26]

On 25 November 1938, the BBC began to broadcast radio appeals for volunteers to come forward who would be willing to foster immigrant Jewish children. Other interested groups in Germany, such as Youth *Aliyah*, quickly linked up with the Refugee Children's Movement and other agencies and ad hoc arrangements were rapidly put together. Lists were drawn up at local levels, transport enquiries were made and orders of priority were argued over. What eventually emerged from this flurry of activity became known as the Kindertransport.

On Saturday, 2 December 1938, just three weeks after *Kristallnacht*, the first Kindertransport group of 196 Jewish child refugees landed at the port of Harwich in Essex. They arrived in a country they knew little or nothing about and were there for reasons that they could probably barely comprehend.[27] The youngsters were mostly from a Jewish orphanage in Berlin that had been attacked, ransacked and burnt down during *Kristallnacht*,[28] and had been hurriedly gathered together the day before.

Their journey to Britain established a template that was copied by most subsequent transports. The refugees were conveyed by train across the German border into Holland and, at the Hook of Holland, near Rotterdam, they caught a ferry to Harwich.[29] From Harwich, they were despatched to Liverpool Street Station for allocation to foster carers. Like future arrivals, they were limited in what they could take with them; usually no more than a small suitcase, with no more than 10 Marks in money, and they all carried an identity tag that recorded the barest of information about them.

Within Britain, vast amounts of money were quickly being raised to receive the children: former Prime Minister Stanley Baldwin had launched an appeal that, by the summer of 1939, had collected over £500,000.[30] Whilst Britain was gearing itself up as a reception centre, further decisions on who would qualify for Kindertransport were being made hundreds of miles away in central Europe.

Future Kindertransport groups were put together in many varied and erratic forms. Some children were chosen by refugee organisations due to their poverty or personal circumstances but, more often than not, it was the parents who had to do all the work to get their children on the transport lists. Their chances of succeeding may well have been boosted if their child was a member of a Zionist youth organisation but, more importantly, they had to have the financial means to independently provide the £50 surety per child that might be the key to British entry.

Many of the new arrivals at Liverpool Street Station, especially in the first few months of Kindertransport, were matched with the volunteer foster carers who had offered their services. The initial reaction to the call for volunteers was good but inevitably over time the number of fostering offers began to dry up, even though the numbers of refugees continued unabated. Consequently, many arrivals on the Kindertransport were filed towards waiting coaches or taxis for transport to a designated hostel or reception centre where they would await relocation. Initially, two summer holiday camps at Dovercourt in Essex and Pakefield in Suffolk, both closed for the winter, were used to house arrivals, but they were soon full. More and more reception and distribution centres were required and were also quickly bursting at the seams.

Arieh Handler, now in London, had been considering how he could continue to contribute towards *Aliyah* in the face of mounting difficulties. His new office, described by one journalist as 'the Clapham Junction for the Zionist movement',[31] was flooded with enquiries and desperate requests from central Europe for help but getting youngsters to Palestine was becoming extremely difficult. He was aware that increasing numbers of Kindertransport arrivals were being held in temporary camps, a situation which was not sustainable. He was also picking up on the increasing frustration being felt by *Bachad* and Youth *Aliyah*. Both these organisations wanted to avoid the need for Jewish youngsters arriving in Britain to be fostered by Gentiles wherever possible, fearing that the children's Jewishness and desire for *Aliyah* might be dulled by Christian influences. This concern was still being aired in February 1940, six months after the outbreak of war, when a writer in *Bachad*'s own journal asked, 'could adequate hostels not have been arranged for before evacuation began?' and then referred to the failure as a 'neglect of duty' and a 'communal incompetence'.[32]

The criticism was slightly harsh. *Bachad* and Arieh Handler were attempting to create solutions for all of these problems. Establishing kibbutzim in Britain was too great a challenge, but setting up smaller *Hachsharot* (agricultural training centres) was much more feasible. Consequently, *Bachad* was actively on the lookout for suitable properties and by the late summer of 1939 a few small *Hachsharot* had been established. The template for each of these centres was for the youngsters to run them independently and cooperatively, in a kibbutz-like fashion, whilst finding work on local farms to develop their agricultural know-how. Education would be provided peer-to-peer and often included nothing more than teaching each other Hebrew or English. However, establishing even such small centres was far from easy, and not cheap, as very specialised locations with the correct facilities were required.

The first was created in March 1939 at Castleton near Rochdale, housing thirty young Jews. This was followed in April by a centre for forty youngsters in north London and in June another by Millisle in County Down, Northern Ireland, comprising of thirty-five boys and girls. Other early centres included Whittingehame Farm School in East Lothian, initially home to forty-five refugees and sponsored by the Balfour family; one in Ipswich (number of residents unclear); and another in Richborough in Kent which housed fifty older boys. The only centre to have more than fifty residents, and thus by far the largest, was Great Engeham Farm in Kent with 134 children. The smallest had just nine residents, all from Poland.[33]

These early *Hachsharot* were deemed to be generally successful but within *Bachad* there was some debate about the associated costs of running these centres. An alternative, and significantly cheaper, experimental model was trialled in Glasgow in July 1939 whereby a small house, known as a *Beth Chalutz*, was procured to accommodate thirteen children. Three of them, all girls, managed the housekeeping and cooking, whilst the ten boys worked by day on farms near the city. Their education was provided by leaders from within Glasgow's existing Jewish population.

Two significant figures on *Bachad*'s national executive were not convinced by either model. Jack Sklan, one of the founders of *Bnei Akiva* in Britain, *Bachad*'s youth wing for those under fourteen, dismissed them all as he did not believe that they provided 'for the proper training of religious children' as they were conceived as non-religious centres. In addition, 'their essentially different outlook on life had made it impossible for them [the children] to be happy and successfully trained.'[34]

The largest centre at Great Engeham typified this concern; there were reports of tensions between the more religiously orthodox youths at the camp, who formed a minority, and the bulk of the young people there who had far less interest in the *Hachshara* idea.

Arieh Handler agreed with Sklan that a *Hachshara* should be built on clear and obvious religious principles, but he was also concerned by another issue. Both models only accommodated relatively small numbers so, whilst helping, they were not significantly easing the wider problem of Jewish youngsters backing up in reception camps. What Arieh favoured was a third model, the creation of a large 'super-centre' with a strong religious as well as agricultural focus. But finding a suitable property for that idea was almost impossible – and it was the main reason this approach had not yet been tried. It would need to be in a rural area and large enough to house many dozens, even hundreds, of young people as well as being a site suitable for rapid transformation into an agricultural training centre. The building would also need to be vacant and available on the cheap, or preferably free. As unfeasible as this all sounded, if one could be found it would be possible to set up a *Bachad* flagship for the entire *Hachsharot* movement which could act as a role model and a template for the creation of others.

If *Bachad* could have imagined the perfect location for the establishment of a flagship *Hachshara*, it might have looked like a large, empty and unwanted castle in rural North Wales.

CHAPTER 2

'A field in the middle of nowhere'

Summer 1939
The gathering of the Gwrych refugees

Great Engeham Farm, near Ashford in Kent, was one of several over-crowded reception centres housing Jewish Kindertransport children who had arrived in Britain from central Europe. The farm had been secured rent-free by Youth *Aliyah* when it was offered to them as a gift following a request for help that they placed in *The Times* newspaper. The centre opened as a *Hachshara* in June 1939, initially with 134 children, and it had even successfully managed to secure emigration to Palestine for a small number of these residents. However, aside from its official residents awaiting their chance to make *Aliyah*, Great Engeham also served as a holding camp for an additional 300 Kindertransport children who were awaiting a more permanent relocation to another *Hachshara* within Britain. For about a third of them, that destination would be Abergele.

Most of these temporary residents were living in great discomfort, housed in large tents providing shelter to eight or more youngsters at a time, or in the compartments of several disused and leaky railway carriages that were rusting in a nearby muddy meadow. The young people at Great Engeham were a disparate collection of children, but within the collective mass were a distinct group of more orthodox Jews with clearer and stronger Zionist ambitions. This group, made up largely of members of either Youth *Aliyah* or *Bnei Akival Bachad*, were under the watchful eye of several adult leaders, or *madrichim* (*madrich* in the singular), including twenty-eight-year-old Eliezer Israel Seligmann, better known by those close to him as Erwin.

As a teenager, Erwin Seligmann had studied at the Academy for the Arts in his home city of Hamburg but after graduation he had chosen a different path, becoming a volunteer and later an instructor in several *Vorbereitungslagers* for both *Bachad* and Youth *Aliyah*. Erwin was a very intelligent man, extremely conscientious and effective in his work. His swift accumulation of agricultural skills and knowledge convinced many that he was actually a farmer by trade rather than an artist. His rise to prominence within *Bachad* circles brought him to the attention of Arieh Handler and they formed a partnership that blossomed; Arieh came to regard Erwin as 'the brains' behind much of what they would later go on to do together.

Erwin arrived in Britain in early 1939 and immediately offered *Bachad* his assistance in the process of creating *Hachsharot* within Britain. As an experienced instructor, he was of great use and by May 1939 he had been installed as part of the leadership group at the Great Engeham camp.[35] Despite being a senior *Bachad madrich*, Erwin was a quiet, reserved and modest man who rarely realised how well-liked he was by those he led. Miriam Sperber, who would later get to know him well at Gwrych Castle, described him as 'a delicate soul. He used to say of himself: I am an ignoramus, but an intelligent one.'[36] He had a very collaborative style of leadership, using discussion to form a consensus wherever possible, and he relied heavily on his own intuition to gauge situations.

However, Erwin did not have to be too intuitive to recognise the rapidly growing problems and tensions at Great Engeham which was having difficulties in trying to be a *Hachshara* and, at the same time, a holding camp for hundreds of youngsters awaiting a place elsewhere. The farm could only provide poor, overcrowded accommodation for the residents they had, and the increasing number of new arrivals by August 1939 was adding significantly to the problem. Most of these new arrivals were members of *Bachad* or Youth *Aliyah* and Erwin recognised that the needs and desires of these more religious Orthodox Jews differed from that of many of the other youngsters at the farm. Consequently, he set up kitchen facilities for his own group to ensure that their food was kosher, but this had the unintended effect of stoking tensions with the *madrichim* of other groups at the farm, who began demanding their own unique facilities. It was clear to him that he and his *Bachad*/Youth *Aliyah* group had to move on, partly because of the rising tensions, but mostly because his group were kicking their heels doing nothing rather than getting on with the task of developing their agricultural training, which they would need to be effective Zionist pioneers in the future. Nevertheless, there was little he could do until he received word from Arieh Handler that a new centre was available.

Arieh's hunt for a large, empty and unwanted building in a rural area had not been going well. Many of the buildings deemed suitable were either in the process of being commandeered by the military authorities or in an area from which young people would have to be evacuated if war broke out. However, he eventually become aware of one property in North Wales, that, on paper at least, seemed to fit the bill perfectly. It was large enough to accommodate the type of numbers that would dwarf any other existing *Hachshara*, potentially 200 or more, and provide him with an opportunity to create the 'flagship' centre he so desired for the entire *Hachsharot* movement.

So, in early August 1939, an optimistic Arieh Handler took a trip to Abergele to take a look at Gwrych Castle, accompanied by his older brother, Dr Julius Handler. Twenty-nine-year-old Julius was a tall, affable, level-headed man with a very easy manner and an ability to effortlessly form friendships wherever he went. Regularly heard humming to himself, Julius was a great lover of music and a talented amateur musician. He had arrived in Britain, probably with Arieh's assistance, earlier in 1939 whilst the British government were still allowing limited adult Jewish immigration for those who satisfied a high threshold. Despite being a fully qualified doctor, having studied in both Germany and Switzerland, Julius fell victim to the British Medical Association's assertions that foreign physicians were insufficiently trained and consequently he was barred from practising medicine. His entry visa only granted him permission to work in agriculture. With limited alternative opportunities, Julius was therefore excited by the possibilities offered by his younger brother's scheme and, although a less zealous Zionist than his sibling, he was fully supportive of Arieh's endeavours and more than happy to offer his help in scouting out Gwrych Castle.

The brothers were both impressed and disappointed in equal measure by what they found in Abergele. In many ways, as Julius later noted, the building was unsuitable 'as a home for 200 children, from the point of view of accommodation and sanitary conditions,' but, on the other hand, it was 'far superior to those in an open camp.'[37] However, given the increasingly limited options, and from the point of view of establishing a *Hachshara* in a rural area, Gwrych Castle appeared to be otherwise ideal.

Lord Dundonald was approached to see whether he would be willing to loan the castle to *Bachad* for housing Jewish refugee children. He seemed happy enough with the idea and even offered to contribute a sum of money towards essential repairs should the project go ahead. However, he also pointed out that permission was not within his gift to grant as he was in the process of offering the castle and the estate to the government: *Bachad* would therefore need to petition them.

A request to the government was duly made and, behind the scenes, a number of influential people began mobilising on Arieh Handler's behalf. Some were working towards influencing the government's decision on whether to grant Gwrych Castle to *Bachad* for use as a refugee training centre, and others were working towards raising the sums of money needed to repair and equip the building, in anticipation of a positive response. Amongst these influencers were the Balfour family and Lord Dundonald himself. Other effective advocates included members of the so-called 'Manchester School' of Zionists, which counted Rebecca Sieff amongst their number. The daughter of the wealthy businessman Michael Marks, the founder of the British retailer Marks and Spencer, Rebecca was President of the Women's International Zionist Organisation and the founder of the Women's Appeal Committee of the Central British Fund for German Jewry, where she had previously forged links with Recha Freier, the founder of Youth *Aliyah*.

Despite there being no certainty of government approval being granted, there was sufficient optimism for Arieh Handler to ask his brother to revisit Abergele and begin preparing the castle for imminent use. In mid-August 1939, two weeks before the outbreak of World War Two, Julius returned to Gwrych Castle with six colleagues from *Bachad*. Amongst them were a couple of handymen who were somewhat taken aback by the size of the task confronting them. Uninhabited for a number of years, the castle was 'in a very dilapidated condition … The only pieces of furniture in the castle were a broken chair and a table. There was no water, no toilets, no sanitary facilities of any kind, no electricity and no money to employ professional help.'[38]

Gwrych Castle sprawled over four floors centred around a small, open courtyard on a sloping hillside. Underneath the main suite of rooms on the ground floor was a basement level that had been designed for the servants to work and live in. It contained fifteen rooms including the kitchen and scullery along with a multitude of storerooms, cellars and servants' bedrooms.

The ground floor contained a large, long, oak-panelled hallway, subdivided into an entrance hall that was accessible from the main forecourt and an inner hall. There were seven other empty rooms off the entrance hall. They had been formerly used as a billiard room, a smoke room, a library, a study, a drawing room, a music room and a dining room. From the inner hall, the base of an impressive, wide marble staircase began its ascent to connect to the two floors above. The first floor was made up of eleven main rooms along with three large dressing rooms, two long picture galleries, a windowless strong room, a bathroom and a toilet. The second floor contained a warren of sixteen smaller bedrooms that led off from two long corridors, along with three bathrooms and two separate toilets.

The sloping hill upon which the castle is built meets the rear of the second floor on the south side. Here, there was a chapel at ground level and a walk-in entrance to the top of the grand, marble staircase which runs down all the way back to the ground floor. The tower on the north elevation contained an extra third level made up of three rooms, known as the Cupola Suite.

Outside of the main building was a collection of towers and external buildings that included a stable block, kennels, laundry and washing facilities, a dairy, a glasshouse and a melon house (so called because of attempts to grow both melons and pineapples within it during the 1840s, though by the twentieth century it served the far less exotic purpose of being the store for the gardener's tools and equipment). In the wider estate stood several structures such as the gamekeeper's lodge and the folly that is Lady Emily's Tower, which is set further to the west along the heavily wooded hillside.

On the surface, it must have appeared to the Handler brothers on their first visit that the castle would easily be able to accommodate 300 people, but a closer inspection had proved that it was not quite that straightforward. For example, three of the main rooms were locked and inaccessible as they had been reserved by Lord Dundonald as storage rooms for unsold furniture left over from when the castle had been mothballed in 1935.[39] In addition, only just over thirty of the first and second floor rooms stood out as being suitable for use as bedrooms and some of those would need to be earmarked for use by Julius Handler, who wanted to establish a first aid room for general day to day consultations and to reserve a couple of other rooms to create an on-site hospital for more serious or long-term medical issues.

This left a possible total of somewhere between twenty and twenty-five rooms that could be utilised as potential bedrooms. With all the young people expected to live at the castle, that would mean that eight to twelve people would need to share each room. To complicate matters further, some of the bedrooms were not in the best condition. A number of walls in the rooms, especially on the second floor, showed clear signs of water damage, which indicated that the roof above was in poor condition and in need of repairs.

How to utilise the communal spaces on the ground floor was also going to present a few problems. The dining room was very large but nowhere near large enough for hundreds of people to use it simultaneously. The adjacent music room and the inner hall were identified for overspill, but this only left five rooms and the entrance hall on the ground floor for use as recreation rooms, teaching rooms and an office. All of this resulted in a rethink of the numbers of children that could be relocated to Gwrych, and a figure closer to 200 rather than 300 was settled upon. Whilst smaller than had been originally hoped, the centre would still be by far the largest *Hachshara* thus far attempted in Britain.

Julius and his small team, including twenty-seven-year-old David Granek,[40] quickly identified several key priorities. Perhaps the most pressing need was to rectify the sanitary arrangements, which they regarded as woeful due to there being an insufficient number of water closet toilets and bathrooms for the amount of people they were hoping to accommodate. The pump that provided the castle's water also seemed to be rather erratic. Sometimes there was no water at all and, when there was, there was very low pressure in various parts of the castle, resulting in a great many taps providing little more than a dribble even when fully opened. This didn't affect the kitchen at least, which received water from the network in nearby Abergele, but the kitchen facilities, although large, were wholly inadequate for turning out food in the quantities that would be needed.

The final major problem was that of heating and lighting. The building had no gas supply. Mains electricity was available but – and it remains an unknown mystery as to exactly why – this would never be used. Presumably, during the early preparation stages, Arieh Handler had decided that the costs were too great, or simply unnecessary.

There was an electricity generator on the site, but it was broken and Julius's team soon formed the opinion that it was not fixable. This had a knock-on effect: a limited central heating system existed within the castle but, given the poor water supply and the lack of electricity to power it, this could not be used either. Therefore, heating would have to come from open fires, primarily burning wood, or, to a lesser extent, coal. Lighting would have to be provided by oil lamps and candles.

Julius's group of seven busied themselves preparing the castle, despite the fact that there was no guarantee that their labours would be worthwhile as it still had not been formally handed over to them. They tirelessly worked at repairing pipes; installing small, internal water pumps to improve circulation and pressure; preparing additional latrines in the castle grounds; and collecting materials such as blankets and bedding.

Julius also made a point of contacting local religious ministers, by way of introducing himself and the proposed group of refugees. The reaction he received was more positive than he had dared hope and one reply included an invitation to meet with members of the Abergele Baptist Chapel. Julius accepted the offer and used the meeting to explain to them the concept of establishing a *Hachshara* at the castle, which was greeted by unexpected enthusiasm. The Baptists wanted to know how best they could assist the new arrivals at Gwrych. As a rule, *Hachsharot* declined charitable donations on the grounds that they were trying to develop self-sufficient communities that could solve problems for themselves. Developing resilience by putting up with hardships was all part of the training expectations and experience. However, the Baptists were earnest in their desire to help and Julius was a pragmatic man so he pointed out that furniture, beds, bedding, lights and candles would be particularly helpful – but, given that they had little themselves, he would be grateful for anything useful.

Edgar Jones, a builder from Abergele, was recruited to assist with some of the repairs that were beyond the skills of the preparation team and from then on, no doubt, the first rumours and questions began to circulate through the local community. Something unusual was going on up at Gwrych. Some locals assumed it had something to do with the preparations that were being made by the government in anticipation of a future conflict, which had become increasingly likely following the German invasion of Czechoslovakia that March. In fact, that same month, the Abergele Urban District Council had approved a proposal to begin converting the caves on the estate into air raid shelters following a report that 'the two lower ones would make a good shelter from high explosive bombs.'[41] Others may have thought that the work and activity at Gwrych was more closely tied to national evacuation preparations. Government publicity for 'Operation Pied Piper', their plans to evacuate tens of thousands of children from urban to rural areas in the event of war, was being issued throughout the summer of 1939 and Abergele was part of a region designated to receive evacuees if necessary. The town had been earmarked to receive nearly 1,400 evacuees if necessary.

On Thursday, 24 August, as the people of Abergele shared rumours and gossip about the activity at the castle, the Emergency Powers (Defence) Act received royal assent. Amongst many other things, the act gave the government the power to requisition property, and the temporary ownership of Gwrych was thus finally transferred over to it from Lord Dundonald. A few days later, on Monday, 28 August, Arieh Handler received confirmation that the government were willing to loan the castle to *Bachad* for free to be used to house Kindertransport children. Excited, Arieh immediately contacted Erwin Seligmann at Great Engeham Farm, instructing him to select an initial group of up to 100 children aged over fourteen to make the journey to Abergele. Erwin, however, was well ahead of the game, and had spent much of the last week drawing up his list in expectation of such an eventuality. To all intents and purposes he was ready to move a large group of children the moment he had the go-ahead and transport could be arranged.

Erwin's preparations were driven partly in response to the growing tensions between his group and the less orthodox groups at Great Engeham, but also by a much greater logic. The likelihood of war was growing and, if that happened, Operation Pied Piper would begin. This was likely to cause severe transport blockages and traffic disruption for a period, which could hamper any attempt to move a large group of refugee youngsters from Kent to Denbighshire. Therefore, he had decided to pre-empt possible trouble by being ready to go the moment he heard from Arieh that a large *Hachshara* site had been secured.

Erwin did not select his youngsters randomly and Arieh later confirmed that there was a process used so that only 'the best boys and girls'[42] were chosen. Erwin almost certainly made his choices based on his impressions of the strength of their Zionism and their suitability for *Aliyah*. Identifying them would have been relatively easy as, by the end of August 1939, most of those eventually selected had been at Great Engeham for at least a week or two – enough time for him, as an experienced *Vorbereitungslager* trainer, to observe some of their strengths and weaknesses. Of the group, about a third of those he chose for Gwrych were members of *Bachad/Bnei Akiva*, and about two thirds were members of Youth *Aliyah*. Most, if not all, of the chosen youngsters had also attended a *Vorbereitungslager* in Germany during the 1930s.[43]

It is also true to say that a fair few of the group selected by Erwin had family connections with prominent Zionists or had relatives who had already made *Aliyah* to Palestine. The strength of Zionism within the original Gwrych cohort was also noted by those who were to join it later. Mimi Schleissner, who came to Gwrych as a fourteen-year-old with a group from Llandough Castle in the summer of 1940, noted that the existing residents were far more religious, more orthodox, and more intent on *Aliyah* than those she was familiar with at Llandough. James Burke was a volunteer at Gwrych who had previously helped to run a small Jewish refugee centre called Barham House, near Ipswich in Suffolk. He also noted the Gwrych youth were more focused and driven than the refugees he had worked with at Barham who, in his opinion, were mostly just biding their time until they turned eighteen, when they could leave and get a job. 'On the whole, the stand work done here [at Gwrych] is higher than at Barh there is less need of supervision because it is done with a willing spirit. Barham House boys were not so politically conscious as the youth at Gwrych Castle.'[44]

There is another reason why Erwin chose a special group for Gwrych: Arieh Handler was a very important figure and although he was also involved in several other projects, this was to be his biggest and it could not afford to fail. Therefore, it is quite arguable that the group selected for Gwrych were a kind of 'elite' set – the flag-wavers for the flagship *Hachshara*, as it were. Imbued with a particularly strong sense of Zionism and sprinkled with a heavy dose of prior training and experience, they were chosen to be the best that *Bachad* and Youth *Aliyah* could offer.

Thus, on Monday, 28 August, the same day that Arieh was informed that Gwrych Castle could be used to house refugees, Erwin confirmed that the eighty-eight children he had selected from Great Engeham would soon be on their way. Amongst them were Jesse Zierler, Herman Rothman, Erich Roper, Wolfgang Billig, Henry Steinberg and Salli Edelnand.

Fourteen-year-old Jesse Zierler from Berlin was one of the tent-dwellers at Great Engeham. He had been earmarked for a Kindertransport in June 1939 but had ended up awaiting his turn at a Youth *Aliyah Vorbereitungslager* in Altona-Blankenese near Hamburg. In spite of the difficulties and upheavals of his young life, Jesse retained a cheeky personality that would later endear him to many at Gwrych Castle. Whilst he was stuck in limbo in Germany and, to pass the time, he and some of his new acquaintances set up a bogus reception committee to have a little fun at the expense of other new arrivals: 'In the guise of an official reception committee, we took down such personal details as what they wished to be served for breakfast, their favourite film stars, and did they possess the regulation number of legs.'[45]

Having finally arrived in Britain during August, Jesse had found himself waiting yet again at Great Engeham. There was very little to do there whilst awaiting notification of a permanent move, and Jesse later remembered whiling away his time participating in childish pranks and other nefarious activities:

There seemed nothing but tents, hundreds of them. And hundreds of children who all ignored our arrival. Ten of us boys were directed to a small tent with ample room to sleep six. Night time brought the inevitable pillow fight. The night patrol outside managed to bring our battle to an abrupt end, pulling out the ground pegs of our tent, which then collapsed. We learned how to erect a tent at night in less than two hours, and too exhausted for further battle fell asleep. The following night saw a repeat performance with very much the same result. On the third night, quite undeterred by punitive measures so far handed out, we planned our counteraction. At the first sign of tent walls slackening, we grabbed hold of the tent pole which now remained upright. After a good ten minutes it became quite clear that none of us was going to get any sleep standing squashed against the pole and by a majority vote we decided to let go. We had become quite expert at erecting our tent in the dark.[46]

At Great Engeham, Jesse encountered the tall and somewhat gangly Herman Rothman, a fellow Berliner and also aged fourteen. This marked the beginning of a friendship that would strengthen at Gwrych Castle. Herman and his family had been spared the direct horror of *Kristallnacht* due to a tip-off from a friendly local police officer relating to the violence that was about to be unleashed, and they had hastily ensured that they were out of the city when events unfolded. However, the young Herman saw the effects upon his return: 'We came back and travelled through Berlin and we saw the havoc that was made of Jewish property. We saw the shops with their glass destroyed and everything looted from these shops. It was a dreadful sight for a child to see all this.'[47]

Herman's uncle, who was married to a German, was arrested and taken to Dachau shortly after *Kristallnacht*, along with nearly 11,000 other Jews. Used as a training centre for SS concentration camp guards, those incarcerated at Dachau experienced violence and intimidation until such time as they could prove that they had made arrangements to emigrate from Germany. Herman's uncle was released prior to his departure for Argentina. His father, a leading Berlin Zionist, somehow initially avoided detention and became actively involved in assisting fellow Jews to leave Germany for Palestine. The family discussed leaving themselves but his father wished to stay to continue his work in helping others.[48] However, he agreed that his two sons should leave the country, a decision encouraged by the family's many non-Jewish German friends. The young Herman had no idea about how his parents had arranged Kindertransport for him but he quite looked forward to it, confident that 'I would see my parents again and everything was fine.'[49]

Herman's journey followed the established template for Kinder-transport refugees of boarding a ferry at the Hook of Holland and he disembarked at Harwich on 24 August 1939. Herman found the jour-ney enjoyable. 'We had a lovely time. We told jokes … I wasn't seasick and I was very happy. Everything was fine and everything looked very promising for me. I had no idea what was in store.'[50]

Herman and his group then travelled to Liverpool Street Station where, to his amazement, 'I saw something I had never seen before. I'd never seen Jewish taxi drivers. In Germany they didn't exist. But in England apparently every Jew seemed to be a taxi driver! They spoke a little Yiddish and I was absolutely surprised how a Jew could be a taxi driver. Everything looked different in England.'[51] From Liverpool Street Station, Herman was relocated to Great Engeham Farm to await a permanent placement.

Erich Roper, a fifteen-year-old Austrian from Vienna, had also ar-rived at Great Engeham from a Kindertransport in August 1939. The short, plumpish Erich, with a mat of thick, floppy, dark hair, had also been taken aback to see Jewish taxi drivers at Liverpool Street Station, especially as one of them unintentionally scared the life out of him. In a broad cockney accent one of the taxi drivers asked Erich, 'Did you come here today?' Erich could speak English quite well but the accent threw him and he heard the question as 'Did you come here to die?'

36

'No,' Erich replied adamantly, 'I came here to live!'[52]

Housed in one of Great Engeham's disused railway carriages, with engraved windows reading 'Non-smokers' or 'Ladies',[53] was fourteen-year-old Wolfgang Billig, from Mannheim in southern Germany. Two weeks before *Kristallnacht*, on 28 October 1938, some 17,000 Jews of Polish descent had been arrested and deported to the German–Polish border as part of 'Operation *Polenaktion*'. Wolfgang's father was amongst them. He could not have known at the time, but Wolfgang would never see him again. On *Kristallnacht* itself, he had witnessed the synagogue in his hometown burn, and watched as the fire engines stood by, not there to quell the blaze but to guard against neighbouring properties being affected by the flames.

Wolfgang had previously attended a six-week agricultural course at a *Vorbereitungslager* as a member of *Bnei Akiva*, the youth wing of *Bachad*, and was thus readily selected for Kindertransport when his mother applied. 'It was a very complex operation, with many organisations working to send children. I was fortunate to be selected for this.'[54] With the benefit of hindsight, he later thought that the selection process was somewhat arbitrary: 'There was someone in each town who played God and they decided who goes and I was chosen and I came.'[55]

At the time, Wolfgang viewed his departure with mixed emotions. As he stood on the railway station platform on 25 July 1939 he was sad but also optimistic and, like Herman, a little excited about his future. However, his departure was ultimately a deeply traumatic moment and something he reflected on long and hard in future years:

> You must imagine a mother sending her only child to England. All she knew is that I was going to England with some youth organisation, not where, not how, not what. It was about under four weeks before the outbreak of World War Two and Jews knew what was coming, because there was six years of experience before that. Put yourself into the shoes of a parent who sent their children out knowing

full well that war is imminent and they would probably not see them again. In fact, and I would say ninety-nine-point-something per cent of children who went with the Kindertransport ... never saw their parents again. You know there were some younger children who said 'What have I done to my mummy and daddy, that they are sending me away? I was a good girl, I was a good boy, why am I sent away?' Can you imagine the cruelty? In the process of being kind it was cruel.[56]

For Wolfgang, the journey to Britain went well and, like others, he was struck by his first experience of his new host country. 'I had never seen pure white sliced bread before and remember distinctly that I told the server that "I don't eat cake for breakfast." That, I hope, may one day be the title of a book if I get round to finishing it.'[57]

Although it would never be published, a young man who did one day manage to finish writing his book was Heinrich Steinberg. Aged sixteen and from Berlin, the blonde-haired Steinberg chose to anglicise his first name to Henry upon his arrival in Britain. Like many others destined for Gwrych, Henry had attended courses at a *Vorbereitungslager* on two occasions during 1939 as a member of *Bachad*. Along with his siblings, his parents then signed him up for Kindertransport, and he left on 20 August 1939. 'I remember my father taking me to the railway station, giving me a hug and a kiss and soon I was caught up in the group of kids who travelled, like me, to England. I knew some of them from my circle of friends, like Adi Better, others from *Hachshara* like Sali Steinbock, who happened to be a friend of Harry Gable.[58] Sali saw Harry ... and yelled "Hey Srullik (Harry's nickname), I want you to meet a new friend of mine." Harry and I have been friends since then.'[59]

Unlike some of the younger travellers, Henry had a clearer political awareness of what his journey meant. He and his group 'just pretty much sat muted and exhausted until we came to the Dutch border.'[60] The crossing of the German border into Holland was a huge relief and invisible tensions drained rapidly from Henry and his group of friends: 'once we were on Dutch soil, we carried on like a bunch of wild monkeys. We slapped each other, hugged, danced, laughed, sang, gathered for prayers, and so on.'[61] Worn out by the whole experience, he then fell asleep on the ferry to Harwich and when he woke up he was in England.

Like a number of refugee children, Henry had a sibling – his younger brother, Emil – who had already arrived in Britain on an earlier transport. And for these children contacting their brothers and sisters upon arrival was a high priority. This was made very difficult by their lack of understanding of their new surroundings and, in many cases, complicated by the language barrier. Henry recalled, 'We were bussed to London where I tried to phone Emil. The operator told me there was no reply. At least I think that is what she said. I did not know any English at the time.'[62]

While in London, Henry and his friends were taken to a restaurant where some locals spoke Yiddish. He recalled how his friend 'Harry was in good spirits and tried to convince people they were related.'[63] Within another twenty-four hours, Henry and his friends, Harry and Adi, were sat in a tent at Great Engeham wondering what their future might hold. For all three, the answer was to be Gwrych Castle.

Salli Edelnand, aged fourteen and from Halberstadt in Germany, had also been fortunate to travel to Britain and to Great Engeham with some friends that he had made at the *Hazkarat Zebi* School in Halberstadt, the only private Jewish elementary school in the former province of Saxony. David Kowalski and Bertel Karmiol arrived with him at Great Engeham in August and they would also go on to be with him at Gwrych Castle. All that Salli possessed had been stuffed into a small suitcase: some clothes, a few family photographs, a couple of books, a bar of soap that his mother had insisted upon him including, and a silver timepiece made by his watchmaker father, which would turn out to be his only inheritance from a family that would be destroyed in the Holocaust. Salli would later recall sitting in one of the large tents in 'a field in the middle of nowhere', contemplating his new life. 'Little did

I guess what was in store for me in a new land when I waved goodbye to my parents and twelve-year-old sister, never to see them again.'[64]

When Erwin Seligmann set about letting his chosen group know that they were shortly to be on the move, the news was greeted with universal delight. Salli was full of excitement: '"A real castle," I thought, "it cannot be true."'[65]

Meanwhile, at the 'real castle', Dr Julius Handler and his team, now bolstered by the arrival of a few more volunteers, were not at all ready to receive their new charges despite all the work they had put in over the last week or two. A stock of basic food supplies and beds were on order but they were not due to arrive for several days. The building itself was still run-down, devoid of any furniture bar a broken table, and short of many other basics. But time had run out; the children were on the way.

Seligmann's swift action and efficiency had surprised everyone. And so, ready or not, the Gwrych Castle *Hachshara* – officially now named the North Wales Agricultural Training School – was, as of 28 August 1939, open for business.

CHAPTER 3

'On a dark night'

30 August–6 September 1939
Arrival at Gwrych Castle

On Wednesday, 30 August 1939, Osias Findling, aged seventeen and from Leipzig, was stood in a field in Kent having an argument with an English truck driver about his suitcase. Known by most people as Ossi, he spoke good English so was able, to a certain extent, to give the driver as good as he got. The other eighty-seven suitcases piled up beside the wagon appeared to be no problem, but the driver had taken exception to the size of Ossi's. Somehow, unlike most Kindertransport youngsters, when Ossi arrived in Britain in July 1939, he had managed to bring with him an unwieldy and oversized wooden suitcase full of personal belongings including books and even a feather duvet.

Following the news that Gwrych Castle could be used to house refugees, Erwin Seligmann had moved quickly and hired a large truck to transport the belongings of the eighty-eight children he had selected to move there. To accompany the suitcases, Seligmann had also selected an 'advance guard' of ten of the older boys to sit in the truck and help to unload them upon arrival in Abergele. It promised to be a very long and uncomfortable journey, with heavy work to do at the end of it. Ossi had been chosen for this dubious honour, though he would have gladly passed up on it if only he could have found a way to get out of it. And now, to make his mood worse, the driver was pointing at his belongings and shouting at him, 'I'm not taking this. I'm only taking suitcases!'[66] All that Ossi possessed that connected him to a family torn apart was inside that case and there was no way he was going to leave it behind. He later recalled his journey to this night: 'My father was not a German citizen. On the night before *Kristallnacht*, he was arrested by the Gestapo. That was the last I saw of my father.'[67] Shortly afterwards, his mother signed him up for the Kindertransport, but not his sibling. 'She wouldn't put my brother down because, she said, "I don't want to lose both my sons on one day."'[68]

He was, therefore, in no mood to back down and, after a few heated words, the driver finally relented and Ossi heaved his case onto the back of the wagon. When interviewed many years later, he did concede that the driver had had a point; it was less of a suitcase and more of a large, wooden chest and, in fact, 'it was quite big'.[69]

That Wednesday afternoon, Ossi and the 'advance guard' departed from Great Engeham to begin their 300-mile trek to Abergele. They were waved off by the main group who were excitedly looking forward to their turn for departure. To their delight, Erwin told them that he had hired two buses and that they would be arriving from North Wales the very next day.

At almost exactly the same time, one of the last Kinderstransport groups to arrive before the war broke out was disembarking at Harwich. They were met by Erich Duchinsky, a Youth *Aliyah* worker who regularly escorted new groups by bus to Liverpool Street Station or Great Engeham Farm. However, he had received some very fresh and unusual instructions. He was to take a bus load of forty children to a wholly new and unknown destination: Gwrych Castle in North Wales.

Also at the same time, although nobody could have known it, the very final Kindertransport to successfully make it safely out of mainland Europe was just setting off in Germany. On it were thirty-one young people whose destiny would also take them to Gwrych Castle.

Amongst them was fifteen-year-old Henry Glanz, the teenager who would, some five weeks later, go window-shopping in Abergele. Born as Hersch Glanz in Kolonia, Poland, in 1924, his family had shortly afterwards migrated to Kiel in Germany which had a small Jewish population of just over 500. To help her young son to fit in better, his mother had chosen a German name to put on his school entry application and thus Hersch became Heinrich Glanz.

The effect of Hitler's accession to power in 1933 hit Kiel quickly and in that same year, when Glanz was just nine years old, two Jewish lawyers in the city were murdered. *Kristallnacht* in 1938 saw the arrest of around twenty per cent of the Jewish male population of Kiel, many of whom were sent to the concentration camp at Sachsenhausen. At this time, Nazi interest was mainly focused on Jewish men rather than women and children and, fearing for his safety, Glanz's father had fled from Kiel and made his way to Belgium and the sanctuary of relatives. It was hoped that his wife, Esther, and three children would secure permission to join him there soon. However, emigration for the family to Belgium proved impossible to arrange and, in the wake of *Kristallnacht*, the persecution of the Jews that remained in Kiel grew ever more serious. Collectively, their property was confiscated and all were forced into 'Jew houses', an early form of ghetto.

Fearing for her children's future, Esther Glanz arranged to get Heinrich on a kibbutzim project in Palestine and she also applied for places on Kindertransport for her two youngest children. However, in early August 1939, Heinrich's visa was cancelled due to British restrictions being placed on immigrant numbers to Palestine, so his mother rapidly switched his name over to the Kindertransport lists. In mid-August, eleven-year-old Gisela Glanz departed for Britain and, just over a week later, it was Heinrich's turn. He had already decided that he would cast off his Germanic name; he was going to Britain and so he would have a British one. He settled on Henry.

Clutching his single suitcase of belongings and accompanied by all that remained of his family in Germany, his mother and ten-year-old brother Joachim, Henry arrived nervously at Kiel train station on the evening of 30 August 1939. There, they were met by Nazi officials who refused to let anyone other than Kindertransportees on to the railway platform. Henry was forced into making his tearful goodbyes at the station entrance. He turned to his mother: 'I was feeling very sad and I asked how soon before she would come. We knew the situation was dangerous but we didn't actually know that there was going to be a war.'[70]

Henry, like the rest of the world, could have had no idea at the time that his Kindertransport was to be the last to successfully escape Germany before the war began. His brother Joachim's turn would never come and his sister was the only family member he would see again. Less than a month later, both Esther and Joachim were deported to a concentration camp near Leipzig. In May 1942, they were moved to the Majdanek extermination camp in Poland. His father was arrested in Belgium after the Nazi invasion in 1940 and he was sent to Auschwitz in October 1942. All of them were killed in the Holocaust.

On the same Kindertransport as Henry Glanz was fourteen-year-old Manfred Alweiss. Manfred was a member of Youth *Aliyah* through whom his mother had belatedly booked a Kindertransport for both him and his younger sister. For a long time, she had viewed Hitler 'as a temporary phenomenon, whose bark would prove to be worse than his bite',[71] but her opinion had changed dramatically after *Kristallnacht* and she began exploring ways of getting her children to safety. By the summer of 1939, Manfred and his sister had already been listed for two transports that had both been cancelled at the last minute, but then, 'In the fourth week of August we were notified that a transport would be organised after all, although only for a reduced number of children. The list included my name but, to our consternation, my sister was not on it.'[72]

Rather than just relying on the space in a suitcase, Manfred had also thought to cram a few extra belongings into a rucksack. During his experience of a course at a Youth *Aliyah Vorbereitungslager*, he had been given some advice, that proved to be somewhat dubious, on what to pack: 'This included a pair of German jackboots. On arrival in

England I was advised to hide these immediately because they would be anathema to English people with memories of the German Army in World War One.'[73]

Like Henry Glanz, Manfred had to say goodbye to his mother and sister outside of Kiel station before he was allowed anywhere near the train. 'Although the thought did not occur to me at the time, and to most of us, it proved to be the last farewell.'[74] The train was packed but the Kindertransportees had reserved seats and Manfred was surprised to find that he and some others had been allocated seats in a rather comfortable compartment.

> This was all the more surprising because the gangways were packed with German army personnel who had to stand (for a long night journey) and who were being mobilised for the conflict which their leadership had evidently already planned. After a while the door of our compartment was opened by a German Army officer who asked, very politely, whether there was a vacant seat, which we affirmed with some trepidation. We soon got talking to him and he turned out to be a sympathetic person. He expressed his great regret that we were made to flee. After this, on this long night journey to Cologne, I fell asleep on his shoulder! A pleasant memory of my last personal contact with a German before the war.[75]

The train was stopped in Cologne where the passengers were inspected by Nazi officials. They would not allow the Kindertransport children to remain on board and cross into Holland, so the children were thrown off and had to spend the night in a Jewish Youth Hostel whilst the organisers and a Dutch refugee charity frantically tried to resolve the impasse.

As Henry Glanz and Manfred Alweiss tried get some sleep in their hostel in the early hours of Thursday, 31 August, the lorry carrying Ossi Findling and the 'advance guard' rumbled up to Gwrych Castle in darkness. It had been a very long, extremely uncomfortable and dull journey and the already grumpy Ossi was not at all impressed with the first view of his new home as he climbed down from the wagon. He was even less impressed when he went inside: 'The castle hadn't been used for about thirty years. The dust was so high it went up to your ankles. We arrived about five o'clock in the morning. We slept on the bare floor but we had to move the dust to find a place to sleep,' he recalled sixty-one years later.[76] Given that Dr Julius Handler and his group had been actively working on preparing the place for well over a week, it was probably not quite as bad as he described, but the fact that he remembered it thus does indicate that the castle was far from ready to receive its new inhabitants.

As Ossi Findling tried to get some sleep, the final Kindertransport group, currently marooned in a hostel near Cologne, were being woken. Manfred Alweiss recalled that 'a courageous lady (a gentile) from the Dutch refugee committee' had turned up with two buses that could take them over the border.

> She personally took charge of us. When we reached the [Dutch] frontier we were confronted by a frontier guard who stood, somewhat dramatically, in the middle of the road, with his rifle raised as if he was about to fire at us. Our plucky lady protector got out and showed our transit papers to the guard. After some consultation, he waved us through, shouting, '*Judenkinder*' (Jew kids) to his comrades. I will never forget the immense feeling of relief which swept through the bus the moment we crossed the border.[77]

On the evening of that Thursday, as the final Kindertransport group raced to the Hook of Holland, the main group of children at Great Engeham also began setting off for their new home. As Erwin Seligmann had promised, two chartered buses had arrived from North Wales, both sporting the green livery of the Crossville bus company that dominated the local transport sector. Accompanied by Seligmann himself, the seventy-eight remaining children excitedly, if nervously, climbed aboard the buses and set off.

At about midnight, as the Crossville buses were making their way through the Midlands, the final Kindertransport group arrived at the Hook of Holland in a very low mood. The delays on their journey had been significant and the final part had been completed by bus rather than the much faster train, so the expectation was that they had arrived too late and had missed the ferry. To their huge surprise, however, the ship was still moored in its berth. The captain had voluntarily delayed his departure by an hour and a half to give them a final chance of getting out of mainland Europe. Had he not done so, it is likely that Henry Glanz, Manfred Alweiss and most of those children on that transport would have perished at the hands of the Nazis during the next few years. Just after midnight, in the early hours of Friday, 1 September 1939, their ferry finally set sail for Britain.

At about the same time, Duchinsky's group of forty children that had been rerouted directly from Harwich finally arrived at Gwrych Castle. Their long and extremely tedious cross-country journey had somehow taken over twenty-four hours and the children were mostly fast asleep when they got there. This was perhaps just as well, for their arrival at their new home was anticlimactic to say the least. Neither Dr Julius Handler's preparation group nor Ossi Findling's advance guard were awake to greet them and neither Duchinsky nor his driver could find their way into the castle. As he recalled:

> The driver banged on the gate, but we couldn't make ourselves heard. So then someone climbed over the gate and found the caretaker, who said that we were at the wrong place and that we had to go to the main gate to be let in. The caretaker was very grumpy at being woken up and we were not made to feel at all welcome. On a dark night, Gwrych was a forbidding place with its high walls and towers and narrow slit windows. Very cold and very gloomy.[78]

As the castle's annoyed caretaker, Bill Price, slid back into his bed, at around 1.40 a.m., shots were being exchanged hundreds of miles away at a German–Polish border point; World War Two was beginning.

A few hours after the arrival of Duchinsky's group, at somewhere between 2 and 3 a.m. on Friday, 1 September 1939, Erwin Seligmann's two Crossville buses arrived in Abergele. It was very dark and a thick fog lay about. Unwittingly, the lead driver missed the main entrance to the castle but, several hundred yards later, pulled over at the Hen Gwrych Lodge near Ty Crwn, Gwrych's old bathing house. The confused children soon found themselves walking along a beach. Realising that an error had been made, Erwin called them back to the buses and they drove around for a little while longer until the drivers finally found the correct entrance. A few weeks later, Seligmann wrote to friends and recalled his initial thoughts upon arrival: 'When our bus reached the main gate, an enormously high tower appeared in view, jutting out of the dark fog at night. We were reminded of one of those towers in the Middle Ages, where the unfortunate prisoners were kept starving.'[79]

At the castle, the new arrivals were greeted with offers of a mysterious concoction that two of the refugees later described as a 'fruit soup' in a cup. Most were grateful, though one of the recipients, fourteen-year-old Sonia Marder, was so disgusted by the fact that the cups were not very clean that she refused to drink it. She was probably further riled when the group were shown to the dining room and told to bed down on the hard floor until dawn. Few actually managed to sleep.

At the same time as Seligmann's group were being offered soup, German Stuka dive bombers were going into action over Poland. Simultaneously, the next Kindertransport was being intercepted by Nazi officials before it reached the Dutch border. None of the children on board made it to Britain. Meanwhile, the ferry with what was now the final Kindertransport group, including Henry Glanz and Manfred Alweiss, was arriving at Harwich. As the tired youngsters disembarked and then travelled onwards to Liverpool Street Station, they began to hear the first rumours that Germany was invading Poland. Manfred noticed that the station in London 'was crowded with evacuees': Operation Pied Piper had already begun to swing into action. He also noticed 'soldiers putting up sandbags'.[80] Manfred, along with Henry Glanz and thirty others of the group were singled out and directed towards a waiting bus. 'We were told that we would immediately proceed to a holding camp in Wales.'[81] Many hours later, at just after midnight on Saturday, 2 September, after a fraught and epic journey across Europe to Britain, they finally arrived in Abergele.

Thanks to the foresight of Erwin Seligmann, and some huge slices of good fortune, the eighty-eight young Jews from Great Engeham, along with seventy-one other children who had arrived on two separate Kindertransports, had all arrived in Abergele safely ahead of any potential disruption to their plans caused by the evacuation programme. Joining them, to help oversee the *Hachshara*, were around fifty young adults, taking the total number at the castle to around 209.

The arrivals had all happened so quickly, and mostly in darkness, so the folk of Abergele had little or no idea that something hugely significant had happened up at the castle. In addition to this, the arrangements had been made privately between Arieh Handler and his associates, the government and Lord Dundonald. The town's focus was thus on the impending arrival of 'a large number of evacuees' due on the Sunday and Monday who, by contrast, received a planned welcome. Arraigned to greet the evacuees was Squire Jacob, the Chairman of the Urban District Council, several councillors and other local worthies, members of the Women's Voluntary Service, a charabanc and over a hundred locals who owned cars, keen to help deliver the 'little ones' to their new billets.[82]

Thus, it was probably with considerable bemusement that a local farm labourer encountered a young Jewish refugee on Saturday, 2 September in what was almost certainly the first encounter between Jew and Gentile in Abergele.

Salli Edelnand had arrived at Gwrych in the early hours of Friday morning as part of Erwin Seligmann's group and just over twenty-four hours later the fourteen-year-old took himself off to explore some of the paths around the castle. Unintentionally, he emerged from the estate at the Nant-y-Bella lodge. Passing by the lodge, he found himself on the winding Tan-y-Gopa Road that runs uphill towards farms and downhill towards the town of Abergele. He knew neither of these things, but chose to continue his exploration by walking downhill. After a brief while, Salli noticed a man walking up the road directly towards him from the direction of the town, wearing wellington boots and chewing tobacco. He recalled the exchange later.

> 'I must practise my English,' I muttered to myself, having learned the language for a short period in the private Jewish school in Germany. 'Goot mornink,' I said in a very crude German accent. He looked at me and after a pause said, '*Bore da, boi bach. Sut 'dachi heddiw?*' [83] to my utter amazement, not realising at the time that Wales existed with its own language and culture.[84]

What Wil Davies, the tobacco-chewing man in the wellies, on his way to work at Tyddyn-uchaf Farm, thought of somebody speaking with a German accent in Abergele is unknown, though he was probably equally as befuddled as the young Salli. However, this seemingly trivial story, and the simple, friendly words exchanged between the two, serve to encapsulate the wider nature of the relationship that was about to blossom between town and castle. The young Jews were curious and desirous to know more, not just about Britain, but also about Abergele and the Welsh, and the folk of Abergele would accept the new foreign refugees on their doorstep with casual equanimity and, in some cases, as friends.

Whilst Salli was accidentally finding his way off of the Gwrych estate, his new colleagues spent much of the day of 2 September taking stock of their new home. 'An enormous, big castle' was how the young Herman Rothman simply remembered his first sight of it.[85] Jesse Zierler was captivated by a building that was actually far younger than he at first thought and, given his sleepless nights on rough ground at

Great Engeham, he was delighted: 'No more collapsing tents! Walls at least fourteen inches thick that had stood for centuries gave us a sense of reassurance.'[86] Wolfgang Billig was also very impressed by his new surroundings, but not for long: 'It was a wonderful castle. It was beautiful, lawns down to the Irish Sea. Lambing I could see. But inside was rotten. We had no sanitation and I don't want to talk about it, because it was awful.'[87] He also quickly discovered that nothing worked: 'There was no electricity and an old generator was broken beyond repair. To call the toilets WCs would have been a misnomer, because the sanitation and drainage system was severely blocked.'[88]

Celia Kreisel, aged sixteen, was disappointed with her new home. 'It was an empty place, an empty castle, very big. And we had very primitive things. And we had orange boxes as tables. And we made do.'[89] Fifteen-year-old Ruth Kessel from Leipzig, who had travelled to Gwrych with Seligmann's group, was utterly delighted and amazed to see her best friend amongst the final group of arrivals and the pair excitedly explored their new home together, only to discover that 'it was a draughty, dilapidated old building … in the middle of nowhere' with very basic facilities.[90]

Unlike Ruth and her friend, Henry Glanz was less interested in exploring on his first day at the castle: he was absolutely shattered. He had arrived at Gwrych in the early hours of that morning, having travelled all the way from Kiel to Abergele as part of the stressful and, as it turned out, final Kindertransport. Apart from a few hours overnight in a hostel near Cologne, he had spent the last couple of days on a combination of trains, ferries and buses, catching sleep but rarely. He felt the desperate need to have a wash, and he was now extremely grateful for his mother's nagging insistence on him packing a bar of soap, but he could find no hot water anywhere in the building to use it. However, it was a bright, warm day, and not far away was the sea, clearly visible from just about anywhere in the castle. He noticed that a number of his fellow refugees had already headed off down to the beach and he decided to join them and bathe, though it took him several frustrating minutes to learn that soap does not work in salt water.

Others wandered around the castle grounds or walked up into the woods on the hillside behind the castle, to take in the magnificent views, whilst one or two of the braver ones, like Salli, dared go beyond the estate boundaries to get a tantalising glimpse of nearby Abergele.

Despite the novelty of their new surroundings, the mood amongst the community was extremely low. Sonia Marder, who had refused her soup due to a dirty cup, recalled that she and her friend spent their first day at Gwrych, and in fact most of the next two weeks, 'pretty much crying. We couldn't look at each other. Every time she looked at me, every time our eyes met, we burst into tears, so finally we decided to turn away from each other.'[91]

There was also not enough food to go around, only what Dr Julius Handler's team had managed to stockpile and a number of items that Erwin Seligmann had loaded onto his buses. To make matters worse there was no easy means of heating food up as, thus far, there had been no success at all in getting the kitchen stove to work. That night, the new community slept once again on bare floors, though a number who had sensibly spent some of the day collecting hay from fields on the estate to fashion for themselves a rudimentary mattress found their beds slightly softened.

On Sunday, 3 September, with Hitler ignoring Prime Minister Neville Chamberlain's ultimatum for him to withdraw from Poland, Britain declared war. Initially, the news spread amongst a small group of the refugees, in the form of a rumour, apparently picked up from Bill Price, the castle's caretaker. However, most of them knew nothing of the news until later that evening when, under the guise of a roll call, Arieh Handler called the community together on the castle forecourt by its main entrance, and broke the news to them. In kind with people across the country, this had a sobering effect on the group at the castle, though they had many reasons for it to cut far deeper.

For some of them, like Wolfgang Billig, the news shattered any belief that they would soon be with their families again. 'My hopes to be soon reunited with my mother who was waiting for the papers to come to England as a domestic servant, were dashed on a day when we all assembled in the square outside the castle's main entrance and Arieh Handler told us that war had broken out and that it may be quite some time before we shall see our parents again.'[92]

Erich Roper captured the mood that the announcement generated amongst the refugees:

> On the forecourt of the castle we came together. We had no eyes for the beautiful picture that nature offered us. We were not savouring the beautiful autumn forest in which our castle was located, we did not go to play in the waves of the ocean that stretched out before us. Our thoughts were with those left behind in Germany, what impact the political events would have on them. It was an unforgettable evening for us. Some were crying, some were serious. The setting sun framed us, it was a glorious evening.[93]

Not all of the refugees shared the sombre mood of the majority. For some, such as Ruth Kessel, 'the news made us really happy. We felt that finally someone was standing up to Hitler.' She and her friend 'rushed down to Abergele to see what was going on, and we found people piling up sandbags.'[94]

That night, many could not sleep, and it was not just because their stomachs were rumbling or because of the bare, hard floors that they had to lie on.

The next day was a tough one for all at the castle. Most were dispirited and deeply anxious about family and loved ones back home. On top of this, they were in a foreign country about which they knew next to nothing, extremely hungry and thoroughly exhausted through lack of sleep. For those who had come from Great Engeham there was a growing feeling that they had traded downwards; the conditions at the farm had not been great but their new home was 'awful' with little in the way of home comforts. By contrast, that same day, the evacuees to the town 'were treated with every consideration and kindness and many residents were not long in unfolding their generosity to the extent of purchasing new clothing and footwear for their young charges.'[95]

Despite these problems and the devastating news of the outbreak of war, there nevertheless remained a naive optimism amongst a few of the refugees that the conflict, and thus their stay at Gwrych Castle, might not be for too long. Herman Rothman was one of these and recalled, 'Children of my age did not understand the full impact of war. It's an experience you learn very much the hard way. For most of us, we thought in any case it's not going to last very long. Two or three months and then there would be peace and everything will be back to normal. That's the impression you have.'[96]

Latching onto this faint and rapidly dwindling optimism, Erwin Seligmann asked David Granek to begin organising the youngsters into working parties and form a more coordinated approach towards the general work of tidying and cleaning the castle in order to make it habitable. This was important, partly because it would give the youngsters something to do to take their minds off things, but also because it was by now apparent to all of them that, regardless of all the efforts made by Julius Handler and despite the outer grandeur of the building and the beauty of their surroundings, their new home was nothing but a dirty, run-down shell. Erwin noted at the time that 'in the beginning there was a lot to be done here. We had to work non-stop from morning till evening to clean inside the castle. This was hard work … We found the rooms in a badly neglected state.'[97]

Many of the children must also have felt extremely lonely, for initially most knew very little of their fellow refugees. This is confirmed by the recollections of Ruth Glasser, a Polish Jew who had arrived in Britain on a Kindertransport earlier that year. Having turned nineteen, she had been found employment by a Jewish agency as a domestic servant at Hendre Bach Farm in Abergele. With no English language skills at all, she was delighted to hear of the arrival of fellow German speaking Jews in Abergele. She made a point of introducing herself and consequently got to know the castle community well. She later commented that, 'The refugees were complete strangers to one another. There were some who spoke only Polish, some came from Latvia and others from Czechoslovakia. The dominant common factor was that all had escaped from Nazi persecution and found a refuge in Abergele.'[98] Although the youngsters spoke a number of languages, any visitor to the castle would have heard German and Yiddish spoken most commonly; the latter was especially prominent on a Saturday, the Jewish Sabbath.

Erwin Seligmann was now, to all intents and purposes, in charge at the castle, at least until Arieh Handler appointed more permanent leaders. He recognised the need for new friendships and bonds to be formed quickly, for the sake of all at Gwrych but also for the sake of establishing the *Hachshara* and developing the project's wider ambitions.

> The crucial thing for a teenager, when he went to a *Hachshara*, was that he left the bounds of the family, for the first time, left his parents, became a member of a community that was wider than the family, but not more binding. There were suddenly quite different laws and other forces that determined him as a person. As soon as one knew his place in the family, one had to conquer his place within the new community. By this, one became more self-sufficient, more mature, ready for *Eretz Yisrael*.[99]

A few of the refugees knew familiar faces from home or had made friends on the Kindertransport. Some fledgling friendships had formed at Great Engeham, such as the one between Jesse Zierler and Herman Rothman. However, most found themselves quite lonely and the hardships that the group were facing were creating strains rather than bonds.

Despite a more structured day, the community once again went to bed that Monday night on hard floors strewn with hay and, once again, they were hungry. It was not clear how much longer this could be sustained. For some of them, it was less than a week since they had slept in their own bed, under the roof of their own family. For others, no matter how uncomfortable the tents and railway carriages had been at Great Enge-ham, they were cushy compared to Gwrych. There was a widespread feeling that the Gwrych *Hachshara* was not really working out.

The following morning, Tuesday, 5 September, the youngsters, like soulless automatons, settled once again into their various cleaning and tidying groups. They had not been at it for very long when everything changed. A convoy of lorries lumbered up to the castle, sporting the livery of Marks and Spencer. The trucks had almost certainly been arranged by Rebecca Sieff, who had helped lobby the British government for *Bachad* to be granted use of the castle just over a week earlier. The lorries were loaded to the brim with all of the bed-frames, mattresses and bedding that the *Hachshara* needed, and one was packed full of food. The refugees fell over themselves to assist in unloading the trucks, moving from one to the other as if they couldn't decide which one to empty first.

Fifty rooms in the main building of the castle had finally been iden-tified and settled upon as bedrooms, even though many of them had damp walls and were not ideal for the purpose. Each was expected, dependent on their size, to accommodate around eight of the young-sters, though in reality many ended up accommodating nearer ten. Boys were allotted the rooms on the top floor and the girls on the floor beneath. Hauling dozens of bed frames and mattresses and carrying bundles of heavy bedding up numerous staircases was tough on the tired community, but the task was carried out with great enthusiasm in the expectation of finally getting a good and comfortable night's sleep.

That Tuesday was to get even better when representatives of the Ab-ergele Baptist Chapel, with whom Julius Handler had met a week or so earlier, appeared at the castle's entrance with several horse-drawn carts overflowing with donations, including a huge collection of benches, tables and kitchen appliances. A group of delighted and grateful youngsters, now no longer apparently tired, swarmed to the carts and began transferring the items inside. As they bade goodbye, the chapel representatives promised to bring much more in the coming weeks.

As if the day could not get any better, Arieh Handler received the wonderful news that another large consignment of furniture items was on the way from London, having been collected and donated by a variety of refugee committees, charities and the Quaker community.

The mood amongst everyone in the castle that night, for the first time since their arrival, was joyous. Prayers were offered in thanks and, with smiles on their faces and with full bellies, the young refugees happily went to bed, some of them early, to try out their new mattresses. Wolfgang Billig remembered that evening as the one when, finally, 'the castle came alive.'[100]

The final group of residents appeared the following day – Wednesday, 6 September. A bus containing another forty-three children, accompanied by two adult assistants, arrived at Gwrych. The children had been selected for transfer from the reception centre at Llandough Castle, near Cowbridge in South Wales. This took the total number of people now at the castle to around 254. This group, it appears, had not been entirely expected and almost immediately there were shortages of everything once again. Erwin Seligmann was dismayed by the temporary setback: 'There were not enough beds and not enough mattresses. Three boys had to sleep on two mattresses. Life was pretty painful.'[101] It would be another two weeks before hastily requested extra beds and mattresses arrived to make up the required numbers (though quite a number of them were double beds requiring many of the youngsters to permanently share sleeping arrangements). However, the mood had lifted so significantly that this was all seen as a minor problem. Had the Llandough group arrived just two days earlier they may have been the straw that broke the camel's back.

CHAPTER 4

'I wanted to do something useful'

September 1939 (Part 1)
Establishing the Gwrych *Hachshara*

For Erwin Seligmann and the Handler brothers, Tuesday, 5 September 1939 changed everything. The entire *Hachshara* project had begun in an understandable rush but, in truth, it had also begun very badly and, given the state of the castle and the lack of basic amenities, it had almost reached the point of collapse. However, the two hundred children they had planned for (henceforth referred to as the *noar*, to differentiate them from their youthful but adult volunteer helpers) had been successfully assembled and they had accumulated some of the essential necessities. The group's leaders could now turn their attention towards getting on with the task of establishing the basic tenets of Britain's largest *Hachshara*.

In addition to the *noar*, a large number of around fifty young adults had also arrived at Gwrych Castle by the end of the first week of September 1939. Running such a large organisation would require both a senior leadership team and a clear operational structure. Despite the overwhelming workload of the previous two weeks, Arieh Handler had been busy assembling both.

To be the overall manager of the Gwrych *Hachshara*, and to guarantee that the *noar* received the necessary agricultural training that they needed, Arieh turned to the ever-faithful and hugely experienced Erwin Seligmann. However, Erwin's role was to be far greater than just overseeing the project; he was to also be responsible for the all-round welfare and well-being of the *noar*. Given his wide-ranging role, it is not surprising that he came to be referred to by the residents with any one of several job titles: headteacher, head counsellor, but more commonly, simply the *madrich*. His calm, caring, friendly and honest nature had already made him very popular amongst the children who had got to know him at Great Engeham and it was to have the same effect at Gwrych Castle. Manfred Alweiss was absolutely convinced that Erwin 'took a personal caring interest in us all, whether orthodox or not.'[102] As Henry Steinberg succinctly put it, he 'made sure that we behaved ourselves, that we did what we were supposed to do'[103] and, given his character, he rarely had to raise his voice; a disappointed look was usually sufficient to reel in the most recalcitrant of youngsters.

Two other very important men, David Smith and Rabbi Sperber, also arrived during that first week of September 1939 to take up roles alongside Seligmann. Smith, a twenty-four-year-old English solicitor, was appointed to manage the business and financial aspects of the refugee centre. It was his role to ensure that the *Hachshara* had sufficient funds, that the funds were allocated effectively and that the project had the resources it needed to operate effectively. It was probably no coincidence on Arieh Handler's behalf that Smith was also a leading member of the organisation known as *Habonim*. *Habonim* (Hebrew for 'The Builders') was a Socialist Zionist movement formed in 1929 which aimed 'to create a space for Jewish children to gain a strong grounding in Jewish culture and the importance of Israel as a focus for the Jewish world'.[104] *Habonim* was responsible for deciding how grants were distributed by the Refugee Children's Movement and the Jewish Agency. Smith would also prove to be effective in influencing the Refugee Children's Movement because he was 'well versed in the mores of Britain ... [and] he often succeeded in squeezing additional money or supplies out of the Refugee committee for our group at the castle.'[105]

However, Arieh Handler's decision to appoint David Smith was not just a cunning political move in order to make use of his connections, nor was it just based on the fact that he possessed a very keen financial and legal mind. David also had experience of playing 'an important part at *Habonim* camps'[106] and a passionate interest in educational provision for Jewish refugees within Britain. He attended many conferences and meetings about this where he demonstrated that, despite his involvement with *Habonim*, he wanted Jewish youth groups to work together rather than argue over what he saw as petty differences between them.[107] His call for a unity of purpose made him a respected figure across all Jewish youth organisations and he had a reputation for being able to find consensus between them. To David Smith, it mattered not whose auspices a refugee was under as they were all Jews. The Gwrych *Hachshara* may have been a *Bachad* project, but there was also a very large number of Youth *Aliyah* members. Differences between various youth movements had been clearly evident when they had been housed together at Great Engeham Farm. Arieh Handler did not want such trivial and distracting arguments to blight his new creation, and Smith's position of neutrality between them would be useful should differences of opinion arise.

His skills as a mediator between different members of the leadership group at Gwrych would also prove important and it was noted that, 'whenever some question of ideological import seemed likely to cause friction, David Smith was one to whom one instinctively turned for advice. In circumstances of varying fortune, he kept his sense of humour.'[108]

In addition to his financial and legal know-how, his useful connections and his ability to pacify any disagreements, Smith also offered the Gwrych *Hachshara* something that nobody else could: with both his demeanour and his impeccable, unaccented English, Smith could provide the project with a thoroughly convincing 'British face'.

Despite the fact that David Smith was to be extremely important in the overall management of the Gwrych *Hachshara*, he was not a regular, visible presence at the castle. He had a home base in nearby Llandudno where he would stay on a regular basis[109] and was also frequently away from the centre for days at a time, often attending meetings to seek grants and donations towards the upkeep of the castle community or as a *Habonim* delegate at various educational conferences. Consequently, he did not become particularly well known by members of the community. Henry Glanz, when asked of his memory of Smith, had little to offer, stating that he 'didn't really know him, but he visited a lot.'[110] Henry Steinberg later recounted that, 'we had a general manager, an Englishman, I don't know if he was Jewish, and he was overall in charge of the entire operation.'[111] Ruth Kessel somewhat vaguely recalled him as, 'a lovely English gentleman, Jewish I think, who was very kind to us. He would arrive with treats and presents for us. One day he came with a new red jumper for me, I was so excited.'[112] Such comments serve to confirm the enigma that was David Smith. He *was* Jewish but, despite appearances, he was not English and nor was his real name David Smith.

David Smith, or more correctly, David Schmidt, had been born in Russia in 1916. His father had been a prominent Menshevik, one of the leading socialist groups involved in the Russian revolutions of 1917. The Mensheviks were soon overtaken by Lenin's Bolsheviks and in 1921, during the Russian Civil War, Menshevism was made illegal. Like many leading Mensheviks, Schmidt's father emigrated and he took himself and his five-year-old son to England to start a new life. One who knew him well at Gwrych Castle noted that Smith 'came from a secular household; his father was a socialist who had come to England from Russia years ago but still believed in Marx and Engels. But Smith blended in well with the group. He was honest, goodhearted, and a fine friend.'[113] Smith's politics were staunchly socialist and possibly even communist but, following in the footsteps of his father, not of the Soviet kind.

The arrival of Smith also meant that things began to start looking up for the previously grumpy Ossi Findling. Not only did Ossi now have a bed at last, but he was also given a new job: 'We had an English manager and I was made his assistant because I spoke better English than most of the other kids. So, I had a cushy job.'[114]

Arieh Handler also needed a leader who could provide the *noar* with the religious education and values that would underpin their training and guide their future. As a sign of the enormous importance of Gwrych as the flagship enterprise of the entire *Hachsharot* movement, the castle community was the only *Hachshara* in Britain to have a permanent, resident rabbi appointed to it.

Rabbi Shmuel (Samuel) Sperber, a Romanian thirty-five-year-old father of two, was placed in charge of all the religious, cultural and educational aspects of the *Hachshara*, and shortly after his arrival at the castle he also voluntarily took over the role of managing public relations with the town of Abergele and the surrounding countryside. Sperber was already held in high regard within Zionist youth movements and was seen by many as something of a spiritual leader. Born in 1904 in Brasov, Transylvania, he had later moved on to Hungary and then Germany, before leaving for Britain in 1933, shortly after Hitler came to power, in order to escape the antisemitism that surrounded him. He enrolled himself in the Law School at the University of London and by the time that the war broke out he was running a *Bachad Yeshiva* school in Cricklewood, London. However, following the evacuation of all of his schoolchildren at the beginning of September 1939, he had effectively become unemployed. Arieh Handler regarded Sperber as the ideal man for Gwrych and immediately offered him a key role at the *Hachshara*. The opportunity was too good to refuse, as his wife, Miriam, recognised fully: 'This was exactly what Rabbi Sperber was looking for – the chance to do something for the war effort and something for the Jewish refugees as well.'[115]

Miriam Sperber, a thirty-seven-year-old teacher, had been born in Kherson in Ukraine and was thus a Russian by birth.[116] Given what she knew of child evacuations via the Kindertransport, she had been reluctant to send her own children off from London as part of Operation Pied Piper, with nothing more than a small suitcase and a label pinned to their coats. Instead, she had contacted a friend in Kent and carried out a personally organised evacuation. Within a couple of days of arriving there she heard from her husband that he was on the move to Abergele and immediately decided to set off to join him with their children, five-year-old Avigail (Abigail) and three-year-old Avigdor (Victor). Miriam effectively became 'the housemother of the castle' and a *madricha* to the girls, being a moral support and comfort to any who were experiencing difficulties.[117]

Although never part of the leadership group, probably because he was not an active member of any particular Zionist group, Dr Julius Handler was a constant part of the venture right from the beginning and Arieh appointed his brother as the community's medical officer. Due to the restrictions placed on his visa, he was not officially allowed to practise medicine in Britain, though there was no reason why his abundant skills could not be utilised for the refugees at Gwrych. Aside from carrying out his duties as medical officer, Julius played a vital role at the *Hachshara* by just being himself; friendly, gregarious and popular, with a natural ability to make people feel good about themselves and to keep their morale up. He was someone who was naturally drawn towards supporting those less fortunate than himself and he 'collected people, due to his caring and kind nature.'[118]

The first week of September also saw the arrival of another extremely important group: the volunteer workers and helpers, from here on referred to as the *chaverim* (*chaver* for singular males and *chavera* for females).[119] The *chaverim* were formed of young adult Jews who had arrived in Britain in the preceding years. Many, like the *noar*, had also arrived on a Kindertransport but had since turned eighteen. Being a *chaver* was voluntary work although it provided a roof over their heads, free food and minor expenses. Therefore, all of the *chaverim* at Gwrych were committed young Zionists hoping to enhance their own chances of making *Aliyah* as well as assisting the *noar* towards the same goal. Many of the *chaverim* at Gwrych Castle were only a few months or years older than most of the *noar* and almost all of them were under the age of twenty-five. All *chaverim* recruited to Gwrych, at least in the early days, were members of *Bachad*. Most came from active, middle-class

Zionist backgrounds, such as Fritz Freier of Breslau, aged eighteen, who was a nephew of Recha Freier, the founder of Youth *Aliyah*. Also amongst them were two young women from Hamburg, nineteen-year-old Eva Carlebach, whose rabbi father had taught Erwin Seligmann when he was a young man, and Hanna Zuntz, aged twenty-three, who was related to the Marks family. Hanna was from Hamburg and became a nanny and nurse to Rabbi Sperber's two young children in addition to serving as an additional *madricha*. Zuntz, who celebrated her twenty-fourth birthday in September 1939, was held in particularly high esteem by the *noar* and was remembered affectionately by Ossi Findling as 'the lady who looked after us all'.[120]

The precise numbers of *chaverim* at Gwrych Castle varied over time as they came and went. Initially there were about fifty of them but by mid-1940 this number had dropped to around thirty. One of those who arrived in September 1939 was Bernhard Wagner, almost certainly the oldest *chaver* to have ever served at the *Hachshara* at the grand old age of thirty-three, but he quickly moved on after gaining a paid job as a gardener at Hafodunos Hall in Llangernyw. Perhaps the most intriguing *chaver* was twenty-three-year-old scientific photographer Alfred Benjamin. What his exact role at Gwrych was is unclear, but it can probably be safely assumed that it had nothing to do with scientific photography. In the summer of 1940, the group would be joined by two British citizens, James Burke and his wife, who were to be unique in being the only non-Jewish members of the *Hachshara*.

The principal leader of the *chaverim* was David Granek, a short and stocky Polish Jew, aged twenty-seven, and one of the original seven that had worked alongside Julius Handler in order to help prepare the castle prior to the arrival of the *noar*. In this role he was also placed in charge of all the work rosters at the castle. Granek became, in effect, a caretaker at the castle and so was responsible for any essential technical construction and repairs, though he had to always seek approval from Bill Price, the official caretaker. To help him in this task Granek received support from twenty-two-year-old *chaver* Salomon Ferber and from local builder Edgar Jones. Salomon and Edgar discovered that they enjoyed each other's company and they hit it off so well that, after the war, Salomon returned to Abergele to pay a visit to his old friend one last time prior to his emigration to the USA in 1947.[121]

Granek had to manage most of the jobs himself through a combination of wartime 'make do and mend' methods but he also utilised working parties of recruits from the *noar* and, more specifically, by directing his *chaverim* towards essential projects. Generally speaking, the approach Granek adopted was to deploy each *chaver*, or small group of *chaverim*, to a key area of responsibility that they would then be held accountable for. Each *chaver* would then have a group of *noar* assigned to them as part of their requirement to carry out additional duties in and around the Gwrych estate. Initially, he faced a degree of reluctance from the *noar*, many of whom, perhaps understandably, did not really want to have any additional duties to perform. Children told what to do, especially if it is something they do not want to do, will often view an authority figure in a less than favourable light but Henry Glanz firmly believed that Granek was a bully who deliberately gave the worst jobs to those he did not like.[122] Henry was not alone in his dislike of Granek and one of the *chaverim*, Julius Hirsch, later hinted at his nature when, in January 1940, he wrote a tongue-in-cheek last will and testament whilst bedridden and feeling under the weather. In it, he decided to leave his boss a whistle so that he would not have to shout quite so much.

Some of the *chaverim* worked closely with *Hachshara*'s leadership team and, as a result, were seen by some of the *noar* as having greater influence in the overall running of the community. For example, closely assisting Miriam Sperber as a deputy *madricha* was Fanny Redner. Redner, from Poland, had attended a Youth *Aliyah Vorbereitungslager* scheme in 1938 as preparation for an intended move to Palestine but she had then missed out due to being over-age when the opportunity finally came. Instead, with the help of a friend, she had managed to emigrate to Britain where she secured employment as a domestic servant with a Jewish family in Cardiff in February 1939. Keen to continue working towards preparing herself for *Aliyah*, Redner had then linked up with *Bachad* in London and was offered the opportunity to join the Gwrych Castle *Hachshara* as a *chavera* and volunteer farm labourer. Other examples include twenty-one-year-old Rachel Blum from Pleschen in Poland, who became David Smith's domestic servant.

Thus, within a week of the first arrivals, Arieh Handler had assembled a first-rate leadership team that dwarfed anything seen at any of the other *Hachsharot* in Britain. With this assembled and a clear structure in place, Erwin Seligmann could now get on with the task of developing the *Hachshara*'s core purpose of providing the *noar* with the agricultural skills they would need to be successful pioneers in *Eretz Yisrael*. To that end, he began looking for work placements on local farms. Although Erwin spoke English well, he usually took David Smith with him in the role of interpreter, and, more importantly, to present the 'British face' to any dubious farmers wondering why a German was knocking on their door. Sometimes the pair also took Julius Handler with them, whose affable nature rarely failed to gain a positive response from people.

Together, the trio visited all of the farms in Abergele, Towyn, Llanddulas and Rhyd y Foel as well as heading further afield to Llanfair Talhaiarn and Llangernyw. One elderly gentleman that stuck out in Dr Julius's mind appeared to be blissfully ignorant not only of the Jews at the castle but of anything happening in the wider world as well: 'In the course of the conversation he asked where the boys came from. I replied, from Germany. He seemed to be pleased and asked me, "How is the old Kaiser getting on?"'[123]

David Smith would explain to local farmers that the Gwrych *Hachshara* was offering them free labour. All they expected in return was for the children to be given meaningful things to do from which they could learn about how to run a successful farm. Naturally, for many local farmers the offer of free labour was a very tempting one, especially given the recent passing of the National Service (Armed Forces) Act on 3 September that required all men aged eighteen to forty-one to register for military service. Not all the young men in the Abergele locality had gone into uniform yet, but many had and gaps in the workforce were already appearing along with the definite prospect of further increased labour shortages over time. Making the offer even more tempting for the farmers, from mid-September 1939, were increased agricultural targets imposed by an emergency 'war cabinet' of the National Farmers' Union (NFU), which wanted to increase the amount of land utilised for food production across Britain. Locally, that demand caused some uproar when Denbighshire was set a target of developing 20,000 more acres of farmland. The Denbighshire branch of the NFU made a complaint that this was both impracticable and unreasonable, especially without additional agricultural workers. John Edwards of Fachell Farm, in near-by Kinmel Bay, summed up the attitude of many local farmers with the disgruntled comment that he 'hoped that farmers were not expected to work like slaves, and that the government would be prepared to give adequate payment for the extra labour involved.'[124] Given the clear need for a major increase in the number of farm labourers, Erwin Seligmann found relatively little difficulty in finding posts for the young Jewish refugees and Dr Julius Handler noted that the refugee children very quickly impressed local farmers, noting that 'they were considered to be honest and trustworthy, and we received many applications for their services.'[125] Consequently, those farmers who were initially reluctant soon changed their stance when they heard good reports about the youngsters on the local grapevine.

Amongst the local employers was Edwin Roberts, the owner of Tyddyn-uchaf Farm which lies over the brow of the hill behind the Gwrych estate. He took on several youngsters, including Salli Edelnand, who, as a result, got to know Wil Davies, the man in the wellies he had encountered on his first foray into Abergele. At least one of the Gwrych refugees worked with the Jersey cowherd of Thomas John Manners and in the dairy at Tan-y-dderwen Farm, on St George's Road. Mr Barrett, running a pre-war residential agricultural training centre at Hafodunos Hall, Llangernyw, also took on a few boys, and even offered a permanent place to fifteen-year-old Robert Weitsch as a trainee gardener.

Some local farmers were willing to pay fair rates for the young labourers but the management team of the *Hachshara*, as a matter of principle, always turned this down. In fact, the refusal of the Gwrych *Hachshara* and its refugees to accept any compensation for their work was widely lauded, to the extent that it even received mention in the national press in October 1939. The *Daily Mirror*, under the headline of 'Alien Boys Resent Pay', reported that at Gwrych, 'Alien children working from dawn to dusk to help Britain grow more food, take offence if they are offered money for what they are doing. That is the spirit of Polish and German boy refugees … they took on the work in the fields as their opportunity to serve the country which gave them haven. Many of them are so earnest about it that they almost resent any farmer's attempt even to give them pocket-money.'[126] This was very much the official line, though in reality many of the youngsters could not resist accepting a variety of cashless backhanders when they were presented. The offer of food was particularly tempting and rarely refused; one young man, who shall remain nameless as it broke all the rules, fell in love with ham sandwiches. The ten boys normally assigned to tend to the Reids' market garden and vegetable plots at Hen Wrych lodge within the estate, were often surreptitiously gifted other items by Mrs Lena Reid. Salli Edelnand recalled that 'All the boys received ten Woodbines each morning … I am sure she felt that we should receive something for our labour as wages could not be paid.'[127] These cigarettes became a useful, if illicit, currency amongst some of the youngsters. As time went on, increasing numbers took less offence at the offer of cash payments, though they mostly kept this very quiet in case Erwin Seligmann found out.

Quite a number of the refugees were also set to work on the Gwrych estate itself, especially the younger or less physically fit ones. Aside from gardening work required at the castle's several lodges, common jobs on the estate included forestry work such as tree felling in the woods; clearing drainage ditches or digging new ones; general tidying and maintenance of the paths and gardens; and repetitive weeding in the nursery where the community was trying to grow its own vegetables following the launch of the nationwide 'Dig for Victory' campaign in October 1939. Some of the older or stronger workers received the dubious reward of a job on a local farm *and* a role back on the estate. Salli Edelnand, for example, did some heavy work at Tyddyn-uchaf as well as carrying out less demanding tasks in the market garden at Hen Wrych lodge.

Those employed in forestry had particularly demanding days. Baruch Spergel was a young Czech Jew and one of just two at Gwrych who had been saved by transports arranged by Sir Nicholas Winton. Later dubbed the 'British Schindler' by elements of the British press, Winton arranged Kindertransport operations from Czechoslovakia, successfully bringing nearly 700 children, mostly Jewish, to safety in Britain. Baruch would later remember his forestry work less than fondly: 'I never worked so hard as there because we had to fell trees ... for wood ... it was a big castle and it was cold in the winter. We had to [work] like back in the Middle Ages.'[128] One of the early tasks given to the forestry team involved digging and clearing stream beds in the vicinity. Another task that had to be quickly addressed was clearing and improving all the various access tracks to and from the castle building as many of the paths were badly overgrown as a result of the site being vacant for fifteen years. One of the castle's main access routes, the pathway leading to Nant-y-Bella lodge, was found to be almost impassable[129] and a small group of several young foresters had to spend over a week hacking through the brambles and bushes to clear it. Their attempts to amuse themselves by pretending that they were hacking a path like machete-wielding jungle explorers soon grew stale as in reality, they were armed with just a couple of saws, and most were actually attacking the foliage with nothing more than cutlery knives borrowed from the kitchen.

Initially, for many of the group, these rural labours came as something of a shock. Although most had some experience of a *Vorbereitungslager* in Germany, the simple fact was that the majority of the inhabitants of Gwrych Castle came from urban backgrounds and city-dwelling families – they were not naturally attuned to the rigours of rural life.

Erwin Seligmann was concerned and recognised that this 'was another crucial moment for the *Hachshara*. City youth went to the countryside. Now they were forced to put themselves in the rural environment.'[130]

Most of the children had limited English, let alone any Welsh, which could have been quite frightening for them when they turned up for work on the farms. Unable to communicate effectively, it would have been easy to assume that local farm labourers would be dismissive of the arrival of agriculturally clueless foreigners, who were potentially threatening their own jobs with their free labour. Herman Rothman was probably not alone in being the centre of attention on his first day at work and, in his case, it turned into an interrogation.

> My first experience with Welsh, ordinary labourers was extraordinary. We were in a big shed. They called everybody in, they sat in a circle, and they said 'you go and sit in the middle of it.' And they fired questions at me, with their Welsh accents. First of all, I thought this was very, very strange. I was taught English and they pronounced things completely differently. I thought people must have taught me the wrong English ... I said I came from Poland. So they said 'Have they got cows in Poland?' So I answered, yes. 'Have they got horses in Poland?' I answered in the affirmative. And they asked, do they do this and that ... I felt very flattered by being the centre of attraction in this cowshed. They were very nice. I can't say I can grumble about the hospitality they extended to me, the Polish worker![131]

The fears of being dismissed by locals were unfounded, and the curious but friendly reaction that the workers showed to Herman was almost universally experienced by those on other farms.

Both Salli Edelnand and Wolfgang Billig were part of the ten-strong Hen Wrych team where the Reid family grew fruit and vegetables for local sale. Lodge work was generally less demanding than farm work and even the most urbanised of the youngsters could adapt to it easily, and even enjoy it – some of the children enjoyed it so much that they volunteered for it. Often this was motivated by avoiding an assignment to a more demanding job, but sometimes it was out of genuine desire.

One such volunteer was Wilhelm Braun from Vienna who, now that he was in Britain, preferred to be referred to as Willy or, more usually, Bill. One of the oldest of the *noar* at seventeen, Bill had witnessed the 'celebrations' following the Nazi *Anschluss* of his country in March 1938 and the rapid rise of antisemitism in Austria as a result:

> They were seizing Jews in the street and beating them. When Hitler's army marched into Vienna on March 13, 1938, almost all Austrians greeted it with great joy. They thought the redeemer had come. I ... had never seen anything like it. The Social Democrats, who had defended human rights, collapsed in one week, one day, one moment. Jews lost everything. They lost any access to law. If you got beaten up, there was nothing you could do about it. If you got robbed, there was nothing you could do about it. You had to feel lucky that they didn't drag you along.[132]

After *Kristallnacht*, which also saw violence in Austria, 'Thousands of men were rounded up and sent to concentration camps ... Most men would come back with hair shorn off their head. Some had their teeth beaten in. They were so afraid that they didn't say a word. They were told, "If you say one word, it's over."'[133]

Arriving in Britain on a Kindertransport in the summer of 1939, Bill Braun had initially been sent to Rowton House, 'a seaman's hostel – a rough place, full of unsavoury characters.'[134] Based at Gwrych Castle, he was in a far happier frame of mind and he thus volunteered for Hen Wrych because 'I ... wanted to do something useful. I knew a little about gardening, so I helped Mr Reid, a gardener who raised flowers and vegetables.'[135]

Overall, Erwin Seligmann did an exceptional job in a very short period of time. Most of the *noar* had agricultural work before the end of the first week of September 1939 and by the time of National Registration on 29 September 1939, everybody at Gwrych was gainfully employed in some way or other with the majority, seventy-five per cent according to Seligmann,[136] working on local farms as 'students' or 'trainees'.[137] A small number had also gained additional voluntary work with local businesses in the town and most also had duties to carry out in and around the Gwrych Castle estate in accordance with Granek's work rosters, which soon proved to be a very unpopular addition to already busy days.

However, a true *Hachshara* was about much more than work, it was also about developing a unified community spirit and a common purpose and, as yet, that was far from being established. The reason why was easy to explain. The youngsters at Gwrych had been through much in the last year and the previous few weeks had seen a combination of long journeys, lack of food, days of hard work and nights of limited sleep. The declaration of war so soon after their arrival at Gwrych had clearly underlined the reasons that lay behind their move to Britain in the first place, and had shattered any optimism that remained that they might be reunited with their families in the near future. It would therefore be reasonable to suggest that most of them, apart from being physically exhausted, would have been utterly bewildered, scared and homesick. An autobiographical novel by *chaver* Alfred Benjamin encapsulated the whirlwind of events, this rapid slide from normality into a living nightmare that many of them would have witnessed before fleeing to Britain:

> My mind goes back in time. The Friday nights, all seven of us brothers sitting with our parents, happily singing, enjoying a meal. The night we stood on our balcony watching masses of people with torch lights marching by, singing songs about killing Jews, the night when Hitler and the Nazis had taken over Germany. Then the arrests of Jews,

the return of our doctor friend, ashes in a box. My parents and brothers fleeing by train. My arrival in Dover, finally fleeing from the German nightmare.[138]

The events of recent months had left Jewish adults in a state of confusion. *Bachad*'s own news journal, *Chayenu*, noted towards the end of 1939 that 'we are horror stricken and dumbfounded, we are torn with pain. We cannot even yet collect our thoughts to ponder on what has happened or to reflect upon events and realise what they all mean to us.'[139]

For Jewish youth, their incomprehension must have been even greater. Most of the children at Gwrych had witnessed or even personally experienced disturbing events in their recent past and the ability of many of them to make sense of it all would have been limited. However, the way that they and their fellow Jews had been treated in their homelands had been the way of things for the last six years which, for many, was nearly half of their lifetime. It had become 'normal' and, unlike the adults, few of them could remember any other time. This meant that many of the youngsters viewed life in a very different way to the adults. Erich Roper, commented that, 'Because we lived in Germany and lived every hour, every minute uncertain about the following day, we became indifferent.'[140] This indifference would have been exacerbated by their arrival at a place they had never heard of and surrounded by people they hardly knew. Inevitably, many of them were utterly clueless as to what was happening to them; their lives had quite literally been turned upside down. In a strange way, however, their indifference 'also had a positive side to it. It helped us to overcome our distress on leaving our natural homes, our families.'[141] The result of all this was a sense of emptiness, maybe even a sense of pointlessness, amongst many of the *noar*.

It is impossible to guess at the psychological state of each of the Gwrych refugees individually, but what they all faced in common was the difficulty of trying to find some sort of normality within a situation that was totally abnormal. It is therefore perhaps unsurprising that Dr

Julius Handler noticed very early on within the group of children that there was a 'poor rapport amongst them'.[142] There was very little that the doctor, Erwin Seligmann or the other leaders at the castle could do about the *noar*'s recent trials and tribulations, but they could do something about their future and that had to become the prime focus. The children at Gwrych were to be the pioneers of the Zionist ideal, the builders of *Eretz Yisrael*, and they had a *Hachshara* to create. To put it bluntly, Erwin and his colleagues had to get a grip, and quickly, or the *Hachshara* would fail.

CHAPTER 5

———

'We had good plans'

September 1939 (Part 2)
Developing the Gwrych *Hachshara*

Arieh Handler's flagship Gwrych project was teetering on the edge. Much had been achieved in such a short time, but the foundations were shallow. If the project was to survive beyond a few weeks, big issues like food and clothing had to be resolved, but even comparatively minor problems such as the lack of furniture needed to be addressed. If the children could not see long-term plans being implemented in their own training centre, why would they believe in the long-term plans – *Aliyah* to *Eretz Yisrael* – being expected of them? If they had farm work but the quality of life in the castle remained inadequate, would they have any chance of snapping out of their indifference and creating the community cohesion that a *Hachshara* needed?

Erwin Seligmann knew that it was vital that the children at the castle developed friendships and bonds and that he had to do something to help speed this up. One of his ideas was to break down the mass of 200 young people into smaller bodies known as *plugoth*[143] to help accelerate the bonding process.

Erwin began dividing the *noar* into three distinct groups, each known as a *pluga*, based loosely on age. The older children of around sixteen or

75

seventeen years old formed the A or *Aleph* group. Those aged fifteen to sixteen were placed in B or *Bet* group. The youngest, aged fourteen to fifteen, were assigned to C group, known as *Gimmel*. Each *pluga* would become the basis for teaching groups, or classes, and many bedroom allocations were rearranged according to group.

As the ages between each *pluga* overlapped, there was a degree of uncertainty amongst the *noar* about how and why they had been selected for one or other of the groups. Herman Rothman believed that their perceived ability with the English language was a factor, which caused him some consternation: 'Simply because I spoke English very well I was promoted to the A group. I wasn't particularly happy because all my friends were with the B group.'[144] Wolfgang Billig had a slightly different view: 'It was done, I believe, according to our maturity level as perceived by Erwin Seligmann ... I think that it was more by accident than design that I was allocated to *Gimmel*.'[145] Both were correct in a way, as it was later admitted that 'their age and the few first impressions that Erwin had of us were really the points of view according to which he divided the groups.'[146]

Regardless of how the groups were created, and despite the reservations of Herman Rothman, they nevertheless proved to have the positive effect that Seligmann had intended. Erika Heisler-Lieberman, placed in *pluga Bet*, found that the changes had a nearly instant effect. She had found life at the castle 'hard, until they organised us ... we were a wild group there until things settled down.'[147] The creation of the *plugoth* also catapulted children of similar ages into the same orbit, helping them to find like-minded people and form friendships which, in some cases, turned out to be lifelong. One group from *pluga Aleph*, who shared the same room, bonded so well that they soon gave themselves a gang name by using their initials – Henry (Steinberg), Adi (Better), Isi (Gewurtz) and Froyum (nickname for Ephraim), and then adding an 'A' (for *Aleph*) to the end – to spell out Haifa, a large city in Palestine.

Erwin Seligmann's next task was to help create the feel of a self-sufficient kibbutz and he felt that this could be aided by assigning people to more specific and meaningful tasks rather than just the general cleaning duties that they had performed during the first week. He recognised that the *Hachshara* needed specialist services such as a laundry, kitchen staff, bootmakers and carpenters. He therefore took another look at the unpopular work rosters created by David Granek. Many of the tired youngsters, now working on local farms for much of the day, felt that these rosters had placed additional and unwanted burdens on them, and this had resulted in their extra duties being carried out half-heartedly or, in many cases, not at all. This, in turn, had caused unnecessary tensions to develop within the community which were negatively affecting the already strained mood within the *noar*. Erwin was aware of the growing angst and he was also aware that much of the frustration stemmed from the way that Granek interacted with people. For example, Granek was also in charge of *pluga Gimmel*, made up of the younger children. One of them, Sonia Marder (who had not settled into the castle at all well since being offered a dirty cup on day one), disliked him so much that she had asked Erwin to transfer her to *pluga Bet*. Henry Glanz and others alleged that Granek had been using his power over the rosters to 'bully' people, which had added to the resistance and belligerence being shown by some of the youngsters. Several of them now effectively declared themselves to be on strike until something was done about it – or about him.

A frustrated Granek appealed to higher authority for support and he received it from Rabbi Sperber. The Rabbi gathered the community together and 'drove home the ethics of work'.[148] Few of the youngsters would dare to argue with the Rabbi and, 'after his talks on the subject, the children vied with each other to complete their assignments.'[149] Erwin had no dispute with the Rabbi's words but he realised that, if the children were only now doing things because they had been *told to*, then something was not quite right. A successful *Hachshara* could not be built on coercion alone.

Erwin therefore put together a plan to restructure the typical day. The *noar* would now be required to work on local farms for half of each day, either mornings or afternoons, then receive three hours of education in the other half, and then have a maximum of four hours a day assigned to a work roster, usually during the evenings. Admittedly, this would leave the children with very little free time but at least it placed a limit on expectations and there was no avoiding the fact that everyone would have to do *some* additional duties if the *Hachshara* was to function properly. The plan received a muted though not resentful response and, on balance, most of the children appeared happier with this than the previous arrangement. Erwin himself chose to set an example by doing some voluntary work on local farms and that seemed to impress most of the community, as well as shutting down anyone contemplating offering a 'but you don't know what it's like' argument.

A typical day soon developed around a familiar pattern: waking up at 5.30 a.m., washing, prayers, roll call and then breakfast.[150] After they'd eaten, the morning farm workers would head off to their various destinations clutching a packed lunch which usually consisted of nothing more than two thick slabs of buttered bread that had been provided by those on the kitchen roster. Those who would be going to work in the afternoon went off to lessons.

For most of the farm workers, their journey entailed a relatively short walk to local farms such as nearby Tyddyn-uchaf or Tan-y-dderwen, though some had a longer trek of up to three or four miles such as those working at Fachell Farm in Kinmel Bay. David Smith soon managed to procure some bicycles which helped speed things up enormously and proved very popular. A few of the *noar* had to travel even longer distances – anything up to around ten miles if they were working near Llangernyw, for example. However, those with longer journeys were often picked up by a farmer's labourer in a horse and cart or by motor transport. Henry Glanz recalled being ferried to and from the castle in trucks much of the time.[151]

Depending on their work location, the morning workers had usually returned to the castle by 2 p.m. at the latest but those expected back later found an extra set of buttered sandwiches had been inserted into their lunch bags. For some, this proved to be quite an incentive. Herman Rothman's farm placement was only for the mornings, but he often volunteered to work overtime in the afternoon just to qualify for the extra sandwiches (and to have an excuse to skip the afternoon lessons). There were others who copied Rothman's little ruse.

As the morning workers returned to the castle they would then go to their lessons, whilst those who had spent the morning in classes picked up their sandwiches and headed off to their farms at about noon. When everyone was back at the castle, usually by around 6 p.m., the work rosters would kick in, requiring their services until 10 p.m., though, in reality, they usually finished an hour or two earlier thanks to tweaks that Erwin made.

Erwin had realised that the unpopular rosters needed to be made fairer and more varied, and that larger teams would enable the work to be done quicker. He therefore asked David Granek to revise and reissue them with the additional intention of moving everybody around to a new task on a monthly cycle so that nobody felt they were stuck in a role they disliked for too long a period of time. That instruction also neatly ended any potential for complaints that they were being picked on by Granek for the least popular tasks. To ensure that everyone was clear on what was required of them, Granek displayed a large work chart in the dining hall which clearly indicated the activity of each refugee. These reissued rosters included a bigger variety of tasks and replaced general cleaning duties with ones that would contribute towards the aim of kibbutz-like self-sufficiency. Duties ranged from doing laundry, estate work or farm work in the neighbourhood, to handicraft work, boot and shoe repairs or special studies.[152] Ruth Kessel, no doubt unaware of Erwin's deeper motives at the time, noted that the alterations helped to deliver what he intended: 'the older teenagers at Gwrych Castle ran the place, and it was a bit like a commune ... along the lines of a kibbutz. We all had our delegated jobs and we kept to our rotas and routines very strictly.'[153]

Part of Erwin's new approach also entailed the setting up of various workshops to provide the community with the specialised services or items that it needed. For example, the revised roster now also included work in a new tailor's workshop. A lack of suitable and spare clothing was a major issue for everyone at the castle as all of the *noar* had arrived in the country with nothing more than a small suitcase and whatever they happened to be wearing at the time they began their journey to Britain. It is hard to imagine the difficulties facing the children and their parents just a few months or weeks earlier when they had sat down to decide what could be taken and what would have to be left behind. In many cases, sentimentality probably got the better of practicality, and as a consequence not all of the youngsters had a collection of clothing that was suitable for the conditions of North Wales, especially when the warm summer of 1939 drifted into autumn and winter. Herman Rothman, for example, in a clear victory of youthful passion and optimism over common sense, had taken up valuable space in his suitcase with his pair of beloved spiked running shoes.

Bill Braun was less than impressed with what he saw as German arrogance with regards to clothing choices. He noticed that in general the German children, like Herman Rothman, had packed a wider variety of items and had higher quality clothing than the poorer Austrian children like him. To both his amazement and derision, some of the Germans had even brought suits and other apparel in the latest fashionable styles.[154]

Charitable donations of clothing were occasionally delivered to the castle by concerned members of the local community but more often than not they were cast-offs or of limited practical use. Consequently, the leaders of the *Hachshara* had to initiate some novel ideas to solve the clothing issue for themselves. Initially two *chaverim* were deployed to be tailors, making up clothing from fabrics purchased on the cheap as well as repairing damaged garments and coming up with clever ways of recycling items that were beyond immediate repair. Through necessity the number of tailors grew over time into a team of twelve *chaverim* and *noar* who became quite efficient at turning out brand new, bespoke blouses, shirts, skirts, dresses, trousers and more. Amongst the *chaver-*

im working in the tailors' workshop would probably have been Meta Khan, who had been a seamstress back in her 'normal' life, and Ruth Muller from Vienna, who had been a trainee dressmaker.

Given the nature of the work that most of the children and young people were required to do, there was also a constant battle to keep their clothing freshly laundered. In the days before washing machines, this was a lengthy and gruelling process that often seemed never-ending. In total, David Granek eventually had to deploy twenty *noar* and *chaverim* at a time to laundry services – around ten per cent of the entire community. There was an identifiable laundry room within the castle but it was not designed for keeping 200 people's clothes clean and, to make matters significantly worse, the boiler was temperamental and often just plain useless. When it did operate properly, it was hampered by the castle's less-than-efficient and low-pressure water supply, necessitating large numbers of children regularly being sent to the kitchen to fill buckets with water and lug them back. Miriam Sperber recalled that 'the laundry room was no picnic either, as you had to wash the clothes in cold water.'[155] The residents soon encountered the additional and almost impossible conundrum of how to dry wet clothing during an often wet Welsh winter; and, if that wasn't enough, there was always masses of sorting, ironing and folding as well as inspecting the clothes so that damaged items could be whisked off to the tailors for running repairs. Reading the new roster in the dining room when it went up, and discovering that they had been assigned to the laundry for the next month, was always cause for children to offer a muttered curse or two.

Suitable footwear was also a problem. Most children had arrived with one or two pairs of shoes at most and some of those were not at all suitable for agricultural work (such as Rothman's running shoes). David Granek wanted to set up a cobblers' workshop but not a single member of the *Hachshara* had any experience in this area and there were no dedicated tools or equipment. For once, the *Hachshara*'s leadership had to accept that they were out of their depth and had no choice but to use the expertise of cobblers in Abergele. Two willing *chaverim* had been assigned as prospective bootmakers and, after they had carried shoes down into town for repair, they no doubt eagerly watched the local craftsmen at work in order to pick up hints and tips. With whatever tools they could lay their hands on, the two volunteers experimented and taught themselves how to remove and replace soles as well as how to carry out other repairs and modifications. Once they had figured things out to the best of their ability, they began to teach two others. By the end of September 1940 there was a team of four people operating as effective cobblers at the castle.

One domestic angle that was relatively easy to resolve was keeping everyone's hair neat and tidy. Initially, the children were shepherded to a barber in Abergele, but amongst the group of *chaverim* was an actual hairdresser who chose two of the *noar* to train as assistants, one of whom was fifteen-year-old Tosca Sussmann from Berlin. Before long, the castle had a thriving mini-salon.

Logs were the main source of fuel for heating the large, draughty building, and reflecting the importance of this commodity, eighteen *noar* and *chaverim* at a time were employed for forestry duties as woodcutters as well as working around the estate's woods collecting logs and felling trees. Aside from trying to feed the constant daily heating demands, the forestry workers were also tasked with attempting to build up a stockpile of logs for the winter months. The foresters undoubtedly had hard work to do and Wolfgang Billig regarded this as one of the least popular tasks.[156]

Routine maintenance, on the other hand, was a relatively popular job. As it was an ongoing requirement that could have been hampered by the appearance of a bunch of clueless, fresh-faced individuals every four weeks, two of the more trustworthy *noar*, Erich Roper and Carl Schäfler, were permanently assigned to this task, with two additional *chaverim* 'on call' should they be needed.[157] Their wide-ranging duties included, amongst other things, cleaning gutters, ensuring that black-out curtains and drapes were fitted to all of the castle's many windows (and that they were effective), and carrying coal or logs to the dozens of fireplaces in the castle. The difficulty of heating the castle was a permanent problem for Roper and Schäfler. With the castle's main water pump inoperative most of the time and no electricity, the limited central heating system could not be used. Maintaining warmth at the weekends was a particular problem when the duo, along with the entire community, observed their day of rest: 'as the group were *Mizrachi* you couldn't do any work on the Saturday (the Sabbath) so they let the fires go out.'[158] The pair were also responsible for all of the internal lighting at the castle and all that they had to work with was an insufficient number of kerosene lamps, the use of which was regulated due to the difficulties and costs involved in obtaining paraffin. Overall, Roper and Schäfler had a dangerous as well as an unrewarding job and Miriam Sperber recalled that 'their faces were always somewhat charred.'[159]

To make matters more difficult, the castle was vast and in poor condition, with myriad draughts from decrepit window fittings, walls with gaps in the mortar and roofs lacking slates. Many of the fireplaces had chimneys in desperate need of a good clean; smoke from the fires often circulated within the building rather than disappearing up the stacks. Often, the only way to get the smoke out of rooms was to open the windows but, once done, the heat generated by the fires simply vanished along with the smoke. Additionally, this could also only be done during daylight, as between sunset and sunrise windows had to be kept heavily draped in keeping with the demands of wartime blackout regulations. Ultimately, the need to retain heat usually won, especially during the harsh winter of 1939–40, and many of the children would remember their first few months at the castle as a time of living in perpetual semi-darkness whilst coughing as they moved between smoke-filled rooms.

Although items of furniture had been donated by the Abergele Baptist Chapel and some London charities, there was still a paucity so a carpentry workshop was also established on site by Granek with the intention of solving that problem. It was on record that 'Alfred Kallner opened the carpentry shop in this cozy bungalow with two *chaverim*.'[160] There is no bungalow at Gwrych, so it may be assumed that the workshop had been created in one of the single-storey outbuildings. The tasks facing nineteen-year-old Kallner in the early days were quite wide-ranging and difficult, but he did his best 'as far as can be done without tools and glue.'[161] The community was particularly short of tables and chairs and the castle leadership were keen to receive broken or discarded items from the local community which Kallner then did his best to repair. One of the *noar* carpenters, Wolfgang Billig, recalled that they became quite inventive: 'We had a woodwork area where, among other things, they built bedside tables from wooden boxes in which some of our provisions arrived.'[162] To add to Kallner's woes, 'even the setting of glass panes was the work of the carpenter.'[163] Without sufficient resources, and presumably feeling overworked and undervalued, Kallner left the Gwrych Castle *Hachshara* almost immediately – certainly before early October 1939.[164] His timing was somewhat unfortunate for, as soon as he had packed his bags and left, most of the problems he had encountered were resolved. A delivery was made from London.

> Who would have believed that there came a big box of tools from London and soon afterwards the carpentry turned into a [real] carpentry, uniting with metalworking and painting. The first major piece [to be made] was the *Seder* [rituals during *Pesach* or Passover] table. This was followed by a new era. The labour forces were increased from two to five *chaverim*. They procured work desks and the ban on using new wood was overturned.[165]

After Kallner left, Roper and Schäfler worked alongside the five carpentry *chaverim* (among them probably twenty-three-year-old Julius Hirsch, who had studied carpentry in Italy before coming to Britain). Work was now run on a day-by-day basis by Isi Gruenbaum. Despite their best efforts, Kallner's skills were sorely missed, and it was not until the middle of 1940 that a new *chaver*, Martin Steinberger, arrived as his long-term replacement. Nevertheless, the carpentry soon expanded by adding two senior workers to operate as locksmiths, in addition to several workers who were co-opted into painting duties or metal-working. Wolfgang Billig was one of those chosen to be elevated from the carpentry to become one of the locksmiths.

> After having a stint of sawing wood, I was transferred to the locksmith shop, a very important task, because there were many outhouses and other areas that were locked and we had to get them open without breaking the doors. To that end I made a number of skeleton keys of varying sizes to open all the doors. I actually brought them into our marriage, until my wife made me destroy them for fear of being found and thought to be the tools of my trade as burglar.[166]

The little hive of activity that was the carpentry was neatly captured in its daily form by one of the refugees, Vera (her surname is unfortunately not recorded), in a description she wrote for the yearbook of September 1940.

> We go over a yard where we already hear the noise of sawing and hammering from the carpentry … we see ourselves in front of a door with lumber, and a sign saying 'Carpenter' cut out of plywood. The *chaverim* stand at the tables in blue aprons. One is planing, another hammering on a box, the third is on the glue pot under which the water is steaming. One turns many times the grindstone [to sharpen tools and knives]. Around the walls, chairs to repair, the eternal plague of the carpentry. *Chaverim* often come up to visit them. What is this work? The same thing has to be done on a daily basis; sweeping, rubbing, wiping, brushing, and then again from the beginning and then again. In addition to that comes the everlasting search for their equipment, which resumes every morning.[167]

The work rosters also assigned a large team to the kitchen. The kitchen at Gwrych Castle was large, with several anterooms, and designed to easily generate food for up to about thirty people at a time. The problem for David Granek was that he had around seven times that number to feed. In addition, the main stove in the kitchen was useless and the chimney was blocked. From both the stove and the chimney, thick smoke poured back into the kitchen, making working conditions nearly impossible and quite dangerous. The oven was fuelled by coal (or logs when coal was unavailable) 'which made an awful sooty mess. Dark and dank, smoke filled the kitchen.'[168] Several of the *chaverim* assigned to kitchen duties quickly fell ill from the toxic fumes that filled the room. For the first three months, the *chaverim* and *noar* had to simply accept and endure the terrible and injurious conditions, for it was not until November 1939 that a new stove was secured and installed and the chimney properly cleaned.

However, sorting out the stove and chimney was, to some extent, an easy issue to resolve compared to the problem of actually preparing and cooking food for the castle's residents. None of the *chaverim*, willing as they were, were chefs or knew anything much about the challenges and complications of mass catering. Initially, Granek chose Moritz Friedler of Vienna as the *chaver* in charge of sorting out that particular issue, which was quite a task for somebody who had just turned twenty-one. Friedler was a Youth *Aliyah* member and had been beaten up during *Kristallnacht* before he had escaped to Britain with his cousin, and later joined the Gwrych community in the hope of helping others. He did his best to get to grips with a role that was completely unfamiliar to him but he was out of his depth. For some time the mainstay of the kitchen's culinary expertise and output was often little more than squelchy dishes of milky potatoes that many of the children just disinterestedly stirred with their spoons, eating it because they had to rather than because they wanted to.

Celia Kreisel, who was rostered to the kitchen staff, was aware that the amount of food available was relatively plentiful but very limited in scope; aside from the potato slop 'we had bread, butter, jams and some meat, some eggs and porridge'.[169] Sonia Marder, who had been fussy over the soup she had been offered on the day of her arrival, remained belligerent and when she was offered bread with margarine she declined it, only to be scolded by a *chaver* who asked, 'Where do you think you are, a hotel?'[170] Nevertheless, she later recalled, as did most of the Gwrych residents, that whilst the food was simple, repetitive and uninspiring, she was never hungry.

Things did improve a little over time and after a while even kosher meat became available. A butcher in St Asaph, some six miles away from Abergele, had a Jewish colleague and friend in Liverpool and was happy to receive and store occasional deliveries on the *Hachshara's* behalf until such time as David Smith could drive over in his car to collect the items.

David Granek also assigned a *chaver* to the pantry, and it was their job to maintain accurate inventories of the food stored there and to keep it as well stocked as possible. This was a thankless task given that money was limited and it became increasingly difficult as wartime supplies grew scarcer, especially after food rationing was introduced in January 1940. The job had an up-side for one young refugee: Adi Better was assigned to this task whilst recovering from an injury sustained from doing forestry work – he had stood on the wrong side of a tree whilst it fell and it caught his arm – and he found that he could help himself to a few items whilst nobody was looking and 'amend' the inventory accordingly.

And then there was the problem of the meal service itself. As the Handler brothers had recognised during their initial visit, the dining room was too small for everyone to use at the same time and thus they would have to seat an overspill of people in the adjacent music room and hall. There also weren't enough plates and cutlery.[171] They possessed 100 slates (rather than plates) and only half the amount of the cutlery and cups required. Serving meals to groups via a staggered timetable was the only solution, so initially in September 1939 three separate sittings were created. With the experience of practice this was reduced to two just a few weeks later and by the end of 1939 the *chaverim* had come up with, and established, a rolling service that allowed for used slates and cutlery to be cleaned and recycled sufficiently quickly to prevent hold-ups and queues. Despite the success of this latter approach, it remained a mystery to Granek and the kitchen *chaverim* just how and why so much cutlery regularly seemed to vanish into thin air.[172]

Two *chaverim* were always placed on 'sentry' duty in the dining room. Their task was to ensure that proper order was maintained, that the room was kept clean and tidy and that the residents ate quickly enough to allow their slates and cutlery to be recycled for those still waiting. More importantly, they were also there to monitor that food was not being wasted. For those surreptitiously accepting edible offerings from their agricultural employers, it was particularly important to return an empty slate so as not to arouse any suspicions.

Twelve *noar* at any one time were assigned to house-cleaning duties, a job which was only assigned to girls and was generally regarded as one of the least popular roles. This duty was overseen by Miriam Sperber, in one of her many roles as a *chavera*. She reminded each new group of girls that it was extremely important to maintain a clean house as it would create a good impression should visitors arrive, which they did on occasion. Their shift was up to four hours per day, carrying out what was widely regarded as a series of tedious and boring tasks. The most arduous and repetitive part of this work was the necessity to regularly clean, scrub and wax or oil the many wooden floors around the castle. Due to its scale and the increasing cost and difficulty of obtaining the necessary materials, the building was subdivided so that the whole thing could be done top to bottom within a monthly cycle with minimum waste. The marble staircase, the showpiece of the castle's interior, was earmarked for special attention by Miriam Sperber. This caused particular annoyance as Mimi Schleissner remembered: 'We had a crew every day to scrub those steps. The whole thing was ridiculous.'[173]

Despite the lectures on work ethics given by Rabbi Sperber, and the revised rosters, many of the children still engaged in avoidance tactics and none more so than those assigned to housekeeping. Miriam Sperber recalled, 'There were no less than fifty rooms and many staircases and halls. It was not easy to keep that place clean, especially once the rainy season started and everyone came in with filthy boots. I had several girls whom I could call upon to help. I gave each one a set cleaning up task, and they were none too happy with me. Often I would find the cleaning materials scattered, the job undone, and the girl nowhere to be found.'[174]

To work alongside Miriam Sperber to help spruce up the castle, two *chaverim* were assigned to painting duties, one of whom already had several years' worth of experience as a painter and decorator in civilian life, and a small number of *noar* were assigned to assist them.

Overall, the changes to the work rosters and the creation of a variety of new tasks that rotated monthly, were generally well received. They also went a long way towards making the *Hachshara* more self-sufficient and helping to create the feeling of something like a kibbutz at Gwrych.

With Erwin Seligmann and David Granek adapting the working side of the day, Rabbi Sperber had the task of developing the educational aspects of daily life at the castle. Education was provided for three hours a day, from Monday to Thursday, and divided into morning and afternoon sessions to be attended before or after work on local farms. Both sessions were delivered to three separate classes simultaneously, with the children generally split into their *Aleph, Bet* and *Gimmel* groups. Those three hours of education were spent on a regular diet of Jewish religious studies, Jewish history and the learning of English. It was not long before the pupils began to get bored with the repetitive and constricted scope of the curriculum and they soon began agitating for wider variety with art, art history, music and general history amongst the most popular demands. However, Rabbi Sperber's chief concern was developing religious education and he was reluctant to diversify the content.

Meanwhile, Dr Julius Handler made a start on providing the necessary health care that the community would need. He recognised from his very first visit that the quality of the water supply at the castle was going to be a fundamental problem to resolve if he were to have any chance of establishing a satisfactory regime of health and hygiene for the *noar* and *chaverim*. He and his initial team of seven had worked hard prior to the arrival of the first children, repairing leaking pipes and installing additional water pumps. The team had noted very early on that the existing main paraffin-powered pump which fed water to the castle was woefully insufficient. It may have been perfectly acceptable when originally installed, in fact it had been quite a 'state of the art' item at the time, but it was designed to supply water to a much smaller household and was inadequate for the demands it now faced.[175] Fifteen years of neglect had also rendered it highly unreliable. Julius's team managed to get the pump going again but it was to prove irritating beyond belief. Even on the rare occasions when the pump inexplicably worked as intended, the pressure was feeble. The cost for installing a new pump was £150, a figure that was just too high to be considered.[176] Thus, the water supply problem remained as an ongoing annoyance and inconvenience that would never be properly solved. In September 1940, one member of the community summed up the frustrations it continued to cause:

> A report about our kibbutz without mentioning the pump, which is a 'mystery' to everyone coming to this castle, would be incomplete. Supposed to supply water to the whole house, but actually only intended for twenty people, it is more often standing still than working, every day there being a different defect, and the result: there is no water in the whole house, and people are continually running down to the kitchen (which is receiving water from Abergele) armed with basins, pails or jugs, from early in the morning till late at night. Two people are working at the pump in 'normal' times, but nothing can be done to guarantee a proper regulation, not even a new, expensive meter would do the trick. And yet the first question on being woken in the morning is, 'Is the water running?'[177]

On the positive side, at least there was water – on occasions – and it was clean and pure.

Improving the sanitary arrangements of the castle was another urgent issue for Julius. Washing, bathing and lavatory arrangements within Gwrych Castle were deemed to be quite advanced when they were installed in the nineteenth century but by 1939 they were archaic and, although numerous facilities existed, they were designed for a much smaller number of people. One of the first new things Julius had installed was a shower bath (another would be added in the autumn of 1940).

Within a fortnight of the opening of the *Hachshara*, the toilet facilities had become a very serious issue. As Miriam Sperber later recalled, 'The toilets, which originally served the Lord's family of six and about twenty servants, could not accommodate 150 young people and their counsellors. They were soon blocked up and presented a clear and urgent danger to health of epidemic proportions.'[178] An investigation into the problem began. The situation was serious and it came to a head at the time of Rosh Hashanah, the Jewish New Year, which that year fell on 13–15 September 1939. From the beginning, the leadership team had been keen to establish the correct levels of religious observance, including clear rules on when members of the community were and, more importantly, were not allowed to work. Unfortunately, Rosh Hashanah was one of those times. However, Julius's concern for the health risk that the blocked sanitation presented convinced Rabbi Sperber to allow for a compromise. Miriam Sperber recalled: 'For this reason, my husband permitted them to open the stoppages on Rosh Hashanah itself, providing that the work was done by volunteers. The very best boys and their instructors came forward.'[179]

One of the 'best boys' who volunteered was Wolfgang Billig who, shortly afterwards, regretted his enthusiasm. 'Halfway down the sloping meadow was a manhole which held the key to the blocked drains. I went down there to see if I could find out what was happening. When I opened the manhole, everything spurted into my face. It was terrible.'[180] He nevertheless became a hero for resolving the problem.

To take pressure off the toilets within the castle and hopefully prevent the issue reoccurring, eight new military-style earthen latrines known as 'field toilets' were also dug in the grounds to complement the proper ones within.

Julius also had to turn his attention to the ongoing medical needs of the community. He was acutely aware that 200 people sleeping cheek by jowl in overcrowded bedrooms and living in a cold, damp, poorly ventilated building that was regularly filled with toxic fumes from the kitchen, was a recipe for disaster. If he was to have any chance of keeping on top of this, he needed a good plan for general practice medicine. With this in mind, he selected the Cupola Suite, the three rooms in the tower of the north elevation, as suitable to be utilised as a hospital. Isolated, to some extent, from the rest of the castle, the suite provided quiet and comfortable surroundings coupled with a magnificent and therapeutic view out over the Irish Sea and along the sweeping coastline between Rhyl and Colwyn Bay. The suite was subdivided into two wards, one for boys and one for girls, each with their own dedicated kitchen, bathroom and toilet facilities. To add to the ambience, Julius himself would frequently be found on the stairs leading to the medical rooms, playing music on his violin to keep both his patients and staff entertained.

Unfortunately, it soon became apparent that his choice of location was not altogether a good one. They discovered that the roof in this part of the building leaked badly and, in wet weather, water ran down the internal walls. Patches of damp grew quickly. It was not until the summer of 1940, following repeated requests and complaints, that the 13th Earl of Dundonald and government authorities took the issue seriously enough to carry out some much-needed roof repairs to this part of the building.

Initially Julius chose two female *chaverim* as nurses, both of whom 'had hospital training and experience'.[181] Rivka Alterman was an experienced nurse in civilian life 'and concerned herself with the health problems at the castle'[182] as well as helping out as a *chavera* in the kitchens. The nurses were very busy from the off, as many of the children had arrived already unwell. Bladder and kidney disorders appeared surprisingly common and many general colds and earaches were also encountered in the early days. The fact that the *noar* were not 'accustomed to the food of this country and communal cooking' was seen as responsible for 'a certain amount of indigestion'.[183] No doubt, the initial sanitation problems did not help either. The shortage of appropriate clothing was also deemed to be a contributory factor to the prevalence of colds. It was also later noted that, 'The children's powers of resistance had been diminished by the physical, mental and psychological shock they had sustained prior to their arrival to this country.'[184] The health needs of the *noar* meant that the nursing staff had to be quickly expanded to six, which proved extremely fortuitous when the castle's residents fell prey to an infection of German measles over the winter of 1939–40.

Establishing good medical care came with a great expense and there was no avoiding the fact that good medical care and facilities could not be done cheaply. Julius began using all of his natural charm to woo the local medical community in the hope of securing additional help. This would prove to be extremely successful. He turned to David Smith, who was in charge of resourcing the *Hachshara*, for help.

Despite Smith's skills in squeezing extra grants from the Refugee Children's Movement and the Jewish Agency to maintain and run the Gwrych community, he also had to turn to other sources to fully fund the flagship *Hachshara*, if it were to stand as an example to others. Fortunately, they benefitted from the interest of several rich Zionist philanthropists. Ossi Findling, in his role as assistant to David Smith, was aware of the many the levels of support that the training centre received. 'We were very well supported. Basically by two families. The Marks and Spencer families. They sent all the beds and all the equipment. But the Jewish Committee were very helpful … with [providing] beds and bedding, mattresses and food. I think a lot of it was from Marks and Spencer. There was [also] a man called David Gestetner who started a duplicating firm. He was a very religious man. He put in a big effort to make us comfortable. I think he paid a lot for the food.'[185]

The Marks and Spencer and Gestetner links both came via a rather circuitous and fortuitous connection to *chavera* Hanna Zuntz. Zuntz was related to the incredibly wealthy Gestetner family who made significant donations. She was also related to Israel Moses Sieff, a very wealthy Jewish businessman, Chair of the Political and Economic Planning think tank, and a leading Zionist. He was also on the executive committee of *Hachsharath Hanoar* (the British Council of the Young Pioneer Movement for Palestine) which was providing much of the funding for Youth *Aliyah* centres in Britain.[186] Sieff, in turn, was a relative of the wealthy Marks family and of course Rebecca Sieff, who had played a part in helping secure permission from the government for Gwrych Castle to be used as a refugee centre in the first place. It was through these connections that the Marks and Spencer company made significant donations to the *Hachshara* as well as providing the contents of the convoy of lorries that had delivered masses of essential supplies within the first week of the *Hachshara's* opening.

By the end of September 1939, the empty shell of Gwrych had thus been transformed into a hive of activity. As Dr Julius Handler put it, 'The dilapidated, rotting castle came to life again.'[187]

That very first month at the castle was also laden with three significant religious events. Following Rosh Hashanah, the castle community celebrated Yom Kippur, the 'day of atonement' and holiest day of the Jewish year, on 23 September. Traditionally this would involve a full day of prayer and fasting, and no doubt Rabbi Sperber ensured that the occasion was observed dutifully. The end of September saw the beginning of *Sukkot*, a week-long harvest festival during which work around the estate, and on local farms, was partially suspended.

Arieh Handler was so pleased with the progress, and confident enough in the abilities of Seligmann, Smith and Sperber, that at the end of the month he decided to return to London to devote his energies to other *Hachsharot* being developed in Britain. The Gwrych *Hachshara* would, however, remain close to his heart and he made a point of returning for a stay every three months or so.

Within a few weeks of arrival, the youngsters had clearly structured days with an established daily work routine. A defined set of expectations was also forming. Having arrived at Gwrych Castle in a state of bewilderment, they were now actively engaged in preparing themselves for the part they were destined to play in the future creation of *Eretz Yisrael*. Erich Roper, who had noted that he and many others had arrived in Abergele in a mood of 'indifference', began to notice that some in the group were becoming energised by the activities they were now involved in. 'After our arrival here we began to release ourselves from the burden which held us back when we were growing up in Hitler's Germany. We had good plans and we wanted to begin a new life. Our desire was to cast off our apathy, to become people, to achieve justice, Socialism, so to speak, in the world.'[188] For some, the chaos and darkness of their lives in recent months and years was starting to be replaced by a more predictable and secure environment, and their heavily disrupted world was beginning to hold the prospect of a better future.

Nevertheless, the transformation was still built on fragile foundations and the future success of the Gwrych *Hachshara* was by no means certain by the end of September 1939. The bonding process and the creation of a united group had begun but it was far from complete and would take a little time yet to fully form. Most worryingly of all, despite the faith placed in him by Arieh Handler and his success in finding work for his youngsters, Erwin Seligmann was deeply unhappy. He had stayed in close touch with the Great Engeham authorities and by the end of September he was asking lots of questions about his old camp, in particular 'Is my successor a success?'[189] He had loved his role there and, in private it seems, he had been quite reluctant to take up the Gwrych posting and only did so because of his loyalty to Arieh Handler. In a postscript to a private letter to close friends in late September 1939, he confided his true despair: 'I cannot stand it here in the castle any longer. I do not wish to live here any longer. You will surely ask me why? I cannot really give you a proper answer because I do not know the reason myself. All I know is that I cannot stand it any longer.'[190]

CHAPTER 6

'I didn't tell them I was German'

October–November 1939
Aliens, football and meeting the neighbours

Despite Erwin Seligmann's personal misery, his efforts had helped to foster the beginnings of a new optimism amongst the 200 young Jews at Gwrych. He had achieved this through a focus on work and developing community cohesion, helping his charges to build shields that protected them from the traumas of their recent past and distracted them from the fears about what was happening in Germany. This was helped, as one of the *noar* noted, by being 'out in the country, which was a different ball-game because you couldn't tell there was a war on – being in North Wales.'[191] But no shield could keep the war at bay for long. It had the potential to end the whole project. Erwin and the castle community would have to face up to it together.

On the day that Britain declared war, over 70,000 Germans and Austrians living in Britain instantly became classed as 'enemy aliens'. Fearful that a number of 'enemies within' could lie amongst this large group of 'aliens', the government had moved quickly on plans to identify just who those people might be and then to intern them if necessary. By late September 1939, the Aliens Department of the Home Office had set up tribunal panels across the country. Headed by government officials and local representatives, these tribunals were charged with the task of assessing the level of risk that any local aliens over the age of sixteen presented and whether they were a genuine refugee or had the potential to be a Nazi sympathiser. The tribunal would then classify everyone that passed before them as a category A, B or C alien. Category A aliens were deemed to be a potential threat to national security and were to be interned immediately. Category B aliens were exempted from internment but, as there were some doubts about where their loyalties lay, they were made subject to certain stipulated restrictions. These restrictions varied in type, but often included travel limitations and measures to reduce any potential security threat, such as a ban on the ownership of a radio receiver. Category C aliens were deemed to be of no threat at all and were exempt from both internment and any restrictions.

Arieh Handler, as an adult German, feared internment. He may have been concerned that his former, albeit very uncomfortable, relationships with senior Nazis such as Eichmann, could be easily misunderstood by a British tribunal. He had recently left Gwrych to return to his desk at Woburn House in London, home of the Board of Deputies of British Jews. There he combined his work on behalf of *Bachad*, Youth *Aliyah* and the Jewish Agency, whilst simultaneously offering his services as a volunteer fire watcher should the *Luftwaffe* raid the capital. Fearing the worst, he decided to pre-empt the inevitable and packed two suitcases before trudging along to St John's Wood police station to hand himself in. After making some initial enquiries, the police received a message directly from the Home Office, following representations made on his behalf by Rebecca Sieff, with instructions to categorise him as a class C alien. With a dismissive shrug, the police officer who delivered the news told Handler that 'they say that you are better outside than inside, so you'd better go home.'[192] In fact, Arieh was deemed so 'safe' that over the coming weeks and months he was occasionally contacted by the police to ask his opinion of other individuals facing a tribunal.

At Gwrych Castle, around half of the refugees were under the age of sixteen and thus not required to face an assessment. However, the other half of the *noar* and all of the *chaverim* of German or Austrian origin would have to face a tribunal, and the examinations began during October 1939.

Those from the Gwrych Castle *Hachshara* who were called before a tribunal had to make their way thirty-five miles to Caernarfon to be assessed in front of the presiding officer, H. Walter Samuel. The first to go was *chaver* Hermann Eliahu Israel Blum, who appeared before the tribunal on Wednesday, 4 October 1939. Despite being a student rabbi and therefore just about the least likely person one could imagine as a potential Nazi sympathiser, he was categorised as class B and thus placed under certain restrictions. Just over a week later, on Friday, 13 October, three more members of the Gwrych *Hachshara*, Dr Julius Handler, Bill Braun and sixteen-year-old Edmund Schnitzer from Wattenscheid, Germany, travelled to Caernarfon for their tribunals. Julius and Bill were both categorised as class C and thus released from any further consideration, whereas Edmund was placed under class B restrictions. On Wednesday, 18 October 1939, six more members of the community, five of whom were *chaverim*, had to present themselves before H. Walter Samuel in Caernarfon. The six included two twenty-two-year-olds: Pauline [Karo] Gerson from Stuttgart and Ruth Muller from Vienna. Also judged was twenty-year-old Selma Horovitz from Frankfurt, who had been hastily signed up for Kindertransport by her parents just before her eighteenth birthday, when one of her father's clients had taken their own life out of fear of Nazi reprisals. Nineteen-year-old *chavera* Eva Carlebach and sixteen-year-old Oskar Urmann, both from Hamburg, and eighteen-year-old Caecilie Donner from Vienna made up the remainder of the contingent that stood before Mr Samuel. All were categorised class C and released without restrictions.[193]

The Gwrych community heaved a huge sigh of relief at the results of these early tribunals. There was shock and dismay that a couple of the residents had been classified as B, but not a single one had been interned and the vast majority had been given a metaphorical 'clean bill of health'.[194] Had it been anything otherwise, the entire project would likely have collapsed.

By the beginning of October, the community had fallen into a comfortingly familiar and predictable daily routine; a combination of farm work, education and rostered duties made up the weekdays, with Saturday, the Shabbat, a day of rest. Breakfast on Shabbat, at least in the early days, consisted of nothing more exciting than slabs of bread with some butter, although butter was a rare treat normally reserved for the sandwiches made for the farm workers, whereas those on site had to make to do with margarine. On Shabbat, there was butter for all. Nevertheless, Sonia Marder recalls, the children 'wanted to put something on the bread and butter but we had nothing, so we used to take onions and slice them up and we ate bread and butter with onions, and I want to tell you something, 180 children eating bread and butter with onions in a dining room with their counsellors, it smelled to high heaven but nobody cared.'[195]

For many youngsters, Sundays were also relatively quiet as they were not expected for work on local farms (though many did help out at the farms on Sundays when required). Often the only work they did on that day was related to the duty rosters but all of that left them very little time for leisure. Despite this, intensive efforts were made by the leadership team 'to keep those children occupied'.[196] Some of those activities were a little underwhelming for a group of teenagers, such as being marched en masse to the hunting lodge to watch the sun rise or set. Children being children, they proved themselves quite capable of finding distractions without any real requirement for help from the adults.

However, Erwin Seligmann was driven by the desire to help form bonds within the *noar* and he assumed that organised activities were one of the best ways to achieve this. He may also have been motivated by the hope of keeping the youngsters quiet for, as Henry Glanz recalled, 'we were up to no good a lot of the time.'[197] The activities may also have been to provide alternative distractions to those who might otherwise sneak off into Abergele. Whilst they were not actively encouraged to mix with the locals, restrictions on their movement were reasonably lax and the braver ones, often surreptitiously, during September and

October 1939, made their way into town. Salli Edelnand, as already noted, had wandered off and encountered his first local within a few hours of his arrival, and it was during early October that Henry Glanz and some friends made their first foray into town and had their terrifying encounter with PC Sam Williams whilst window-shopping.

Organising activities was also a useful way of providing the *noar* with distractions from the reality of the increasingly disturbing news about the progress of the war. Poland had surrendered on 27 September and two days later the Nazis and the Soviets had divided their spoils, resulting in two million Polish Jews now being in Nazi hands. In early October the deportation of Jews from Vienna began. A number of those at Gwrych had Polish or Viennese backgrounds, and therefore had family members who would have been caught up in these events.

Mizrachi and other Jewish organisations were, no doubt, extremely aware of what was happening in mainland Europe, and the likes of Arieh Handler and other members of the Gwrych leadership group would have been well informed. The children, too, were not ignorant of the news. Henry Steinberg noted that, 'We were pretty isolated from the outside world but were fully aware that the troubled world was still out there.'[198]

Erwin Seligmann frequently provided interested youngsters with the latest war news. He was acutely aware of the concern many of the children had for loved ones at home as well as being wise to the fact that many were getting snippets of news in personal letters that often left out the more disturbing developments. Without wishing to increase their concerns unduly, Erwin believed that the children had a right to be kept up to date with what was happening in the war if they wanted to know. Besides, many of them knew some aspects of how Jews were being treated. Henry Steinberg said, 'We knew about concentration camps as they existed before the war.'[199] Often a group would gather around Erwin as he read to them from British newspapers and provided them with other updates on the situation in mainland Europe. One member of the *noar* recalled one of those evenings:

In the semi-dark, I recognise a familiar silhouette of a head. Especially the glasses of a somewhat 'upright' person. Erwin! Who would miss out on the opportunity to live here? Erwin starts again with a political overview. He describes the fighting situation in the Russian–Finnish border area [the Soviet Union attacked Finland on 30 November 1939], speaks of Germany, of Sweden, Holland and Belgium and their precautions. Questions are raised. How is Italy? What will America do? What will the other small states do? Erwin answers all questions. Eli Freier and Osias Findling bring news from *The Jewish Chronicle* about Poland. Destruction, executions, imprisonment, coercive measures, etc. A bitter fate for this considerable part of the Jewish people. Silence. Several minutes pass. It is already long night. But no one is able to break the prevailing, almost solemn mood.[200]

Although the news that Erwin gave was rarely comforting, he was highly respected for his honesty.

Arieh Handler, on his frequent visits to the castle, would host what Henry Glanz recalled as 'press conferences', where he would provide a detailed update on the progress of the war, also primarily based on news from British newspapers. With hindsight, Henry believed that Arieh's presentations played down the dire straits Britain was sinking into – especially in 1940 after the evacuation of the British Army from Dunkirk – to shore up potentially wavering morale amongst the castle community. However, neither Henry nor others could have known that at the time. As far as they were concerned the news they received was real, and sometimes far too real for comfort; Henry was particularly struck by Arieh mentioning a British bombing raid on his home city of Kiel.[201]

Despite the restrictions and difficulties created by the war, many of the youngsters were still in contact with parents, family and friends by letter. The vast majority of these contained nothing more than personal and family news, but the horror of what was beginning to happen in

Nazi-dominated Europe must have permeated these communications to some extent. However, the children's parents and the *Hachshara* adults may often have spared the youngsters the more worrying details. Henry Glanz believed that his father self-censored his communications[202] and Henry Steinberg, looking back over fifty years later, believed that, in their monthly exchange of letters, his father was, 'inclined to pretend that some bad things aren't really existing … he did not at all elaborate.'[203]

Ossi Findling was able to maintain contact with his mother, who had found refuge with relatives in Belgium. They wrote to each other on a monthly basis, until Belgium was invaded by the Nazis in May 1940. His memory of the contents of that correspondence was that it was generally dominated by quite typical maternal concern and that the bigger issues were downplayed: 'They [his family] wrote that conditions weren't very good but that they were alright. She [his mother] only wanted to know how I am. Have you got underwear, have you got this, have you got that? Have you got enough food?'[204]

Initially, most of the direct mail that could be maintained was done via the International Red Cross, but this was not at all straightforward. At a cost of 2 ½ shillings, each child was permitted just one letter per month, consisting of no more than twenty-five words, including the address. As one Gwrych refugee commented, 'What can you say? "I am well. Hope you are well." And that's about it.'[205]

Once the deportations of Jews began on the continent, direct mail from Wales to their homelands was no longer possible. Some used third parties to maintain contact. Herman Rothman managed to stay in touch with his parents for quite some time, through an address in neutral Sweden that had been given to him by another of the Gwrych refugees. Henry Glanz sent his letters to relatives in the USA (neutral until December 1941) who then posted them on to Europe on his behalf. Replies followed the same path but in reverse.[206] This circuitous route may have been another reason why many of his father's letters lacked detail: 'I had a feeling my father censored some of my letters, because he didn't want the Germans to know I was in England.'[207]

Even when things were at their darkest, many parents probably spared their children from some of the details. Via the International Red Cross, Salli Edelnand wrote to his father in Halberstadt frequently and he received regular, if delayed, replies in return. Most of these letters were simple news exchanges with family gossip updates that gave little hint of what was truly happening at home. Salli managed to maintain contact until well after he had left Gwrych, receiving what turned out to be a final brief message from his father via the International Red Cross on 14 April 1942; the message had been despatched in February but within days of sending it both of his parents and his younger sister had been deported to the Warsaw ghetto where they would die in unrecorded circumstances. 'Beloved Salli! We were really happy about the message. We are healthy. Write immediately, we wait. Countless greetings and kisses from parents and sister. Israel Edelnand. February 27 1942.'[208]

Henry Glanz received what proved to be his last letter from his mother when he was later living in London. Dated 21 October 1941, his mother's final words were written to both him and his sister Gisela, with whom Henry had managed to reunite by that time: 'My beloved dear children, always hold together in love and faithfulness, and God will bless you. Papa writes often and wants us to come to Brussels, but unfortunately we cannot. Farewell, my dearest beloved children, we wish you all the best and ask God for a speedy reunion.'[209] Seven months later, Henry's mother and brother were murdered in a Polish extermination camp. His father was sent to Auschwitz a year after Henry had received his last letter from his mother.

Some parents were a little more honest. Having exchanged several letters with home via his contact in Sweden, Herman Rothman received some extremely upsetting news from his mother in October 1939: 'she sounded – I could see in the letter, the tone of it – absolutely distraught, by saying that my father was arrested and put into the concentration camp of Sachsenhausen … I took this letter into the lavatory and for the first time I burst out crying. I always kept myself as manly as possible, not showing my emotions. In this case I did not want to show my emotions in public. I knew that is the end for my father.'[210]

Herman's attempt to conceal his despair in one of the toilet rooms of the castle probably did not go unnoticed but it may have gone unremarked upon. When asked, years later, whether any of the children talked about what was happening at home, one resident commented, 'I don't know if the subject ever came up. I don't know if we ever talked about our parents. They were out of our life.'[211] However, Henry Glanz, when asked about the general mood of the *noar* in this regard, recalled things differently. Not everyone kept things to themselves, he remembered, 'some couldn't talk about anything else apart from their parents. Some were happy. Some were miserable.'[212] Erika Heisler-Lieberman was amongst the latter group. She was in contact with home, but it had never occurred to her to bring photos of her family with her to Britain and, as a result, she felt 'very lonely, extremely lonely'.[213]

Although some, like Herman Rothman, attempted to erect for themselves a barrier to reality, they all knew that every letter received had the power to be magically uplifting or utterly devastating. As Henry Steinberg recalled, 'Inside the castle we were very supportive of one another. We were concerned with everyday existence but we were also very apprehensive as to what was happening to everybody's family members still in Germany. Here and there somebody was informed that a family member died at the hand of the Germans. It was very traumatic for all who knew that person, but most of us felt that no news was good news. But there was always bad news for someone.'[214]

For some, that bad news was particularly terrible. In the spring of 1940, Isi Peterseil received a brief note via the Red Cross from his mother: she had received the ashes of his father, who had not been seen since being arrested during the Austrian *Anschluss* of 1938. Isi heard nothing further from her and only learned many years later that she had been burned alive in Radomysl, Poland, in 1943.

Another to receive the terrible news that a family member had died was a young girl from Kiel, Henry Glanz's hometown.[215] He recalled that 'She had information from the Red Cross, that her father was murdered in a *KZ*.[216] Her mind snapped, and Erwin [Seligmann] arranged for her to be admitted to a hospital in Birmingham. I visited her there about a year later. It was very distressing, she did not recognise me.'[217]

The castle leadership had recognised early on that strong bonds and friendships between the children would be important. They would provide support mechanisms for each other to help them move on from what they had been through but also for what they would face in the future. One of the youngsters, known only as Drori, wrote: 'The greatest bond between people is friendship ... a real friendship, once sealed, will never break ... Friendship is a goal; something to give to one another in order to perfect oneself.'[218]

For many it was the mutual sharing of information from home that developed those relationships far more than any of the distracting activities the leadership offered. It was also at those moments of receiving bad news from home that those bonds of friendship were at their most vital. Henry Glanz continued to visit the broken girl from Kiel who had been sent to Birmingham until the final days of her life, which ended in a care home some sixty years later. She never recovered from the trauma of that letter and she never recognised Henry.

Nevertheless, not everything was bleak and many of the children quickly began to find ways of distracting and entertaining themselves. When Dr Julius Handler had first arrived in August 1939, the only items of furniture in the castle were a broken chair and a table. Before the Marks and Spencer and Baptist Chapel donations poured in, this table had already been put to good use by the irrepressible Jesse Zierler and some of his new friends. He recalled, 'A flat-topped wooden contraption, richly carved on all four sides, graced the first-floor landing. It might well have been designed for resting the coffin of a recently departed member of the family. From our point of view, it now served a far better purpose as a ping-pong table, being of almost regulation height and size. It very soon became the venue for inter-group and inter-room tournaments, and greatly improved the overall standard of table tennis, but not doing much to maintain the antique's appearance.'[219]

Using bats they had fashioned for themselves out of bits of wood, ping-pong became perhaps one of the most popular sporting activities amongst the *noar*. Unfortunately for them, the *chaverim* were also keen on the game and they often abused their superior status by dominating time on the makeshift table. This resulted in many arguments over the next few months until it was finally settled in January 1940 by a challenge tournament between the *noar* and the *chaverim*. Who won is, unfortunately, unclear.

It was also common to see the *chaverim* indulging in volleyball. Playing the sport was the brainchild of the carpenter Alfred Kallner. Although we do not know for certain, he probably did little more than create a playing area by stretching some string between two wooden posts stuck into the ground. Following Kallner's early departure from the castle, volleyball organisation was taken over by all-round sportsman Jack Adler who arranged several inter-*plugoth* tournaments.

Table tennis and volleyball were by no means the only sports the youngsters enjoyed. Initially, the greatest hindrance to them was that they had no access to any sporting equipment unless, like Herman Rothman and his running spikes, they had brought it with them. Therefore, the ingenuity shown by Jesse Zierler repurposing the neglected table had to be the model for other sporting endeavours. It was not long before the children had developed ways of participating in various forms of athletics in the castle grounds. A variety of running, jumping and throwing activities were quickly and easily set up and most proved very popular.

And then there was football. Some argue that the sport is an international language and Henry Glanz discovered early on in his time in Abergele that there could be some truth in this cliché. His first real encounter with local boys of a similar age came when he was walking near the Abergele National School on Market Street and stopped to watch some boys playing football on a patch of grass nearby. Henry was asked if he wanted to join in and was beckoned into the game with no real quizzing of who he was or why he had a strange accent.[220]

Up at the *Hachshara*, having gained a ball from some donation or other,[221] flatter areas near the castle soon found themselves festooned with discarded jackets as goalposts as the boys took to spontaneous games. In next to no time, football competitions between the *plugoth* were arranged and, inevitably, thoughts turned towards having a Castle First XI team. By early October 1939, the team was formed, calling themselves simply 'Gwrych Castle'. The team was primarily made up from the Kindertransport youths, but it was augmented with a few of the younger *chaverim*. Henry Glanz, who liked to play as a defender, was disappointed not to make the team; a decision he puts down to the influence of a rather arrogant goalkeeper who claimed he was so good that he did not need a defence in front of him.[222]

The goalkeeper's arrogance was swiftly shattered by the result of their first game in October 1939, which was played away against the National School. The school were a player short so Gwrych Castle FC, with a player spare, graciously 'loaned' Mondek Winczelberg to their opponents. In a game described as 'cleanly contested',[223] the National School thrashed the refugees 8–0.

Exactly who else Gwrych Castle FC played and when, is sadly unknown, but by the end of December 1939 they had played their fifth game against local sides and won all bar their first match. Their fourth victory was against a team from the Abergele Sanatorium. All that survives on record about that match is a note that someone called Mulli scored the second goal and Jack Adler scored the third.[224] Gary Lineker's famous quote that 'football is a simple game. Twenty-two men chase a ball for ninety minutes and at the end, the Germans always win' seems to have had sound historical precedents.

Playing chess was another popular pastime and the children also often amused themselves with a variety of their own invented games. The castle was ideal for games of hide and seek, which could go on for hours. However, the leadership also had to ensure that there were other distractions available, especially for those who were less inclined towards games, sporting activities or just joining in with things in general. For example, religious observance was a key part of the ethos of the community and thus the daily life of the *Hachshara* and also provided a series of events for all to participate in. Rabbi Sperber ensured that everything possible was run in strictly orthodox fashion. Every Friday evening, once the sun had set, dutifully observed preparations for Shabbat began. Most of the community thoroughly enjoyed the evening, especially Herman Rothman: 'Every member could read fluent Hebrew and we conducted the services. Very lovely services. They thought I had a fairly good voice [Jewish services or prayers are often sung] and very often I was taken to lead the services. I felt uplifted.'[225]

Saturdays – Shabbat – were particularly looked forward to. Work of any kind was not permitted and the most routine of tasks such as the lighting of fires, even on the coldest of days, was put to one side. The only person who appeared to be annoyed by this was the local milkman, Mr Morrison, who received no help that day and consequently had to make numerous trips down to the cellar laden with heavy bottles.[226] Many, of course, used Shabbat as intended, but many also used it as a chance to get out and about beyond the confines of the castle. Walks in the local hills or down into Abergele were popular and, on warmer, drier days, many would spend much of the day on the beach.

By the end of October 1939, a few new 'traditions' had been established at the castle and one of them took place every Saturday night. The day's events would culminate in a well-attended dance, during which 'no one was left out, every girl was invited to dance',[227] and music was provided in whatever form possible – often by Dr Julius Handler.

Julius's passion for music was shared by several of the youngsters and one or two had, somehow, brought their own instruments with them from home. While occasional donations from the local community were often politely declined, they were happily and eagerly accepted if they included a musical instrument. So Julius proposed to set up an orchestra. Within twelve hours of a request for players appearing alongside the work roster in the dining room, half a dozen or so youngsters had volunteered. It was more of a band than an orchestra in the early days, but nobody seemed to mind. Julius played his beloved violin and later on his sibling Arieh also somehow acquired an accordion which he donated to the orchestra. Herman Rothman, who could also play the violin, took a leading role in the project, and it took his mind off the recent news of his father's arrest and detention at Sachsenhausen. 'Being occupied with that took my mind away from any other things. It was, in actual fact, for my benefit that I formed this music group. I never forgot my parents of course, I was always worried about them, but it made it a bit easier to have a cultural life.'[228]

In the hope of impressing the Handler brothers, the orchestra made time to practise and improve whenever possible. However, they had their limitations and desperately needed guidance. A request for a music teacher was put out and before long, a young female *chavera*, and gifted violinist, Henny Prilutsky, had been selected for occasional visits. Arieh Handler was almost certainly directly involved in this decision as he had met Henny in Berlin in 1938 before leaving Germany. Both had been members of the same choir and Arieh had quickly fallen in love, even though his shyness meant that his 'adoration was not immediately obvious'.[229] However, Henny 'did not take any particular notice of him. There were other young men ... Arieh pretended he was not interested in girls. He was too busy with his serious work of getting Jews out of Germany.'[230] Nevertheless a courtship of sorts had developed between the two of them, only to be swiftly ended when Arieh found himself stranded in Jerusalem and unable to return home following the events of *Kristallnacht*. Henny eventually managed to leave Germany with a visa arranged through Youth *Aliyah* in August 1939 and gained a job as a domestic servant in London. Arieh met up with her again after completing the first phase of the setting up of the Gwrych *Hachshara*, restarting communications under the guise of having concerns for the welfare of Henny's younger sister who was at a smaller *Bachad Hachshara* in Scotland.

Henny had a 'striking personality ... tall, slim, tastefully dressed, she exuded a sense of confidence bolstered by a discreet irony and distinctive sense of humour. Any bombastic statement by Arieh could easily be punctured by a gentle, ironic intervention accompanied by a slight smile. Arieh appeared for a considerable time to have been at a loss on how to win this pretty, artistic girl.'[231]

Henny was acutely aware of Arieh's befuddlement and tried to entice him out of it by inviting him to meet with her twice weekly for singing sessions. Rather than be encouraged, Arieh became more 'hesitant, apparently doubting his singing prowess.'[232] In reality, he was unsure as to whether Henny would accept him, causing bemusement amongst his circle of male friends as 'this was not the confident Arieh'[233] they knew.

Although it's not certain, one night at the height of the Blitz may have played a part in Arieh resolving to seize the moment. As a volunteer fire watcher whilst in London, he witnessed scenes of death and destruction on a regular basis, and one night during that terrible ordeal he finally summoned up the courage to ask Henny to be his wife. Henny, of course, accepted. When the news broke, it was greeted by the delight of all at Gwrych Castle.

Theirs was not the only romance in the air. *Chaver* David Granek and *chavera* Selly Neufeld began a relationship that would result in them marrying in the spring of 1941 and two of the *noar*, Gerhard Drukarz and Herthel Flaschmann, began a courtship that led to their marriage in 1947. There were also a number of short-lived romances during the two years that the centre was open and many more where the feelings were largely one-sided and never developed beyond an unrequited or undeclared infatuation. Henry Glanz grew very keen on a girl one year older than himself, but he was far too shy to ever tell her.[234]

In October 1939, three of the *noar*, Erich Roper, Bill Braun and Bernhard Liwerant had got together to produce a community newsletter, which they intended to publish on a monthly basis. *Der Daat Hachshara* contained a mix of notices from the castle leadership, polemical pieces of a Zionist nature and a roundup of recent events within the community, as well as submissions from *chaverim* and *noar* alike. Due to paper shortages and the difficulties of reproduction, just a handful of copies of the first edition were produced, but it wasn't long before the publication's popularity saw it having to expand its print-run.

When they started out, it would have been in the minds of the three budding journalists to have something ready in time for a major occasion that was energising everyone at the castle. Having beaten off bids from several other Jewish youth refugee centres, the flagship Gwrych *Hachshara* had been chosen to host the first *Pegisha* of the *Bachad* in Britain during the weekend of 27–29 October 1939.

This *Pegisha* was a major get-together of representatives from eleven *Hachsharot* from around the country as well as being attended by various *Bachad* VIPs. It was held partly for social reasons and to celebrate a unity between the various *Hachsharot*, but more importantly, it was a chance to cement their common purpose as well as to discuss the problems that they mutually faced with the hope of sharing good practice and finding solutions. That the honour was handed to the movement's 'youngest *Hachshara*' showed the importance of Gwrych as a beacon for the *Bachad* mission.

The Gwrych delegates at the *Pegisha*, along with their counterparts from the other centres, held discussions about various organisational issues as well as comparing and contrasting their differing educational programmes. They discussed the role of the *chaverim* and the problems they faced, particularly in terms of their own personal and financial support as unpaid volunteers. There was also a recognition of the difficulties in recruiting further *chaverim* who generally preferred to stay in or near London. No doubt, the Gwrych delegates had in mind the very recent departure of Alfred Kallner from the carpentry shop and the ongoing issue of not having a proper chef to run the kitchen. The discussion resulted in some criticisms for Arieh Handler to consider, the main one being *Bachad*'s refusal to offer any financial incentive to the *chaverim*. Whether Arieh and *Bachad* did something with this suggestion is not entirely clear but it does seem likely for, during 1940, both the vacant roles of carpenter and chef at Gwrych were filled.

Nevertheless, the *Pegisha* was deemed to have been a great success and, by the time of its conclusion, the consensus was that it had helped the various communities represented at the conference 'to define our path for the future in a single-minded manner.'[235] The *Pegisha* also gave the visiting delegates a glimpse of the approach being taken by their flagship enterprise. Certainly, Jack Sklan, who attended the meeting as a *Bachad* executive member, was impressed by what he saw at Gwrych and soon afterwards he wrote an article for the movement's newsletter in which he extolled its virtues as the model centre: 'the sight of some 150 youngsters sitting down to a meal after a day's work in the fields, their faces showing a little of their happiness, is really something inspiring to the beholder. More especially so when one realises that this is no ordinary refugee hostel, but a place which is preparing young people for a future life.'[236]

The *Pegisha* also stimulated a greater political awareness amongst many of the refugees at the castle. Some already held strong political views and Erwin Seligmann would often spend time with small groups, encouraging and provoking debates to help them develop their understanding. He also encouraged the youngsters to form and attend a regular student council meeting, known as the *Assefah*, where they could air their questions and concerns about the running of the *Hachshara*.

Early meetings of the *Assefah* were dominated by volatile discussions about creating and raising a *kupa*, a collective fund from which the *noar* could access some 'spending money'. By the end of 1939, more and more children had become brave enough to consider wandering in and out of Abergele in their spare time, but many still did not. This was partly because, once they had arrived in town, there was little they could do without money to spend. Some, with family or friends outside of Nazi-controlled territories, received occasional postal orders that could be cashed at Abergele Post Office, a responsible job carried out by one of the older *noar*, Leopold Chajes, every week or two. Some even opened savings accounts at the Post Office. However, the majority of the *noar* were not in this position and standing around in the town looking into shops that sold sweets, chocolate and other goodies was a doleful experience for teenagers with no money in their pockets. This was made much worse by the fact that their Welsh peers on the farms, who had mostly left school at the age of fourteen, were getting paid for their labour. The Jewish teenagers were working on the very same farms but they were not being paid a penny.

Between their arrival and the end of November 1939, the relationship between those at the *Hachshara* and the local community of Abergele continued to grow, but cautiously at first. The refugees' initial arrival had been rushed. Arrangements had been made directly between *Bachad*, the government and Lord Dundonald, with no input from or communication with the local community. To put it simply, 200 people at the castle had appeared as if from nowhere and, quite literally, overnight.

For the first two or three months, most members of the community at Gwrych rarely strayed beyond the estate or their allotted farms. This was partly out of fear of how they might be treated by the locals, not just because they were used to antisemitism, but because most of them were German and from the country that Britain was currently at war with. As Miriam Sperber said, 'the presence of a large group of refugees who spoke German and were engaged in who knows what at the castle' had the potential to prove 'very upsetting to the local Welshmen'.[237]

Herman Rothman was acutely aware of the issue. On his first day at work, when he was quizzed by Welsh farm hands, he told them that he was Polish. 'I didn't tell them I was German. That would have been absolutely murderous, they would have killed me.'[238]

There was an additional reason why the children remained wary of the town in their early days at the castle, and that was that they were deterred from going. *Bachad* wanted its members to accept and develop the spirit of communal engagement that would later be expected in a kibbutz in *Eretz Yisrael*. The whole point of the *Hachsharot* movement was to prepare and train their youth for *Aliyah*. They could ill afford for the young people in their centres to become too involved with their current local communities as that ran the danger of them becoming assimilated and losing that clear focus. Most other *Hachsharot* accepted that view and they very much kept themselves to themselves. However, at Gwrych

Castle, Arieh Handler wanted to attempt something a little different and he promoted a middle way. He explained to Erwin Seligmann and the leadership team that he wanted the *Hachshara* to 'remain isolated' but at the same time 'they should be part of the community.'[239] In essence, Arieh wanted the Gwrych *Hachshara* to develop a very good relationship with the local community but to also retain a respectful distance from it.

Quite how that difficult balancing act could be achieved was not immediately clear but Rabbi Sperber enthusiastically volunteered to lead the way as the castle's public relations maestro. According to his wife, Sperber 'wanted to draw closer to the local people in order to explain that these young people hated Germany no less' than they did.[240] He believed that such a pathway could be successfully negotiated if the castle community could present itself as proudly Jewish but at the same time 'normal' in the eyes of the locals. In an attempt to achieve this, he decided to make regular appearances in the town and to be seen doing completely ordinary and typical things. One of his most bemusing attempts to demonstrate this involved going to the local pubs in the evening, just as many of the townsmen did. The experience soon proved somewhat awkward for all concerned, though, as the Rabbi wasn't really one for alcohol and the regulars felt uncomfortable drinking heavily in front of a man of the cloth. Completely contrary to his good intentions he often found himself stood in corners and looking out of place in the pubs he visited. Sperber soon realised that he was just listening in to people's conversations rather than being part of them and, fearing that this could be mistaken as the behaviour of a foreign spy, the Rabbi soon stopped going to pubs.

Something that worked better was enrolling his five-year-old daughter, Avigail, at the National School. She quickly fitted in well, possibly helped by the presence of two older Jewish children who had both arrived in the town as evacuees, and soon began picking up the Welsh language, including learning the Welsh national anthem which she was delighted to sing every morning. Ultimately it was the children of the *Hachshara* that would create Arieh's desired connection between

Gwrych Castle and the town. It had been the children sneaking off to explore Abergele at beginning of October 1939 that effectively alerted locals to the presence of the group of Germans at the castle. After PC Sam Williams and his colleagues arrived at the castle with cake a few days after their encounter with Henry Glanz and his friends, a message was sent to both communities. The local residents were assured that there was nothing to fear from the 'Germans at the castle' and the refugees learned that leaving the confines of the castle estate was maybe not quite as dangerous as they had first feared. Refugee pioneers quickly discovered that the locals were not antisemitic and that most were actually quite friendly. It was a far cry from what they had been used to back home and, as word got around amongst the children that Abergele was a safe place to go, more and more of them confronted their personal anxieties and went to look around.

A plan was developed by Seligmann, Smith and Rabbi Sperber as they recognised that some of the children were going to sneak into town whether they approved of it or not. They put together an organised rota of who could go down and when. In the early days, due to their own fears and an understandable reluctance to be alone, the refugees usually appeared in small, quiet groups. They would be nervously trying not to attract attention and, as a result, end up standing out like a sore thumb. Julius Handler noted that, 'their isolation would only be exaggerated by their custom of always moving about in tightly knit groups.'[241] Even so, the little groups found they were welcome in Abergele[242] and their presence soon became unremarkable, especially as familiarity grew.

Most of the castle residents got to know locals of a similar age through working on the farms, and bumping into them in town would lead to nods of recognition and even conversations. Local boys playing football were always happy to let the Jewish boys join in, especially as stories of their ability began to circulate once Gwrych Castle FC began hammering all opposition.

Another reason the group were always welcome in Abergele was that they were polite and courteous to a fault. Good manners had been reinforced with all Kindertransport children right from their initial arrival in the country. After disembarking from the ferries at Harwich, every Kindertransportee had been handed a little note in both German and English written by J. H. Hertz, the Chief Rabbi, stressing the importance of good behaviour: 'You are a Jewish child and ... often the whole Jewish people are judged by the actions of any one of us.'[243] At the castle, good manners and politeness were expected by Seligmann, Smith and Rabbi Sperber. The children took all of this very seriously and bent over backwards to give a good impression even if it that sometimes resulted in their behaviour being so formal as to be somewhat comical. Before the hairdressing 'salon' at the castle was fully up to speed, David Smith had come to an arrangement with D. Hywel Roberts, a local barber, to receive groups of six children at a time and then to invoice him at the castle. Julius Handler wrote to a friend to explain that 'After the haircut each youth would stand firmly to attention and say "Mr Smith will pay!"'[244]

Little by little, through the autumn and early winter of 1939, a good relationship between the town and the castle grew and the positive reception from the local community was even noted in *Bachad*'s national journal.[245] By and large, the relationship had developed in line with Arieh Handler's plan and, by the end of November 1939, the Gwrych *Hachshara* had established itself *within* the local community whilst not becoming *part* of the local community. This was just as well, because the strength of that developing relationship was about to be very seriously tested.

CHAPTER 7

'An old bowler hat'

December 1939–February 1940
Blackouts, winter and *The Wizard of Oz*

Although a long way from the main hub of the war, the North Wales coastline was in fact a front line of sorts. Huge amounts of shipping were going to and fro daily between the major port of Liverpool and Ireland, or out into the Atlantic and far beyond. German U-boat attacks on ships around Anglesey had occurred during the Great War and enemy submarines were patrolling in the Irish Sea once again. Both U29 and U33 had been laying mines, one of which was suspected of having caused the loss of a ship near Liverpool on 2 February 1940. Ten days later, U33 was sunk by a depth-charge attack in the North Channel entrance to the Irish Sea between Scotland and Northern Ireland, and on 3 March 1940 a ship outbound from Liverpool was sunk by U41 off the southern Irish coast, before the submarine itself was hunted and sunk by the destroyer HMS *Antelope*. As a consequence, twin-engined Avro Anson maritime patrol aircraft of Coastal Command were a regular sight in the skies over the sea north of Abergele.

Having a friendly spy on land, providing landing parties with information, or sending signals, would be a positive boon to any U-boat commander patrolling the North Wales coast. Unsurprisingly, therefore, unfounded rumours that a German spy was active in the local area had already begun to circulate before the end of 1939 and well before the nationwide 'spy fever' of spring 1940 that would significantly enhance such fears.

So, it was inevitable that a very small number of locals might be wary of the refugees at the castle, regardless of the early rulings of the Caernarfon 'enemy aliens' tribunals and the efforts of Rabbi Sperber and others to develop good relationships with the local community. For a small minority, perhaps susceptible to conspiracy theories, there was always the *possibility* that the refugees at the castle might not be all that they appeared and may even be a threat. What if the suspected enemy agent in the area had burrowed themselves into their ranks?

Gwrych has a magnificent view of the entire coastline from Colwyn Bay to Rhyl, and visible on the horizon to the west is Anglesey and to the east, Liverpool. On a particularly clear day, the Isle of Man to the north can be discerned. In December 1939, strange lights were seen at the castle, further stoking rumours among the suspicious minority. Could the mysterious lights be somebody signalling to a U-boat out in the bay? Some forty years later the rumours that circulated as a result of this odd sighting were still being given some credence by a local historian who wrote that 'Mrs Williams, [of] Cae Bedw, still retains a schoolgirl memory that a relation of hers had seen lights flashing out to sea from the rocks above Tan yr Ogof.[246] Were they indeed, as supposed, signals to a German U-boat in Abergele Bay? Had there been a Nazi infiltrator among the refugees? We shall not know the answer until those sworn to secrecy are allowed to tell what they know.'[247]

In reality, the only accurate part of this account is that the incident raised some concerns at the time. The far less fanciful truth was that a simple, though admittedly dangerous, mistake had been made by the group at Gwrych Castle.

On 6 December 1939, the refugee community began to celebrate Chanukah, the eight-day winter 'festival of lights' marked by the daily lighting of a new candle on a menorah which, traditionally, would be placed in a window. However, the castle residents knew that this was not possible as there were strict blackout regulations in place for the hours of darkness, designed to deny enemy bombers any glimpse of what lay below them to aid their navigation. Air Raid Patrol (ARP) wardens and special constables went around Abergele and the district at night checking that windows were sufficiently covered to prevent chinks of light escaping. The punishment for breaking the rules was a fine that could potentially rise to £500[248] or result in up to two years' imprisonment. The most favoured ways of complying with the blackout requirements was to hang heavy, dark curtains over the window frame aperture or, for a simpler and cheaper alternative, to apply an opaque black paint directly on to the window glass. Both of these approaches were being utilised, as best as possible, at the castle. The problem was that there were scores of windows to cover, many of which were an unusual shape. Undeterred, David Smith had already procured a large number of heavy drapes, with more ordered and on the way.

The castle's leadership team were well briefed on the blackout regulations and expectations and had participated in the town's air raid training exercise on Wednesday, 13 December, when all the sirens in Denbighshire had been sounded to test the readiness of local precautions. PC Sam Williams had continued to visit and on one recent visit during Chanukah, he had issued admonishments to them for minor violations of the blackout rules. There was, therefore, little excuse when, just four days later, a window was left uncovered. A number of locals reported seeing a light up at the Gwrych Castle estate, prompting another visit by PC Williams who, on this occasion, was in a far less friendly mood.

On Saturday, 6 January 1940, David Smith stood at Abergele Police Court before Superintendent Tomkins and its chairman Lord Clwyd, to answer a charge of breaching the blackout regulations on behalf of the castle management. It was alleged that on the night of Sunday, 17 December 1939, as many as seventeen people had reported visible lights on the top floor of the castle's main building and from its tower room (almost certainly therefore from the boys' quarters and Dr Julius Handler's hospital suite). The lights were also seen by a patrolling special constable and by PC Sam Williams himself, who both immediately made their way up to the castle to investigate. PC Williams stated in court that prior to the night in question, he had noticed lights at the castle on two separate occasions in the previous weeks and that on his visits he had met with both Rabbi Sperber and David Smith to issue them with relevant advice and warnings. On this third occasion he felt the need to act more formally. He went on to explain that, by the time he had arrived at the castle, the lights were no longer visible and that he had been greeted by Rabbi Sperber who, somewhat disingenuously, had attempted to claim that the constable must have been mistaken. PC Williams had asked to inspect the upper floor where he caught boys red-handed in two rooms still displaying lights without an apparent care in the world. In the tower he had also found an extinguished kerosene lamp that was still very hot to the touch. A shamefaced Rabbi Sperber had then admitted to all of the lights in question.

Rabbi Sperber had been originally summoned to appear at the court, but David Smith had appeared on his behalf due to it being a Saturday and thus Shabbat. Smith claimed that the Rabbi was deeply 'distressed over the whole affair' and that 'they had enormous difficulty in blacking-out the windows owing to their peculiar nature and shape.'[249] He further stated that 'blackout material purchased for the window had been left in a bus by one of the refugees. Everything humanly possible had been done to comply with the regulations.'[250] Smith fully accepted the truth of the allegation, however, and admitted that the castle community were, indeed, guilty as charged. All he could offer was a sincere apology and an explanation that a simple mistake had been made. Colonel Hughes, of Kinmel Hall, and a member of the court, interceded on behalf of the Gwrych community, claiming that he had been a visitor to the castle just the night before and had noticed that the unusual shape of the windows rendered it very difficult to black them out successfully. Another member of the court dismissed these concerns, arguing that the law was clear and that the debate around oddly shaped windows was irrelevant. Superintendent Tomkins was, however, sympathetic to the arguments advanced and suggested that the community no longer use the upper tower room at night as 'the lights from this room can be seen far out at sea and also from the main coast road.'[251] He went on to say that he 'knew the refugees were poor'[252] but he and Lord Clwyd had no choice other than to find the *Hachshara* guilty and, as a result, the castle community was fined £5.[253]

The refugees had settled in quietly but effectively at Gwrych Castle over the previous four months, and during that time they had been easily accepted by the vast majority of people in the local community. However, Tomkins's comments about their lights being visible from the sea were reported in a local newspaper, and may have unintentionally fed a few locals with more fertile imaginations the idea that something dubious could have been afoot at the castle. The vast majority of the Abergele community would, however, have shrugged the whole incident off. The fact was that the folk of Abergele, generally, were not taking the blackout or fear of an enemy raid anything like seriously enough, despite the fact that the local ARP Committee had been formed in 1938 and publicity about the dangers of an air raid had abounded since then. The Denbighshire ARP gas van had made an appearance in the town in February 1939 for locals to try out gas respirators, and on 24 July they took part in a full-scale air raid training exercise which was deemed to be a great success. On the back of this, by the summer of 1939 just over a hundred members of the community had been trained up as wardens and between 24 and 26 August they issued gas masks to all of the town's residents.

The first real test of all these preparations had come just a few days after the outbreak of war in September 1939, when the large air raid siren in Pentre Mawr park had sounded. The alert was quickly proved to be a false alarm, but as the siren wailed nobody knew this. Instead of the prepared response to the sound of a siren, it was almost universally ignored by the town's population. Robert Griffiths, a teenager in the town, had forgotten to carry his gas mask and, in a panic, he began to run home to get it as 'four men who were standing in the entrance of the market hall started jeering and laughing at me.'[254]

The local newspaper reported multiple blackout infringements during the first few weeks of the war, many of which resulted in equal or larger fines. In mid-October, several weeks before the Gwrych *Hachshara* was summoned to the police court, even an Abergele Urban District Councillor, Hugh Thomas, had been found guilty of breaking the rules. As he was handed his fine he could only offer the court the sheepish comment that 'his memory had betrayed him for once ... he forgot to switch off the light.'[255] The week before David Smith appeared before the court, the Abergele Sanatorium and Dr Lindley of the Rheuma Spa in Abergele, both large buildings with numerous windows like Gwrych Castle, had also each been fined £5 for breaking the rules.[256] In the sanatorium's case it was not just a chink of light that had been the problem; pretty much the whole place was lit up.

The lax attitude towards the blackout was a great irritation to Superintendent Tomkins. A few weeks earlier he had been particularly angry at a local for drunkenly driving in a zig-zag manner during the blackout. He became positively apoplectic at the man's explanation that he had *not* had too much to drink and only 'became dazed and dizzy when he left the public house for the open air.' Lord Clwyd threw an £11 fine and a five-year driving disqualification at him.[257] In June 1940, Tomkins issued a warning to all residents of the town, stating that he was so fed up with the amount of police time being wasted on blackout infringements that his men would no longer bother to give warnings and that he would prosecute every single time.

Despite this, local attitudes changed very little; at a police court three months later, in early September 1940, Lord Clwyd heard a further twenty-four cases and issued £44 in fines. As late as 1941, one unbowed resident responded to the police court with the disgruntled comment that 'it was all so paltry ... I have been fined once. You will have to fine me again,' before saying her accusers were no better than the Nazis.[258]

Councillor Locke, a member of the Civil Defence Committee, exhorted people to carry gas masks, whilst simultaneously admitting that 'he himself was one of the culprits'[259] who routinely failed to do so, and acknowledged that the compliant attitude of law-abiding children was showing him up.

There were two other reasons for the devil-may-care attitude being shown towards the blackout by many in the town. The first was that the siren in Pentre Mawr park was genuinely inaudible to many on the fringes of the neighbourhood and this, in turn, encouraged many others to disingenuously claim they could not hear it either. This issue prompted an exasperated exchange at a meeting of the Civil Defence Committee, where it was suggested that even if there were twelve sirens somebody would have the barefaced cheek to claim that they had heard nothing.

The second, and far more serious, reason was a very visible degree of in-fighting or resistance from the organisations most heavily involved in applying the rules. Councillor Tom Leigh was at constant loggerheads with the council-appointed Civil Defence Committee and frequently critical of Councillor Foulkes, the man they had appointed to lead the town's ARP Wardens. At a fiery meeting in late March 1940, Leigh accused them of all being part of a cosy and ineffectual clique and demanded an overhaul of the committee's membership, claiming that the issue was a 'burning' one for the town. In a somewhat childish response, a member of the committee proposed that Leigh should take over, with one councillor sarcastically stating that he appeared to be 'an adept in this work'.[260] Another, perhaps more bluntly, referred to Leigh as 'like a boy just leaving school, but by the way he is going on, he will soon be the boss of the show.'[261]

Leigh declined the opportunity but, within a couple of months, he was 'again on the warpath'[262] after the Civil Defence Committee scheduled future meetings for times when they knew he would not be able to attend. He accused the committee of wasting time 'quibbling about a little badge or fancy armlet for a few individuals'[263] rather than focusing on more important issues such as the two planned public air raid shelters which, some ten months into the war, had still not been built, let alone a proposed one for 'the little kiddies at the National School'.[264] He said he would be personally whipping up a gang of volunteers to build the shelters if the committee continued to prevaricate. Another member, exasperated by Leigh, claimed that 'one got a little tired of destructive criticism of ARP work ... Mr Leigh simply came along to the monthly meeting and threw stones at things which he did not understand.'[265] Councillor Squire Jacob was equally blunt: 'It is all very well Mr Leigh poking his nose in some "gossip heaps" in the town and bringing his "muck" into this chamber. He is simply listening to outside twaddle and brings the filth here.'[266]

At the same time as their leaders publicly displayed their disunity, one group of ARP wardens, feeding off the fact that squabbles seemed to be the order of the day, refused to carry out their night duties in an argument over nothing more than the positioning of a telephone that they found to be inconvenient.

The issues and tensions were never clearly resolved and one year later, in the summer of 1941, even the Abergele Urban District Fire Brigade, knowing the potential consequences of an enemy bombing raid better than most, refused to obey national orders to paint over their bright red appliances with a less visible battleship grey, and threatened to resign en masse if forced to comply. Their threat proved effective and they were given permission to retain their red livery.

For all these reasons, the *Hachshara*'s blackout infringement caused relatively little comment. Even more conveniently for the castle community, in the same week that Smith stood before the court, the usually low-crime Abergele had been treated to two sensational cases that were the talk of the town. The first involved a local shepherd who, over a period of several months, had arranged for the disappearance of as many as ninety sheep from flocks under his care in a profitable dabble with the black market. For this, he received a sentence of six months' imprisonment with hard labour. The second case involved two shady characters from Chapel Street who had been accused of stealing council property when they had been found to be in possession of several wooden benches that had recently disappeared from the Tower Hill footpath. In court the pair creatively pleaded guilty to *taking* the benches but not guilty to *stealing* them. Unable to discern the difference, Lord Clwyd handed each a 10-shilling fine.

It was abundantly clear to most in Abergele that there was no enemy spy ensconced at Gwrych Castle, but at an official level the examinations of 'enemy aliens' were still proceeding. Despite it being Shabbat, a further three *chaverim* from the Gwrych *Hachshara* were summoned to appear before the Caernarfon 'enemy aliens' tribunal on Saturday, 16 December: twenty-three-year-old Hanna Zuntz from Hamburg; twenty-one-year-old Rachel Blum, the sister of student rabbi Hermann Blum, from Poland; and nineteen-year-old Milli Koenigshoefer from Breslau. As with almost all the others that had gone before them, each was categorised as class C and thus declared to be of no threat. A few weeks later, Erwin Seligmann along with eight more members of the Gwrych *Hachshara* travelled to Caernarfon to face their tribunals. Schimon Tempel, aged twenty-one from Pardubitz, Czechoslovakia, was the only one placed in the class B category. Seligmann and all of the others were categorised as class C.

Any objective locals following the proceedings of the tribunals would have easily concluded that there was no alien threat from the Jewish community at Gwrych Castle. Not a single one of the Gwrych refugees had been interned and the vast majority had been categorised as class C. In addition to this, over the Christmas period of December 1939 to January 1940, several of the older teenagers from the castle signed up to join the town's ARP service and nearly twenty of the community were chosen for new employment locally under the aegis of the government's Ministry of Labour, to work on various civil defence projects in the area. What those projects were is not entirely clear, due to security censorship, but labourers were needed on a variety of small military sites in the area such as the anti-aircraft searchlight position in the fields to the east of the ARP Control Room at Pentre Mawr in the town, or the radar masts at

Bodelwyddan. There was also work under way along the coastline, readying it to resist any enemy invasion force. All this was evidence that the Abergele community, in general, had formed a very clear impression that the refugee group were harmless. They seemed pleasant enough, they clearly worked hard, and they generally kept themselves to themselves.

The castle leadership were nevertheless acutely aware that their recent indiscretion regarding the blackout regulations would have set some tongues wagging in the town. Erich Roper and Carl Schäfler, who had been responsible for checking that blackout curtains were drawn properly, received admonishments. They also reviewed their procedures in an effort to ensure that there would be no repeat of the error. However, the castle was large and had many windows, so the internal review came to the very honest conclusion that there was not much more that they could do other than to buy more drapes and be ever more vigilant in checking the windows were covered at night.

Suitably chastened by events under his watch, Erich Roper, one of the editors of the monthly castle newsletter, ensured that the February 1940 edition included reminders of the need for everyone to take responsibility. He also printed a letter from a Mr Williams, an English Jew on the Council for German Jewry, reminding readers of a recent article in the *Daily Sketch* that had referred to 'notorious Jews'. The letter took pains to point out how such indiscretions as had happened at Gwrych Castle played easily into the hands of antisemites and those keen to point fingers at 'aliens'. Williams concluded his letter with the hope 'that my lines will help to finally improve the state of this castle and to achieve a proper blackout and therefore to live up to the law of our country.'[267] This sobering rebuke from the Council for German Jewry and the slap on the wrist issued by the British legal system at the Abergele Police Court served to focus minds at the castle but, unfortunately, not enough to prevent a further breach of the blackout regulations later in 1940.

Rabbi Sperber felt it was important to step up the public relations campaign given the recent blackout embarrassment, and a perfect opportunity presented itself almost immediately. On Saturday, 30 December 1939, the Abergele Urban District Council and the local, 200-strong Women's Voluntary Service (WVS), which had been founded the previous March, organised a Christmas party at the Church House on Groes Lwyd for around a hundred children who had been evacuated to the town from Merseyside. The Reverend Joseph Ellis turned up dressed as Santa Claus and distributed gifts provided by the WVS. Regardless of the event being the high point of the Christian calendar, Dr Julius Handler was sent to make an appearance and he provided impromptu entertainment by playing tunes on an accordion that he had borrowed from the castle's orchestra. His attendance delighted many, and a sign of the importance of his appearance was that it was even reported in the *Liverpool Daily Post* newspaper.[268] So impressed was somebody at the Church House with his performance that he 'was invited to join the local music society which gave frequent concerts in various parts of North Wales, and ... also entertained soldiers on training in Wales.'[269] Julius's love of music was never far from the fore, and he took full advantage of any opportunities available to him, especially if they simultaneously allowed him to get more involved in the local social life.

Arieh Handler also helped build relationships that Christmas. As the festivities drew near, he arranged for the children to write and deliver hundreds of Christmas cards to the more prominent citizens of Abergele and to those who had offered help or kindness towards the *Hachshara*. Some of those people were even invited to the castle for tea. Amongst them was local dentist Robert Pye and his wife Mary, who would later recall that, whilst sat on unsteady camp beds, Julius had happily entertained them by playing his beloved violin. Mary Pye kept her Christmas card from the *Hachshara* for the rest of her life.

Rabbi Sperber also played his part. After his unsuccessful visits to the local pubs, he began trying to court friendships with local church and chapel leaders, as Julius Handler had done so successfully in the early days, in order to explain his position to them and break down any unnecessary religious barriers.[270]

This approach fared much better and he struck up friendships with some.[271] He was particularly well received by Reverend Cooper of the English Presbyterian Church in Pensarn who had formerly lived for some time in Poland and was secretary of the International Hebrew Christian Alliance. A few months later, in June 1940, Cooper presented a well-attended lecture for local people on the subject of 'Israel's Affliction and Christian Compassion'.

Another of Sperber's new clerical friends, although sadly unidentified in the surviving records, even turned to him for his help with a personal problem. Rabbi Sperber agreed to help and what happened next quickly entered the local gossip stream, briefly turning the Rabbi into a local celebrity and simultaneously, by association, enhancing the reputation of all of the Jews at the castle. As Miriam Sperber recalled:

> They [the priest's family] were a family of pacifists and had one son who had refused to be [registered for service] … Instead, he was serving with the Merchant Navy. Whenever he received leave he would come home. They had been expecting him for days now, and he had not arrived. He used to come home even if it was only for several hours. The boy's mother was now worried sick and lay in bed all the time, unable to function. Would the rabbi be so kind as to visit the priest's wife and try to encourage her? The priest led my husband into the bedroom, where his wife lay listless. 'My dear,' said the priest, 'a Jewish rabbi is here to see you. He is a religious man who helps many that suffer, and he would like to speak with you.' The woman burst out in bitter cries. Immediately my husband said, 'Don't worry, your son is alive and well. He will be home shortly, and then you will all come and visit me.' The woman sat up suddenly, looking around the room in disbelief. My husband had spoken with such assurance that she had come alive. When he returned home he said to me, 'I don't know what came over me, but

I had no other choice. She was so pitiful.' Several days later one of the boys came to tell me that a priest and his family were waiting to see the rabbi downstairs. My husband descended, whereupon he saw the pastor, his wife, and son. Soon after the rabbi's visit, the son had turned up at home. They were here to express their gratefulness for the prophetic announcement he had brought them.[272]

Rabbi Sperber made no claims to be a prophet, but this was not the only example of him displaying a curious ability to predict things with accuracy and he gained something of a reputation as a result.

Meanwhile, the children continued working on local farms, attending lessons and carrying out their duties at the *Hachshara*. Ever increasing numbers of them visited Abergele during the winter of 1939–40; their tentative visits in small groups during September and October had turned into more confident visits, with many going alone by November. Their politeness continued to impress those who encountered them and probably did more to develop the relationship than anything the *Hachshara's* leaders were doing. Through the children, a proper bond between town and castle was now starting to form. Mayor Wartski of Bangor, completely independent of the whole Gwrych Castle project, was extremely positive about what he witnessed on a visit to Abergele in February 1940: 'I am very impressed by the manner in which Gwrych Castle, with its 190 young men and women refugees, is being conducted; they are maintaining excellent relationships with their neighbourhood.'[273]

Some of the young refugees were even venturing further than Abergele. Herman Rothman had been receiving letters from his mother, who was concerned about his lack of suitable winter clothing. She urged him to write to other family members outside of Germany to ask for their support. From Palestine came some second-hand clothing, but far better for Herman was some money that was sent to him by relatives in Argentina. Flush with cash, he went into town alone, then jumped on a bus to Rhyl where he bought himself a new jumper from a department store.

Access to the bicycles that David Smith had procured some time earlier made visiting the town a much easier prospect for many of the children but, although it was only a walk of a mile, some of the *noar* had found other ingenious ways of speeding up their journeys into Abergele. One ruse involved hiding in the back of delivery vans that had pulled up at the castle, only to stealthily disembark when the van got back into the town. Salli Edelnand often took advantage of the visits of baker Dick Edwards, with whom he was forging a friendship: 'I managed to hide in the back of the van when Dick called at the castle and was in a hurry to get home for his tea … I suspect that Dick Edwards knew of my presence in his van all the time. Kind, generous Dick Edwards.'[274]

A major reason that so many of the *noar* wanted to get into Abergele more frequently was the fact that, at long last, they had finally been given some spending money. Through 1939 and into 1940, the *Hachshara* had been relatively well funded by grants from the Refugee Children's Movement, the Jewish Agency and the philanthropic support of several wealthy business families. There were also some significant donations from well-wishers and other Zionist agencies. For example, in December 1939, following an inspection and favourable report by Solomon Eleazer Sklan, the executive committee of the *Mizrachi* Federation awarded £100 'in aid of the work'[275] and, every now and again, sent further donations. Aware of some of these donations, the *Assefah* council had tasked a *chaver* named Rosenblum to negotiate with David Smith about the possibility of using some of the cash to set up a pot of spending money, a *kupa*. At the *Assefah* meeting of January 1940, Rosenblum proudly announced that the *kupa* had now been created with an initial deposit of £18 – the rough equivalent of around £1,000 today. When divvied up equally this would have amounted to the modern equivalent of just over £5 per person.[276] It wasn't much, but those present at the *Assefah* to hear Rosenblum's news were delighted, apart from one grumpy soul who 'then asked why so little writing paper is issued' if there was spare money lying around.[277]

And then there were the backhanders received from the local farmers that many of the *noar* had been squirrelling away. These started as payments in kind, but turned into cash as time went on and those who took it usually went straight into town to spend it. The usual item of choice for most of the children was a Milky Way, which was so different to anything they had encountered back home. The marketing slogan 'The sweet you can eat between meals'[278] also appealed to those eager to avoid anger from a watchful dining room *chaver* should they not be able to finish their food when they got back to the castle. On one occasion, Ruth Kessel and her friends had the windfall of being offered a half a crown and 'bought ourselves as much Cadbury's chocolate as our money would buy.'[279]

If they combined their illicit earnings with their allowance from the *kupa*, many of the youngsters could also afford to visit Abergele's cinema, the Picture Palace – a trip regarded by most as the ultimate treat. Few of the refugees had ever sampled the delights of a cinema before and certainly not since 1935 when German Jews had been banned from attending them. Many began going in small friendship groups or even alone.

Henry Glanz was one of many that had never been to see a movie and his first experience created a lifelong memory. When interviewed seventy-nine years later he could instantly recall the first film he saw in Abergele – *The Wizard of Oz*, which was released in Britain on 26 January 1940. He had absolutely no idea what the story was about as he could not follow most of the dialogue, but he was still awestruck. He could also recall being particularly affected by another movie that he saw in Abergele on its first release in December 1940: Charlie Chaplin's *The Great Dictator*, a satirical condemnation of fascism and Nazism in which the comedian played the dual roles of the Hitleresque dictator and a persecuted Jewish barber.[280]

Mr Parry, who ran the cinema, took a particular liking to the young people from the *Hachshara* and he frequently allowed them in for free, or in return for a small chore. Salli Edelnand benefitted from two free films a week: 'I had to rewind the films in the projection room ready for the next performance. I must say that I enjoyed this job very much indeed as it was certainly very different from my daily chores such as tree felling, gardening and working on the farm.'[281]

In the meantime, daily chores at the castle continued unabated despite a very severe change in the weather as the year came to an end. Temperatures dropped so low locally during that winter that tragedy ensued: three people died in the locality following terrible accidents that were later attributed to the extreme conditions. One of those people was Florence Evans, a twelve-year-old girl in Llanddulas who, on 28 December, had been drawing pictures whilst sitting by the fire in her home. As she stood, her overalls wafted over the flames and within seconds she was ablaze. Hearing a scream, her sister ran into the room, threw a rug around her and eventually smothered the flames. However, the burns were so severe that Florence died shortly afterwards. Just days later, and in very similar circumstances, Elizabeth Roberts, a thirty-six-year-old woman from Peel Street in Abergele, died as a result of severe burns from an open fire at the Bee Hotel, where she worked as a kitchen maid. Recording 'death by misadventure' at the subsequent inquest, Trefor Johnson, the Assistant Deputy Coroner for West Denbighshire, stated: 'This is the third inquest within the last ten days of people being burnt to death I have had to investigate in this district, and it is a very serious position. In the three cases the victims have been females. It is quite possible that the cold weather has induced people, mostly women, to go near a fire, in fact too near, and clothing of females is, of course, much more liable to catch fire.'[282]

The winter became colder. On 17 January 1940, the River Thames froze for the first time since 1888 and soon afterwards, on 26 January, severe ice and snow storms blighted the whole country. At Gwrych, the hours worked by those assigned to forestry work were increased substantially to collect more wood to burn on the castle's open fires but, despite their efforts, there was never enough. The cold conditions weren't helped by the refugees' lack of suitable winter clothes, again, despite the best efforts of the tailors' workshop. Many resorted to gathering in huddled groups to share what little warmth they could generate between themselves. Some, such as Herman Rothman, could raise the cash to go and buy themselves something more suitable, but most could not, or had chosen instead to spend their hard-earned money on chocolate and a movie.

The residents of Abergele were united in their sympathy for the plight of the young people at the castle and they collected and donated piles of second-hand clothing. In response to the Arctic conditions, the WVS had been furiously knitting and had produced over 3,000 socks and mittens for evacuees in the area over the previous weeks. They decided to gift 1,000 of them to the Gwrych Castle *Hachshara*.[283] A group of local women gifted something far more appreciated by many of the children: 'One day they came and they told us to line up outside the dining room and as we got into the dining room on either side stood one of these ladies handing out chocolate bars.'[284] Some of the children struggled with the moral dilemma this posed for them as – despite the fact that many were already accepting gifts and money from the people they worked for – they were still repeatedly told not to accept charitable donations, and here they were being presented with those right in front of the castle leadership. A few defied authority and accepted the gift, others stayed true to the principle and politely declined the chocolate. Some also declined to select clothing from the donations for themselves for similar reasons, though their quandary was quickly overcome if they saw something that caught their eye. Sonia Marder saw 'a pleated skirt, and I wanted that skirt, and I went over and I said, "Can I have it?" And they were only too happy to give it to me. I wore that skirt. I was totally out of place, but I liked it!'[285]

The piles of clothing were augmented by a second major donation that had been collected by the Llandudno Women's Zionist and Welfare Society. The excited children immediately and enthusiastically began to sort through this new collection and were given the freedom to do as they liked with items within it. However, enthusiasm soon waned once they began rifling through the piles and slowly came to the realisation that the well-intended donors of Llandudno had contributed an awful lot of things that were of no use in keeping them warm. The donation included 'flimsy dresses and high-heeled shoes'.[286] Nevertheless, this generous but thoroughly impractical donation proved to be a positive boon in providing hours of indoor entertainment and amusement as the children messed around dressing up. Jesse Zierler was thrilled that 'An old bowler hat took a fancy to me. It fitted like a glove and we became virtually inseparable. I did take it off at night!'[287] It also gave some bright spark the idea of running a costume competition and parade. This was to be arranged to coincide with Purim, on 23 March 1940, a festival that commemorates the survival of Jews in ancient Persia who had been threatened with death, and is often celebrated with fun and games and the wearing of fancy dress. Fortunately, the Llandudno society also gave a more useful cash donation of £104 and 1 shilling, some of which went towards the *kupa*.

The huge castle estate and the rural nature of the district afforded many opportunities for a nature ramble and one was proposed by *chavera* Eva Carlebach, which a number of the children signed up to despite the freezing weather conditions. One of the ramblers provided an account of the day.

> We were in such a good mood. We went past the hunting lodge and lookout tower and over the grotto. From there we decided to climb down ... From there we went along the main road to Llanddulas [neighbouring village]. After Llanddulas ... we rested and played various games and talked with each other. We went on to climb another hill again ... and when you looked down it made you dizzy. It was too difficult to climb right down. We tried it on all fours and just sat down and slid down. It was a very funny picture how down the steep slope we slipped and ended up in a farmyard. We had a terrible thirst and so we asked the

farmer for some water ... Frozen, with great hunger and thirst, we got back to the castle.[288]

Sports also continued during the freezing winter. During January the rivalry between the *noar* and *chaverim* over the table-tennis table began to abate after someone in the carpentry suggested building a second, purpose-built one.

Gwrych Castle FC took to the field for their sixth game. Their fixtures were now being referred to, with tongues firmly stuck in cheeks, as 'internationals'. Once again, the Abergele Sanatorium provided the opposition. After a delayed kick-off, the game of two twenty-five-minute halves got under way. The sanatorium's team scored almost straight away but, following a Gwrych attack and a fine save from the opposition goalkeeper, a refugee named Lachs knocked in the rebound to pull the game back to 1:1. The rest of the first half 'went back and forth'[289] with Gwrych conceding a second goal. The half-time inquest noted that the sanitorium had the better team, no doubt causing a few heated arguments about how Gwrych could turn the deficit around. Whatever plans were made appear to have made little difference; the sanatorium continued to apply pressure in the second half, winning a succession of corners from which a Gwrych defender, Edmund Schnitzer, 'excelled' by heading everything safely away. Then with just three minutes of the game remaining, Isi Zolmanotz got his head on to the end of a Gwrych corner and the ball flew into the sanatorium's net through a crowded goal mouth. The result was a somewhat fortunate 2:2 draw.[290]

Meanwhile, the harsh winter was creating additional problems for Dr Julius Handler and his nursing team which he had recently expanded to six due to increased demand. They were busy dealing with many cases of German measles and tonsillitis. The latter had become a prevalent issue, prompting Julius to make disinfecting mouthwashes available to whoever wanted them, 'unfortunately without the desired success. The bottles and their contents were hardly touched.'[291]

By February 1940, Julius was stating that, for various health reasons, as many as twenty of the residents at a time were ill and unable to work, which was particularly problematic in a kibbutz that required everyone to work. The *chaverim*, too, were experiencing varying degrees of ill health and there was considerable anxiety amongst the castle's inhabitants when one of them, Benno Sternheim, had a nasty fall on the ice. Despite initial concerns, his injuries proved to be minor and he was back at work just a few days later.

This was when twenty-three-year-old *chaver* Julius Hirsch found himself lying ill in the castle infirmary. It was here that, with nothing much else to do, he decided to amuse himself by writing his last will and testament and then submitting it to Erich Roper for publication in the monthly newsletter. It sheds some light on characters and relationships at the *Hachshara* that freezing winter. The document stated:

A comb and a brush for Dr Handler.

A bit of soap to Rebecca [surname unknown] so that she can wash her hands again after she has massaged Mondek's [Winczelberg] feet.

A shaver for Karo [Pauline] Gerson and Eva Carlebach.

Uscher Dürst, with the duty to say daily a psalm for my soul.

A few pants for Mondek Winczelberg. It would be advisable, to extend the life of the pants, to add trouser pockets.

To the *chaverim* who want to be further trained in craftsmanship, I leave a nail cleaner (as screwdriver).

Erwin Seligmann, the man who is forever cold, a few woollen stockings that he can tie around his neck as a necessity.

A whistle, for David Granek, to stop him shouting.

My corpse, to be displayed for eight days in David Granek's
greenhouse so that every *chaver* may say goodbye to my
mortal remains.

As I breathe my life out for Zionism, Erich Roper is allowed
to say a word of farewell to me, in return for which I leave
him my gas mask.

The rest of you, I ask to remember me as one who lived and
died for them. However, if I do not die, this last assignment
does not come into force.[292]

Hirsch made a full and not unexpected recovery from his 'death bed',
but the numbers falling ill was still of great concern to Dr Handler,
who took the matter so seriously that he began to believe that the issue
was a personal failure. He was also concerned by the introduction of
rationing on 8 January 1940. Although this only applied to bacon,
butter and sugar, and thus was unlikely to cause any great complications for the castle community, it was a worrying sign that potential
further restrictions may lie ahead. The Gwrych kitchen was not turning
out particularly good food as things stood and there was still no proper
cook amongst the *chaverim* so there was a distinct likelihood that the
situation was liable to get worse.

For all of these reasons, Julius redoubled his efforts to develop bene-
ficial contacts amongst the regional medical community. This included
Llewelyn Morgan, the local dispensing chemist and optician at the
Medical Hall on Market Street in Abergele, who often delivered medical
supplies to the castle. Julius also personally arranged a direct link with

the West Denbighshire Hospital in Colwyn Bay which, in response, assisted in setting up a very valuable and well-equipped dispensary at the castle. The hospital also loaned him medical instruments for basic treatments as well as allowing him to have access to an operating theatre if there was ever a need for him to carry out minor surgical procedures. In addition, the hospital also generously offered to properly train three of his new nurses. The *Hachshara* and the sanatorium had been developing a good bond through their organised football matches, something Julius built on, and through this relationship, he was allowed to arrange for every child at the castle to have a chest X-ray.[293] Julius also introduced a routine of providing the children with regular medical examinations and frequent weight checks, combined with the compilation of proper medical records. A Jewish dentist, Dr Etlinger, was sent to the castle for a three-month stay to examine, and treat if necessary, every child.

Julius also offered voluntary first aid lessons as an evening class and utilised the *Hachshara*'s newsletter to provide the entire community with sensible, if perhaps obvious, health and hygiene advice such as the need to clean their teeth twice daily and to wash regularly, regardless of the lack of hot water.

But despite the freezing weather and general ill health, there was growing excitement amongst the castle community about the *Kongress* – a mock election that had been proposed by Erwin Seligmann. Over a two-week campaign period, various youngsters set up three political parties, created manifestos, recruited followers and canvassed voters. The castle was covered in a variety of chalked slogans and political propaganda posters, which agents from a rival party often erased or removed, replacing them with their own. On the late afternoon of Shabbat, 6 January – but before dark so as not to run the risk of breaking the blackout regulations again – the culmination of the electioneering began. Erich Roper recounted that 'the height of the preparations was reached with the torchlight procession … where everybody really participated. It was talked about by all parties from left to right. Most of the masses demonstrated … to prove their existence.'[294] As part of the fun, some of the demonstrators began throwing water at each other and 'it was late into the night until the camp came to rest.'[295] The great debate was due to begin the following day at 4 p.m. and 'on Sunday morning, the house was really like a polling station. Everything, even floors and stairs, was provided with inscriptions, some of which were quite humorous. The only ones who did not like these inscriptions were [the team in charge of] housekeeping [that month] – easy to explain.'[296]

Despite the jovial nature of the preparations for the debate, the question that Erwin had posed for the youngsters to vote on was an extremely serious one: the task of the *Kongress* was 'to solve the Jewish question'. It was a question that did not have the same sinister overtones that it would have exactly one year later, at the Wansee Conference in January 1941 where the Nazis would resolve upon genocide as being the 'Final Solution' to 'the Jewish question'. 'The Jewish question', at least in the way that Erwin intended it, was wholly different. To him, and indeed to most Jews, the question was a long-standing one about how the Jewish people fitted into the world, given that they had no nation state to call their own. Despite his success in developing the *Hachshara* after the incredibly difficult opening weeks, Erwin had remained concerned that the community had not yet developed a common purpose or vision. Debating this question, if it could be managed carefully, could go a long way towards doing that.

Three possible answers dominated the debate amongst the castle community. The first was that 'the Jewish question' could ultimately only be solved by the creation of a unique Jewish homeland, an *Eretz Yisrael*. The second was that Jews would simply have to accept the reality of continuing as enclave communities within other nations. The third was that the Jewish people should assimilate themselves more fully into their host communities. On a micro scale, this was a genuine question for how the Jewish community at the castle should relate to the town of Abergele. That the days preceding the *Kongress* – where such a serious question would be considered – were filled with processions, humorous propaganda and water fights serves to indicate not just the naivety and innocence of the youngsters at Gwrych, but also to remind us of the quite unbelievable conclusions that the Nazis were willing to contemplate.

The Gwrych youngsters filled the main hall of the castle for the great debate, many sporting the chosen colours of their preferred parties. At 5 p.m., an hour later than advertised, the event began, signalled with three strikes of a metal bucket standing in as a gong. Erwin opened the proceedings with a short speech, and then invited the leaders of the three parties to outline their response to 'the Jewish question'.

Representing the Communist Party was 'Comrade' Ossi Findling. His 'boss', David Smith, (whose father it might be recalled had been a Russian revolutionary), had made it very clear in the build-up to the day, and on the day itself, that he fully backed Ossi's position and the Communist party. With such an influential supporter in his corner, Ossi confidently rose to deliver his message to his fellow refugees, arguing for a classless society because if a 'socially just society exists, then there is no longer a Jewish question.'[297]

Erich Roper, known by all to be a close associate of Rabbi Sperber, then rose to speak at great length on behalf of his party, The Zionist Association. Erich put forward a lengthy but carefully crafted and articulate argument for the need for a Jewish homeland as the only solution to 'the Jewish question'. The somewhat biased Zionist audience greeted his conclusion with loud applause.

Samuelis Geller, representing the Association of English Townspeople of Jewish Faith, then spoke to offer a contrasting view that was never likely to find much favour on a Zionist *Hachshara*. In fact, the seventeen-year-old – who did not have the backing of anyone on the castle's leadership team – was likely to stir up trouble with his assault on traditional Jewish culture and his proposed solution of assimilation into the host culture when he stated that 'we reject Zionism because ... it awakens antisemitism.'

Questions and debate then followed, during which David Smith chipped in with some strong, revolutionary criticisms of organised religion and even – with a heavy dose of humour – incited the audience 'to get on the streets of Abergele and call the workers there. Workers of all countries, unite!'

Findling, Roper and Geller each added further comments on their chosen themes and other ideas were then taken from the audience. Taken as a whole, they revealed not just the articulate intelligence of the castle community, but also the fact that there was, as Erwin Seligmann had suspected, no clear agreement on what Zionism actually stood for within the group.

After a while, Erwin intervened and asked the audience to vote. In truth, it had been fairly obvious from the start that Erich Roper's Zionist Association was going to win, and the public vote very quickly confirmed the inevitable. Erwin then concluded events by summing up the key and common arguments that had been raised in the form of a resolution. This house, he affirmed, had provided the answer to 'the Jewish question', and it was thus: 'a Jewish nation in the Jewish land, whose economic form is socialist and whose culture is Torah culture.' The resolution was unanimously accepted.

Back in September, Erwin Seligmann had been on the verge of re-signing from Gwrych for reasons that he could not fully express, even to friends. However, one of the issues that seemed to frustrate him was the slow progress being made in embedding the true *Hachshara* spirit that appeared to be eluding the Gwrych enterprise. Now, by encourag-ing debate, he had united the whole castle behind a single vision; and it was the one that both he and *Bachad* subscribed to.

The refugees themselves had also evolved; the confused, scared and disunited youth that had arrived in September 1939 were developing into a coherent, tight-knit group with an astute political awareness. Erwin Seligmann's *Kongress* had completed the transformation and, at the same time, provided the *noar* with an agreed vision.

One demonstration of that growing unity was the increasing popu-larity of *Der Daat Hachshara*. In February 1940, one of the newsletter's creators, Erich Roper, wrote in his editorial that, 'When we started to write a ... newspaper five months ago, we mainly tried to publish a paper ... for light reading ... management is not our main task, but nevertheless *Der Daat Hachshara* ... is still worth it. However, there are not enough to go round, so therefore, we have decided to publish [print] the newspaper from now on fifty times [copies] so that each room gets an issue.'[298] Despite the shortage of suitable paper, the producers delivered on their promise over the coming months and, sometime around April 1940, the process was substantially aided by the donation of a new duplicating machine from the generous Gestetner family.[299]

The increased popularity of the newsletter, and the suggestion that it was subtly moving its content away from light reading and more into issues of the overall management of the *Hachshara* is telling. The *noar* were starting to exhibit a collective strength that was also being exercised through the *Assefah*, which had forced the leadership into listening to their demands for a *kupa*.

During that winter, the *noar* successfully forced more change. Their original division into three *plugoth, Aleph, Bet* and *Gimmel*, had been based loosely on age but also largely on first impressions, and it had formed the basis for the teaching classes since September. Many of the children had been confused or annoyed by their own placement from the beginning, like Herman Rothman, who was placed in *Aleph* despite being chronologically more akin to Bet: 'The A group had discussions which were far beyond me. They all seemed to be very grown up.'[300] These debates within the A group were often a heady and heated mix of ideological politics and philosophy tempered with arguments as to how Zionism did, or did not, fit into the present or future world. It is, perhaps, of little surprise that a fifteen-year-old observed this with a mixture of both awe and incomprehension. As a result of representations made at the *Assefah*, Erwin Seligmann and Rabbi Sperber agreed to a slight reorganisation of the groups.

Rabbi Sperber was also forced to acknowledge the growing criticism of his educational provision. Many of the *noar* were increasingly bored by their lessons but their previous complaints had been rebuffed.

Through the *Assefah* of January 1940 they agitated more formally for some fundamental changes. However Rabbi Sperber still refused to consider making any substantive alterations. This was not due to stubbornness but a conviction that the curriculum he was providing was correct. One of the fundamental aspects of the Gwrych *Hachshara* that marked it as different to those that preceded it was that the *noar*'s religious training had to be equally as important as their agricultural training. *Bachad* was convinced that the destiny of its members currently outside of Palestine 'would be determined ... by the character of [their] Judaism.'[301] One of the enshrined aims of *Bachad* as an organisation was to create an *Eretz Yisrael* where the social order would be determined 'in accordance with the principle of justice and morality enshrined in the Torah, in the light of which all its problems are to be solved.'[302] Sperber agreed with this view and believed that there was little point in youngsters preparing themselves for *Eretz Yisrael* if, upon arrival, their mindset was not fully aligned with their purpose.

In reality however, Sperber was providing a curriculum that went above and beyond what Mr A. Baum, *Bachad*'s executive member for education, was demanding as a minimum within its *Hachsharot*. Baum argued, in the spring of 1940, that to achieve a 'wholehearted, even fanatical, belief in the urgent need to work unceasingly for the rehabilitation of our people',[303] the *noar* should have at least one evening per week given over to educational work. Sperber was providing four half-days. Baum wanted classes in both Hebrew and cultural understanding, which would include such things as Jewish Studies and Jewish History. Once again, Sperber was providing both and more.

However, the *noar* knew nothing of this. They simply wanted greater variety and they were no longer as acquiescent as they had been. They brought their complaints up again at the February *Assefah* and Sperber, once more, refused to adapt the focus. Recognising the growing frustration amongst the children, a willing *chaver* independently set up a drawing workshop as a voluntary class for youngsters to attend in their limited spare time if they so wished. The Rabbi did not prevent the *chaver* from doing this but his disapproval was noted. At the same time, Dr Julius Handler had already introduced a voluntary class of his own, on first aid. This was done in an effort to improve general healthcare but some saw it as another challenge to Sperber's authority and as a green light for the rebel *chaver*. With Rabbi Sperber being challenged, and some of the *chaverim* starting to do their own thing without approval, there were signs of a fundamental shift in authority at the castle. The recent minor demonstrations were the first indications of cracks developing in the previously united leadership group.

The January *Assefah* had also provided another hint that all was not united at senior leadership level. Erwin Seligmann had kept his personal unhappiness at Gwrych a secret from everyone. He had, despite this, made an enormous success of the organisation but it now appeared that he was losing his authority. The *Assefah* raised the question as to why a lock had been placed on the pantry door, suggesting that this showed a lack of trust in them. Erwin replied that the lock would be removed after *Pesach*, the Passover festival in April, implying that food was being stored for the event. Nevertheless, he clearly recognised that the issue had irritated the youngsters and he told them that 'if it was up to him then the whole control system could be abolished.'[304] If it was not up to him, then who was in charge? But one week later, that question faded into unimportance as the castle community faced a near catastrophe.

At 3 a.m. on Monday morning, 29 January 1940, some of the residents awoke coughing. Isi Gruenbaum, the *chaver* on duty, was doing his rounds and some kind of sixth sense kicked in – something was not quite right. He began rousing people from their beds as a precaution. Many grumbled, ignored Gruenbaum's exhortations and pulled their blankets over the heads until someone shouted '*Feuer!*' from one of the boys' bedrooms on the top floor. This quickly focused minds and a full evacuation of the castle began.

Three of the *chaverim* went in search of the fire, including Felix Kollmann, from Vienna, and Hersh Lerner. Fire was a constant danger at the castle, either from one of the many open fireplaces or from the kerosene lamps and, concerned by this, twenty-one-year-old Lerner had been experimenting throughout the early winter of 1939–40 with a home-made 'fire engine'. Quite where he got the necessary materials and how he intended to supply it from a very temperamental and low-pressure water system is unclear and no description of his invention survives, beyond it being some sort of water cylinder with a short hose mounted on a trolley that could be pulled around. Just one week earlier, Lerner had impressed everyone by successfully demonstrating his invention on a controlled fire somewhere in the castle's grounds.

Kollmann ran off to fetch buckets of water but before he could return to the upper floor bedroom where the fire had broken out with two of them, Lerner had collected his 'fire engine' and was busily spraying the flames. Kollmann emptied his buckets on to the fire and then turned to assist Lerner. In the meantime, David Smith and Julius Handler had also arrived at the scene, having telephoned the Abergele Urban District Fire Brigade. Lerner's device proved effective though, and the fire was extinguished within thirty minutes, before the fire engine had arrived and before the flames could spread beyond the bedroom or cause too much damage. Shortly afterwards, a policeman also arrived at the castle and, with the firemen, began an investigation into the cause of the fire. They pointed the finger of blame firmly at a kerosene lamp. The group of boys who occupied the room, as punishment for their negligence, were ordered to spend the next few hours clearing up the mess that had been made.

The winter of 1939–40 had seen the Gwrych *Hachshara* come to life. The *noar* had transformed themselves into a stronger, more united, spirited and purposeful community who were forming a genuine bond with the people of Abergele. In turn, locals had established that the members of the *Hachshara* were of no threat to them at all and started to see them, increasingly, as part of the town's fabric. Although slight cracks in the leadership were starting to appear, as yet, they were not causing any major issue. It seemed to everyone that the Gwrych *Hachshara* was going from strength to strength and the spring of 1940 promised much.

CHAPTER 8

'Leck mich am arsch'

March–April 1940
Learning Welsh, fancy dress,
the 'naughty' boys and girls, and a car crash

The Gwrych *Hachshara* was a mere eight months old, but it was already becoming everything it was designed to be. There was something undefinably uplifting in the ethos and atmosphere of the place and, as a result, less effort now needed to be expended on creating the camaraderie of a kibbutz lifestyle. The children could, for the first time in a long time – if ever, given how young some of them were – begin to relax and enjoy life as it was. They could behave a little more like 'normal' teenagers. They were developing their agricultural know-how, too, and could begin to reap the rewards of their efforts as well as deepen their connections with Abergele. The spring of 1940 would prove to be the best and most harmonious time the majority would experience at the castle. Their optimism for the prospect of a better future was finally evolving from theory into practice and this was epitomised by the news that Miriam Sperber was pregnant. The prospect of a new life at the castle now had a literal representative.

The positives within the community spilled beyond it; the *Hachshara* was also benefitting the local area. The 200 or so young people working

146

on the farms had provided cover for the increasing numbers of labourers joining the forces and had thus played a significant part in not only maintaining but also boosting the local agricultural economy as part of its contribution towards the increased production quotas. Many of the refugees were also providing free labour for local businesses and, through the *kupa*, most of the children were also spending money in local shops and supporting the cinema. A study by Youth *Aliyah* concluded that 'the nearby village of Abergele was economically stimulated by the youngsters' arrival; the children substantially augmented the village population.'[305]

The refugees had also proven themselves to be willing and flexible workers with the ability to learn quickly. Because they were inexperienced, the agricultural work allotted to them in the early days was often quite menial, such as digging drainage ditches, mowing grass, clearing out cowsheds or pigsties, lifting potatoes and picking soft fruits or flowers in the market gardens. However, as their experience grew, and trust in them developed, local farmers often widened their duties. After spending some time doing little else but digging, Herman Rothman remembered that he became trusted enough to be given more responsibility and independence: 'I got to take the horses out and feed them, and take the cows out and feed them. I liked to work with the horses. That was an interesting job. I had to take horses to have shoes put on and then ride two or three miles back. I was very conscientious and I worked very, very hard. I thought hard work would mean progress for me. I was fairly exhausted when I came home, but I kept fit. And I made friends with the farmers. Most were very nice.'[306]

After a time of carrying out basic jobs, Henry Glanz also received a promotion from his employer and he was allowed to milk the cows. For his first attempt, the nervous Henry was given a huge black cow to practise on. Having filled half of his bucket successfully, he then accidentally knocked it over, wasting the entire contents. Henry got a good telling-off as a result but, over time, he became a proficient cow milker. Later on, he was promoted again. This time he was recruited into a cattle-breeding programme during April 1940. This led to some embarrassment. On one occasion, his activities were being watched closely by a young, female farm worker from Abergele whom Henry found very attractive. The bull he was in charge of appeared to be disinterested or confused by the task before it, and a red-faced Henry had to encourage it to perform its duty whilst the girl smiled over at him.[307]

So efficient had some of the workers become that, in April 1940, ten of the older boys were selected for relocation to a *Hachshara* farm in Rossett, between Wrexham and Chester, operating under the aegis of *Bachad* and the University College of North Wales Agricultural Department. At Rossett they received higher-level training as well as imparting some of their knowledge to other *Hachshara* members. In recognition of their skills they were paid agricultural minimum rates.

The majority of the young Jews got on extremely well with their agricultural 'employers', most of whom, as Herman Rothman commented, 'were very nice'. By and large, the farmers regarded their young 'employees' as efficient, hard-working, serious and responsible. In fact, the refugees were almost doing *too* good a job as they became increasingly sought after. By the spring of 1940, the *Hachshara* found itself unable to satisfy the growing demand from farmers for extra workers.

Whilst most had a good working relationship with the local farmers they were sent to work for, there were, of course, exceptions. *Chavera* Fanny Redner worked in the kitchen of one farmer, 'but I didn't do it for long because he was very difficult, and in fact he nearly killed somebody.'[308] It can also be argued that young Jewish refugees in agricultural training centres were exploited, and there is some truth in this.[309] Fritz Deutsch (later known as Fred Dunstan), a Youth *Aliyah* leader, was posted at the Braunton Farm *Hachshara* in Devon. He noted that 'The working conditions on the farm are very hard ... the work consists mainly in the picking of flowers. The workers have to spend their time in a bent down position not only in the open but also in rather low greenhouses, where one cannot stand upright at all. This has to be done for ten to twelve hours every day, there is only one half hour for lunch … You cannot possibly call this a *Hachshara*. It is exploitation of child labour.'[310] The work that many of the Gwrych refugees had to do was undoubtedly equally as hard, but the hours were nowhere near as long as those at Braunton and there is also no evidence at all of any exploitation on any of the local farms at which youngsters were employed.[311] Instead, Herman Rothman recalled that local farmers, despite differences between them, showed kindness to their new employees: 'I always found a difference between an English farmer and a Welsh farmer, not in detriment, they had different ways. The characteristic difference between English farmers and Welsh farmers were to me very apparent. English farmers were more liberal; Welsh farmers were not. They [the English farmers] were very nice to me, some, because I spoke English, engaged me with conversation and so on.'[312]

Some of the refugees soon figured out a way to really impress the more 'illiberal' Welsh farmers. Henry Glanz 'found that we got away with murder if you spoke to them in Welsh, so we learnt as much Welsh as we could.'[313] Salli Edelnand, after several months at Tyddyn-uchaf Farm, came to the firm conclusion that the English he had learned at home in Halberstadt was quite different to the language he was now actually hearing. This was partly down to the accent and partly down to the fact that many of the farm labourers he encountered spoke Welsh or, even more confusingly, uttered sentences that happily mixed the two languages together. Therefore Salli, like Henry and many others, also began to take the trouble to learn some Welsh. His main tutor was his new friend Wil Davies who, he remembers, also taught him 'some swear words, and … took the greatest delight in listening to me when I tried to repeat them.'[314]

Wil Davies was not the only person to take advantage of the linguistic naivety of the castle youngsters. Henry Glanz often worked with a few young boys from Abergele at the Reids' market garden at Hen Wrych, and one of them taught his Jewish peers a few unsavoury phrases. From 23 June 1940, a new, twice-daily BBC radio broadcast, *Music While You Work*, became very popular across the country and this frequently became the background soundtrack for the Hen Wrych work team. With the help of the local boy, Henry and the team happily learned to sing the 'Colonel Bogey March' with the alternative lyrics of 'Hitler has only got one ball'.[315]

Locals would frequently smile at the refugees' attempts at either English or Welsh. On one occasion, the *Hachshara's* designated ARP warden met with his equivalents from the town and, unintentionally, introduced himself as an aeroplane. For a long time he had no idea why his fellow wardens had all burst out with laughter. Another youngster got into a fuddle when he went into a shop and asked to buy some chocolate, to which the shopkeeper responded by saying 'Good morning' – no doubt hinting that this was the polite thing for a customer to say *before* attempting to purchase anything. The confused youngster replied that he did not want to buy a 'good morning', he wanted to buy chocolate. Bad pronunciations could certainly raise a laugh, but sometimes children would attempt to grapple for a word that was totally unfamiliar to them, and this was often funnier to observe than to correct. One boy caused much amusement for the farm labourers he was working with as he did not know the word 'gloves'. Instead he had, logically, adapted the literal translation from his native German and happily went around referring to them as 'hand shoes'. The labourers made no attempt to correct him for many months.[316]

However, language disparities could sometimes play into the hands of the castle residents when they were on local farms. They could talk openly with their fellow refugees about anything they wanted, in either German or Yiddish, fully certain that Welsh farm labourers wouldn't understand them. Whilst maintaining a fixed smile, they could moan or curse when they were unhappy, without their employer or fellow labourers knowing anything about it.

Aside from farm work, some of the older refugees and *chaverim* also looked for part-time work in the local area, either to earn a little money or purely out of curiosity. Many of the boys had an obsession with all things automotive and a small group volunteered themselves for work at Slater and Wheeler's garage in the town, partly out of personal interest but also to gain valuable experience in mechanics for a future life in Palestine. Wolfgang Billig and another boy were taken on as compositors at Robert Jones's printing works next to the Bee Hotel on Market Street after the original employees had left to join the army. For a year they helped to print the weekly local newspaper *The Abergele Visitor*.[317] One of the *noar*, Leon Manela, a unique individual at the castle as he was Spanish, spent some of his time working as a dustbin-man in the town.[318] Quite how he got the role remains unclear but it appears that he volunteered himself to the town council as, quite simply, 'he enjoyed it'.[319] Many years afterwards, Henry Glanz found himself in Jerusalem and, hearing a voice that sounded familiar, he turned to see Manela, still working as a refuse collector and still enjoying it.

Many of the children became friendly with local businessmen who had dealings with the castle. Wolfgang Billig got on so well with the milkman, Mr Morrison, that he was soon effectively 'employed' by him as an additional driver. He recalled, 'I already knew how to drive in Germany and sometimes in Wales I would take the milkman's car. You didn't need a licence – all the drivers were in the army and there was no one left.'[320] In Wolfgang's case, this additional experience proved invaluable when, a little time later, he joined the British Army as a driver of DUKW amphibious vehicles. He drove one onto a beach in Normandy on D-Day in 1944. Salli Edelnand also learned to drive through his relationship with Dick Edwards, who owned a bakery in Llanddulas. 'He delivered to the castle daily in a rather tatty old van which would never pass an MOT test today,' he remembered. 'I often helped him to unload and as a reward he allowed me to drive his van from the castle along the drive to Appleby's lodge [Nant-y-Bella]. What a thrill that was for me as a fourteen-year-old boy.'[321]

Not all of the local contacts worked out successfully, however. Aled Ellis, a farmer in Rhyd y Foel, came to the castle to collect kitchen refuse for pigswill for his farm but gave up after three visits due to its poor quality and the fact that it was 'generally laced with an abun-

dance of knives, forks and spoons.'[322] This may help to understand
the mystery of the disappearing cutlery that regularly confused David
Granek and the kitchen *chaverim*, even though it does little to explain
the circumstances behind it; perhaps a member of the kitchen team
covertly diverted them into a bin to reduce the washing-up burden.

Meanwhile, Dr Julius Handler was continuing to do his bit to fulfil
his brother's desire that the *Hachshara* should be a part of the local
community. His work with local medical professionals had not only
benefitted the *Hachshara* community materially but also in terms of
prestige. Julius increasingly found himself moving in more exalted local circles and, in March 1940, he was invited to the inaugural dinner
of the Abergele section of the Special Constabulary which was held at
the Bee Hotel. The guest list of fifty-two local dignitaries included the
chief constable, Superintendent Tomkins, several justices of the peace,
an array of local councillors and Colonel Hughes of Kinmel Hall. One
councillor even raised a toast to Julius.

Julius's efforts to improve sanitation and hygiene at the castle and
thus the health of the Gwrych community were also starting to bear
fruit by the spring of 1940. In April, one visitor commented that he
'was particularly struck by the cleanliness of the place.'[323] An independent doctor from the Jewish Agency, who was invited to carry out a
sample of medical examinations to assess the fitness of the *noar* for
Aliyah, passed every youngster that he randomly selected for his tests.
Local doctors in Abergele, with whom Julius was working closely,
were also impressed, stating that the health of the castle's residents was
actually better than the district generally. The only lingering issue that
they noted was that many of the children were rather pale. This was
attributed to the paucity of vegetables and high levels of fat in their diet
which could be blamed upon food shortages caused by the war.

As the self-confidence of the *Hachshara* grew, so did the number of
invitations extended to the local community. An offer to visit quickly
became a sought-after honour for the folk of Abergele and, by the
spring of 1940, the number of visitors had increased to the point

where there was more of an open-door policy. No doubt some were just hoping to catch a glimpse of the inside of the castle itself, but most visitors also came with offers of assistance – some coming from as far as Liverpool.[324] Other visitors to the castle at this time included Jewish soldiers stationed in North Wales for training, and members of the small local Jewish community. One regular visitor was Ruth Glasser, the Jewish girl who worked at Hendre Bach Farm in Abergele as a domestic servant. She would spend all of what little leisure time she had at the castle, effectively becoming an additional volunteer *chavera*.[325]

But by far the most welcome visitors were residents' relatives. These visits were few and far between, and probably incredibly hard to witness for those whose entire family remained in central Europe. However, a few of the residents had siblings who had also arrived via Kindertransport and who had since reached the age of eighteen or secured a degree of financial independence sufficient enough to allow them to travel to Abergele. One Polish *chavera*, Lies Teppich, looked forward to occasional visits from her boyfriend, German refugee Gunter Heilbrunn and the pair planned to marry in June 1940. A photo of Henry Steinberg with his visiting brother David on bicycles in front of the castle in March 1940 would become a treasured possession in the Steinberg family.

A particularly important visitor in early April 1940 was a Mr Findlay Steele, a representative of Colwyn Bay Social Services. Steele and his organisation were driven by the feeling that, 'since our Government has invited these people to take refuge amongst us, the least we can do as a social service organisation is to try to make their lot a little more comfortable than it is at present, and so give them a good impression of our people and our country.'[326] Dr Julius Handler gave Steele a tour of the *Hachshara* and the pair discussed 'their needs, to make life more tolerable.'[327] Although reluctant to accept charity, Julius recognised the generous and helpful spirit that motivated Steele and openly discussed with him what sort of assistance would be the most useful.

Steele reported back to his committee that 'they [the castle community] had a very monotonous time this winter: except for one or two chess boards they had no games whatever. After working hours, they could only walk about the empty and bare passages, go for outdoor walks or read what few books they had sent them … The furnishings were somewhat sparse and there was a total absence of any real comfort or luxury. There were large trestle dining tables and forms, bare floors and, except for a few efforts of those with artistic temperament, there were no wall decorations.'[328] While a slight exaggeration, Steele's comments serve as a reminder that, despite the efforts made by the leadership team and *chaverim* at the castle, life in Gwrych Castle remained far from ideal, despite appearing lavish from the outside.

To the great delight of many at the *Hachshara*, Steele returned just a few weeks later with a donation of various items of sporting equipment including some more footballs as well as 'table tennis equipment, lawn tennis rackets and balls, cricket gear and any other sports items.'[329] The donation also included a few golf clubs and, although hardly anyone at the castle knew what they were, a small group took themselves off to the golf course on the estate where a handful of friendly, local players taught them the rudiments of the game. Steele also delivered an offer from a Colwyn Bay gentleman to come to the castle and provide cricket coaching.[330] For Julius and his little orchestra, the donation also included something quite magnificent. In addition to a number of stringed instruments, an anonymous but very generous well-wisher from Victoria Park in Colwyn Bay's West End had sent them a piano.

Overwhelmed by the generosity of the donation, Julius penned his sincere thanks to the editors of several local newspapers. 'I need not tell you how grateful we are for these gifts which will do much to relieve the monotony of our existence. Every one of us has been impressed by the contrast between our reception here and the brutality from which, thanks to British hospitality, we have escaped.'[331]

For most of the *noar*, however, it was the table-tennis equipment that caused the greatest delight. With fortuitous timing, the castle's carpentry had just finished making the new second table – which created much excitement until some jobsworth spoiled the mood by pointing out that it had been made thirty centimetres short of regulation length. Nevertheless, to inaugurate it, a tournament was arranged between the B and C *plugoth* which took place in late April, on a day when heavy snow hit the area for a final time after the harsh winter. *Bet pluga* emerged victorious with a score of 8:7. However, their victory was hotly disputed and the argument spilled over into a mass snowball fight outside, during which, despite the fun of it all, a small number of snowballs were thrown with a touch of venom and spite. The *noar* at the *Hachshara* had cultivated an image of being conscientious and polite but 200 teenagers cooped up together in a castle obviously did not always behave with such courtesy, especially at times when they were not in the public eye. The slightly aggressive snowball fight was such an example, albeit a mild one.

The reality was that not all of the children got along with each other. Bill Braun, as an Austrian, was aware of a certain degree of friction between his compatriots and the German boys at the castle. Based on his own observation that most of the Germans had brought better quality and more stylish clothing with them than the Austrians, he believed that they had generally come from wealthier backgrounds. By his own admission, the Austrians 'were totally impoverished and came from the lowest levels of the ghetto society and were absolutely inferior in social standing, in manners, and so on.'[332] As a consequence, he felt that the Germans looked down their noses at them, and he personally felt a little 'oppressed by these rich and well-to-do and superior Germans.'[333]

Henry Glanz recalled that some of the children were involved in bullying each other on occasions. Many of the boys, including himself to his lasting regret, picked on a large boy that they considered to be vastly overweight. They also mimicked the strong accent that marked him out as Berlin's equivalent of a London cockney. Henry also recalled how the boys teased, and probably deeply upset, two female *chaverim* about their facial hair.[334]

More often, however, the bad behaviour was more minor, especially what was witnessed by those beyond the castle walls. Ruth Kessel had 'to admit that occasionally we would go and pinch apples from the local orchard, and we would be chased away by the owner.'[335] The orchard at Hen Wrych belonged to Mr Reid, and his walnut tree was particularly prized by many of the children. Salli Edelnand remembered that 'near Mr Reid's garden was the one and only walnut tree which bore fruit regularly. He jealously guarded this treasured tree and did not think too kindly of us when we attacked it from time to time. However, he just told us not to. He never shouted nor swore at us. A very kind and considerate gentleman.'[336] One suspects that Salli's incursions may have been more successful than those committed by Henry Glanz who, by contrast, recalled Mr Reid as 'a grumpy Scottish man'.[337]

Henry was, by his own admission, one of the 'naughty boys'.[338] He and several friends would occasionally catch a bus to visit Rhyl, Colwyn Bay or Llandudno for a day out, especially if they had received cash backhanders from farmers amounting to more than 9d (the cost of a bus ticket) that week. As the school-leaving age was fourteen at the time, they had to pay adult rates. However, Henry, who was quite small and young-looking for his age, often claimed that he was a child and got away with it. He recalled one driver accepting his plea with a conspiratorial wink and a smile. Then he leaned over to point at the soft moustache that was starting to sprout on Henry's top lip and commented that, despite being ever so young, he really ought to start shaving.[339] One day that spring, Henry also took a fancy towards David Smith's newly purchased car. It was parked on the castle forecourt and, as there appeared to be nobody about, Henry climbed inside with the intention of taking it for a short drive. He got no further than twenty yards before being halted, whereupon he was given an almighty telling-off.[340]

It wasn't just the boys who got into trouble. Mary Auskerin, who arrived at the castle as a fourteen-year-old, recalled that she and some friends 'were very naughty. One Yom Kippur, some of us broke into the pantry in the kitchen and got ourselves something to eat. Just out of sheer devilment. I mean, things were rather boring.'[341]

Amongst the usual suspects was the irrepressible Jesse Zierler and his partner in crime, Herman Rothman. In late April 1940 the duo began planning a raid that had been on their minds for a little while:

> One section of the castle's cellar had been well barricaded by the owners to discourage any unwelcome visitors. As it had also been placed out-of-bounds to us, the time had come for some investigation. Our labours through a long corridor revealed racks carrying hundreds of assorted bottles, covered in thick dust and cobwebs. They had clearly been forgotten by the owner when he moved. The labels showed them containing wine, which by now could have gone off. It made sound sense to sample some of them before getting rid of the lot, in case some of it was still all right. We must have tried dozens without finding one single bad drop. In fact, the wine improved with continuous tasting. Further experimentations brought our judgement to a state of warm appreciation. The less sweet variety seemed fine to wash off the dirt and cobwebs we were all covered in.[342]

Jesse did not refer to the consequences of their actions, but it is highly likely that the pair found themselves stood before Erwin Seligmann to receive a severe dressing-down.

And then there was the day during the spring of 1940 when the castle received yet another in an increasingly long line of important visitors. A dignitary of some description, possibly a mayor, was being introduced by Erwin Seligmann to a group of boys stood in a line. The VIP asked the first of them, as he shook his hand, how he would say 'How do you do?' in their language. The boy replied, '*Leck mich am arsch*' and the worthy gentleman proudly and loudly repeated it back. Erwin visibly flinched. The boy smiled back, prompting the visitor to have the confidence to shuffle down the line and ask each of the boys individually, and with increasing gusto, '*Leck mich am arsch?*'

A red-faced Erwin was unable to intervene without causing huge embarrassment, so had to stand back and listen for several minutes as the dignitary went down the line shaking hands and asking 'Lick my arse?' to each of the sniggering boys.[343]

One of the group went way beyond what might be described as adolescent messing about and challenging boundaries. In the late spring of 1940, one of the older *noar*, Leopold Chajes, was suspected of being involved in theft from the *kupa*. He denied it but a trap was set and he was caught red-handed shortly afterwards. A disappointed and furious Erwin Seligmann expelled the boy from the Gwrych *Hachshara* and had him transferred to a Jewish hostel in Manchester.[344]

Unbeknownst to everyone at the time, Chajes had also recently committed another more serious crime. As part of his duties at Gwrych, Chajes had been responsible for ferrying money and postal orders between the castle and the town Post Office. On 10 February 1940, the counter clerk at Abergele Post Office, Arthur Williams, had reckoned up at the end of the day and had inexplicably found himself short of three 18-shilling postal orders. Initially, little could be done and the poor young clerk had taken the blame and been required to replace the shortfall himself.

However, in May, Chajes attempted to use those same postal orders in Manchester and he was thus easily tracked down. He was arrested on 28 August. Under questioning he initially claimed that he was attempting to cash the orders on behalf of a friend but when pressured to name his friend he crumbled.[345] When charged, Chajes did not argue. He replied simply, 'Yes, that is right. Can I pay the money back?'[346]

He was returned to Abergele to face a specially convened magistrate's court where he pleaded guilty and also asked for two other crimes to be taken into consideration: the theft of a Post Office savings bank book from a fellow Gwrych refugee (though he had made no attempt to use it) and an attempt to steal other postal orders from Abergele Post Office. Chajes was hesitant to explain exactly how he had managed to get three postal orders from the other side of the counter without being seen, but he was adamant that he had acted alone and that he had no accomplice. He wanted to explain to the court that 'I am not a thief. I acted on a sudden impulse, and I can assure you that if you deal with me leniently, nothing of the kind will happen again.'[347]

A somewhat uncomfortable exchange followed. The defence produced a document gained, somehow, from Germany showing that Chajes had no criminal record. The prosecution dismissed the document, claiming that nothing from the Nazi government could be trusted. He may well have been correct, but then showed a staggering ignorance of the circumstances that Jews had faced in Germany, and an equally impressive ability to be selective in what he trusted, when he noted a comment in the document stating that Chajes had spent two weeks in solitary confinement in a Nazi concentration camp after *Kristallnacht*.

The prosecution concluded that Chajes had 'abused, in a very gross manner, the hospitality extended to him in this country.'[348] The defence argued that his behaviour was out of character and 'the young man came from a very respectable family in Poland, and it was a great surprise – in fact it was unbelievable – to his friends that he had done such a thing.' They recommended that 'a good talking to' would suffice as punishment.[349] Similarly, Detective Sergeant Tilley urged the court to deal with Chajes as compassionately as possible, given the young man's circumstances.

The two local magistrates took a serious view of the matter and jailed Chajes for six weeks. Some saw this as harsh but those at the castle, aware of the details behind his expulsion from their community for theft, had little sympathy for their former colleague.

Despite some examples of bullying and the renegade behaviour of Chajes, the group were forming strong friendships. Herman Rothman stated that, 'I enjoyed myself because I was amongst boys and girls of my own age and a little older.'[350] Ruth Kessel noted that 'for most of us this was the first time in our lives that we were living without any interference from, or supervision by, adults – and, despite the sad circumstances that had brought us here, we thrived on this communal

living. Everyone looked out for each other and we built up tremen-
dously strong bonds.'[351] On a visit to the castle in 2008, she recalled
that 'Gwrych Castle was very nice and friendly. People were very kind.
Especially all the girls. We were like a family.'[352]

Back in Spring 1940, the 'family' at Gwrych were also gearing up for
two of the most-anticipated festivals in the Jewish religious calendar,
Purim and *Pesach*. Purim, on 23–24 March that year, had been on
everybody's mind since the Llandudno Women's Zionist & Welfare
Society had donated a pile of useless clothing and somebody had suggested using the contents for a fancy-dress party to coincide with the
festival. A recent, and much-coveted, donation from a local in Abergele
– a large box of chocolates – had given someone else the idea of putting
that up as the prize for the *noar* or *chaver* who could come up with
the best costume. With the time to be inventive, and a reward worth
fighting over, many of the children – particularly the girls – threw
themselves enthusiastically into preparations for the event, fashioning
outfits to turn themselves into queens, princesses, pirates and more.[353]
Some, as always, viewed the mounting hysteria with disdain, being far
too laid-back to involve themselves in such childish antics. Herman
Rothman was always on the lookout for ways to achieve an easier life,
while Jesse Zierler was constantly looking for ways to subvert things for
his own amusement. They mutually decided that the fancy dress competition was beneath them – at least they did until the last moment.
Jesse later recalled how the day went:

> Herman Rothman and I retreated to our room for a well-
> earned rest. I was fast asleep when our *madrich* [Erwin
> Seligmann] looked in and threw us out of bed accompanied
> by a lecture on such matters as failing to fall into the spirit
> of things etc. Given that kind of incentive we made for the
> old clothes cupboard and, with less than ten minutes to
> go, selected two moth-eaten ladies' dresses, two enormous
> wide-brimmed floral hats (once paraded at Ascot before

Queen Victoria) and some other *shmattes* [rags] to form respectable bosoms. A heavy woollen sweater rolled into a bundle was to play the part of a mongrel. We somehow laid our hands on an old rusty bicycle without tyres, brakes or a seat. It did however have a bell that worked loud and clear. Thus kitted out, we entered the packed auditorium which had just about finished applauding the last of the participants. With our appearance all hell broke loose. The outcome was never really in doubt. Waltzing off with our fully deserved box of milk and plain assortment, our popularity with the opposite sex increased beyond belief.[354]

After Purim, the castle community began gearing up for *Pesach*, which would be held between 22 and 30 April. Their mood was considerably heartened by the news that, at long last, a proper chef had been found to take over in the kitchen. Leo Silbermann, aged twenty-five, had been recruited from the *Hachshara* at Manor Farm in Tingrith, Buckinghamshire, where he was one of the *chaverim*. Although he was self-taught rather than a chef by any qualification, he had worked in the kitchen there and knew enough about mass catering to be a valuable recruit for the Gwrych *Hachshara*. David Smith arranged to collect him from Liverpool in his new car.

Smith regularly travelled away from the castle, often to Liverpool or Manchester to pursue issues relating to the *Hachshara*'s finances, though he also often travelled more widely and for other reasons. In December 1939, for example, he had been in London at a Jewish educator's conference, and in late February 1940 he was in Aberystwyth to address the Jewish Students Society on the subject of 'Jewish Peace Aims'.[355] To make life easier, he had purchased himself a second-hand car from a Mr Holden, a teacher at the Abergele Grammar School (the very car that Henry Glanz had recently tried to 'borrow'). Smith was very proud of his new machine but in early April 1940 he had to face the embarrassment of being fined £1 for having an unauthorised mask on his headlights which broke the blackout regulations.[356]

On 9 April 1940, Smith drove to Liverpool to collect Silbermann. The plan was to get him installed in his new home at Gwrych well in time for *Pesach*. Also in the car with him was twenty-three-year-old *chavera* Karo Gerson.[357] On the journey back to Abergele, along the relatively fast and straight road between Northop and Holywell, a sheep strayed onto the road ahead of them.[358] Smith swerved to avoid the sheep but lost control of the car. The car ploughed through a hedge, overturned and rolled down a twenty-three-foot embankment. The car's descent was only halted when it careered into a thick hedgerow and came to rest on its roof. All three were pulled from the vehicle by a passer-by, who then called for an ambulance. The two men were taken to Lluesty Infirmary in Holywell and Gerson was taken to Holywell Cottage Hospital. The injuries to Silbermann and Gerson were fortunately minor and both were soon discharged back to Gwrych. Smith, however, had been very seriously injured and had a suspected fractured spine. Within hours, when his spinal injuries had been confirmed, he was transferred to a hospital in Liverpool for more specialist treatment. Shortly afterwards, he was moved again, this time to a hospital in London for further care.

Hearing of the accident, Erwin Seligmann contacted the hospital in Liverpool and was given the awful news that the doctors held little hope that anything could be done to aid David's recovery. Erwin broke the news of the accident to the residents of the *Hachshara*, but kept the more harrowing part of the prognosis to himself. As already noted, David Smith was not particularly well known by the *noar* at the *Hachshara* and so, despite the news causing some sorrow, especially for Smith's assistant, Ossi Findling, it did not significantly dampen the enthusiasm that was building for *Pesach*.

Pesach, the Passover festival, is one of the most popularly observed Jewish festivals and commemorates the story of the escape from Egyptian slavery as told in the Book of Exodus. One of the requirements of the festival is to avoid leavened bread. In its place, a bread known as *matzah* is made and then baked very rapidly to create a thin, cracker-like bread. The new kitchen stove, installed the previous November, was a significant improvement on the original one but not really up to this particular task so Rabbi Sperber and some of the *chaverim* came up with a simple 'make do and mend' alternative. Using a broken brazier and metal buckets, Sperber improvised a basic outdoor stove. He then gathered the youngsters in one of the castle yards on 22 April, the day before the first day of *Pesach*, to witness the baking of the *matzah* and to hear the *Hamotzi* blessing. After nightfall on the following day, the community gathered for the *Seder* meal around their new table, the first piece that had been specially commissioned from the carpentry workshop. This was the first *Pesach* to be held at the *Hachshara* and for the vast majority of the youngsters it was also their first without their families. As such, it was an even more significant event and was even recorded for posterity by a camera.

The mood amongst the castle community had probably never been better than it was at the time of Purim and *Pesach* but the after-effects of David Smith's accident and imminent developments in the war were about to change everything.

CHAPTER 9

'A very traumatic experience'

May–June 1940
Spy fever and internment

On the same day that David Smith's car had careered off the road near Holywell, Germany had invaded both Denmark and Norway. Denmark was defeated in a day and although Norway would officially resist until June, the inevitably of a similar result was clear early on. Until this moment, the war in the West during the previous eight months had been so low-key that the Americans, still neutral, had termed the whole thing the 'phoney war'.

On the home front in Britain up until now, the war had not had the impact that was initially feared. The threat of *Luftwaffe* bombers darkening the skies had not yet materialised and, by March 1940, over half of the evacuees that had flooded into Abergele in September 1939 had returned home.

A visitor to the town at this time would have noticed very few indications that a war was going on. Many people were still not carrying their gas masks despite the local press regularly exhorting people to do so, and the number of prosecutions for failing to adhere to blackout regulations at night showed little sign of decline. The town's two public air raid shelters, at the junctions of Bridge Street and St George Road, remained theoretical rather than actual. Discussions at council level were more about the planning issues involved than getting on with the task of constructing them.

The war had not been 'phoney' for one Abergele family, however. Charles and Florence Shaw had lost their son, Stephen, when HMS *Royal Oak* was sunk by a U-boat in Scapa Flow, Orkney, in October 1939. Yet, by comparison, at an equivalent point in World War One, eleven men from the locality had been killed. At the same time as mourning the tragic loss of Leading Seaman Shaw, the townsfolk were also basking in the glow of their first war hero: Sergeant Alexander Thomas of the RAF had recently been awarded the Distinguished Flying Medal.

The Gwrych *Hachshara* had played a part in minimising any disruption the war brought to the town. In May 1940, the Abergele Farmer's Union expressed considerable concern at the loss of significant numbers of men who had enlisted into the forces, but were thankful that this had been more than compensated for by the provision of nearly 200 young workers from the castle. The agricultural economy, as a consequence, had therefore been relatively unaffected. Stock sizes and auction prices reported in the local press noted that Abergele cattle, sheep and horse sales in the spring of 1940 were almost identical to those of the year before and other years immediately before the war.

In fact, the effects of war felt so limited that the Abergele Publicity Association was busy planning a joint advertising campaign with the railway companies in a major drive to attract tourists to the town for the summer of 1940. Speaking for the Association back in March 1940, Abergele Urban District Councillor Tom Leigh stated that 'be it peace time or war time the essentiality of holidays is still the same … someone will always have to be on duty, yet it will always be the turn of someone for a holiday.'[359]

The invasions of Denmark and Norway did, however, begin to alter the general public mood towards 'aliens', leading to an increased fear of German spies and more talk of the dangers posed by the possibility of 'fifth columnists'.[360] If such enemies existed, it was argued, they would most likely be found within the 73,000 aliens that the internment tribunals had allowed to remain at large within Britain. Collectively, the tribunals had interned less than one per cent of all aliens and less than nine per cent of the remainder had been placed under category B restrictions. There was now open talk and fear of an enemy 'fifth column' within Britain and a new 'spy fever' rapidly grew.

Following the invasions of Denmark and Norway, the Nazis turned their attention westwards to Holland, Belgium, Luxembourg and France on 10 May 1940. In Britain, Neville Chamberlain resigned and Winston Churchill became Prime Minister. The situation was becoming critical, exacerbating existing concerns over enemy aliens. The next day, the internment of foreigners from Germany or its allies began in coastal areas where a potential invasion force would most likely land. As the *Manchester Guardian* put it on 13 May, 'Refugees are welcome here because they look for Hitler's downfall and are only anxious to assist us, but it would be folly not to assume that Hitler will have tried hard to find some helpers for his parachutists should he send them. No half measures will do. We must make certain of disposing of it [this new danger of the fifth column] quickly.'

If ever there was a moment for the locals to turn upon the Gwrych Castle refugees, most of whom had German or Austrian heritage, this was it. The night light reported at the castle back in December 1939 had caused little damage to the reputation of the Gwrych *Hachshara* or the good relationship it had developed with the local community, but on 14 May 1940, in the midst of this national crisis, it happened again.

At around 10.15 p.m., PC Sam Williams and a special constable noted several lights at the castle. He went inside 'and the boys, upon seeing him, fled in all directions.'[361] Williams ascertained that one of the lights came from a kitchen window, at which there appeared to have been no attempt to adhere to blackout regulations. Other lights were found in the boys' recreation room and three other rooms around the building.

Charged with multiple breaches of the blackout rules, Erwin Seligmann was summoned to the Abergele Police Court to represent the

Hachshara in the absence of David Smith following his car accident. Erwin made no attempt to give any excuse or defence for the centre's conduct and could only offer the court the rather limp comment that the lights had been completely unintentional.[362] The court imposed a fine of £5 and 5 shillings.

Thus far, the members of the *Hachshara* had felt more uncomfortable about their nationalities – being mostly German or Austrian – than their religion. When Herman Rothman had been 'interrogated' by the labourers on his farm on his first day, it had only been his nationality that he had felt the need to hide. Ruth Kessel noted that 'when we were asked where we came from, we felt uncomfortable to admit we were from Germany.'[363] Being Jewish, whenever it had come up, had never been a problem.

Henry Glanz, when asked if he had experienced any antisemitism as a refugee during his time in Abergele, replied, 'I never did. Not in Wales. I did in Birmingham. It really upset me.'[364] Henry Steinberg had a similar recollection: 'I may have encountered a few incidents here or there. I'm sure that there were some people who didn't like us but, to be honest, I do not recall ever having [any incidents].'[365] Ruth Kessel recalled that, 'We never experienced any antisemitism from the local people ... instead of being called a "dirty Jew", as had happened to many of my friends, here we were treated as equals. Secluded in our haven in Wales, this was the first time in years we actually felt safe.'[366]

At the very least, virtually everyone in the town and district could accept the old idiom that 'my enemy's enemy is my friend' and, for most, that had been sufficient reason in itself to welcome the Jewish community with open arms. Salli Edelnand later commented on this aspect of the relationship with the locals: 'The local population realised that all of us were in the same boat, with a common target, an evil enemy who had to be defeated.'[367] Arieh Handler noted that, 'We found in the Welshmen, like later in Scotland too, a lot of understanding for what it means to be a kind of minority group.'[368]

However, there is always a minority who are capable of distorting reality to match their own prejudices, and such people did exist in the area. One year later, in the spring of 1941, former Plaid Cymru Deputy Vice President and President of the Council of the National Eisteddfod of Wales, William John Gruffydd, wrote his editorial column of the Welsh-language paper *Y Llenor*: 'North Wales is full of wealthy, scheming Jews who arrogate to themselves all the resources of the land leaving the native population helpless and impoverished ... And by the way, is it not high time that somebody protested loudly against those Jews who oppress Llandudno, Colwyn Bay, Abergele and the surrounding countryside?'[369]

Gruffydd's views were very much his own and certainly not shared by all Welsh nationalists.[370] They are also impossible to explain from a factual point of view especially as they can only really have been made in reference to the Gwrych *Hachshara*, the creation of which had singlehandedly increased the Jewish population of North Wales by around fifty per cent. Ruth Kessel was thus fairly correct in her later recollection that the local population 'had probably never met a Jew before'.[371] There were established but small and scattered Jewish communities within North Wales, though in no way was the area 'full of wealthy, scheming Jews'. Prior to the arrival of the Gwrych Castle refugees in 1939, there were probably no more than three or four hundred Jews living across the whole of North Wales.[372]

The only notable example of the Jewish population of the region having anything like the sort of influence that might have allowed them to successfully carry out the kind of coup Gruffydd was suggesting, was the Llandudno Women's Zionist & Welfare Society and the fact that the mayor of Bangor was Jewish. In any case, during the early part of the war especially, any shared focus of these individuals and groups was primarily concentrated on the problem of how best they could assist in the settlement of young Jews that had arrived in Britain via the Kindertransport, rather than anything more fanciful. For example, in Llandudno, a Mr and Mrs Rafhael Rosenberg fostered five-year-old Eva Oesterreicher, one of the Czech children saved by Sir Nicholas Winton, and the Sonabend family also played a role in bringing Jewish children from Poland into the area. These were hardly the actions of people intent on a sinister plan to impoverish their neighbours.

That Gruffydd should write such blatantly incorrect nonsense in the editorial of a circulating quarterly, based on no evidence at all, does however suggest that his opinions would have resonated with at least some of his nationalist readers. It is therefore likely that a very small minority of people in the Abergele locality may have agreed with him and believed that the Jewish community at the castle were actively and secretly planning to 'oppress Abergele and the surrounding countryside' as part of some wider Jewish conspiracy. However, the vast majority of townsfolk were not feeling the slightest bit oppressed by the 200 or so youngsters keeping themselves to themselves up at the castle. It is hard to credit Gruffydd's statement with any authority other than being the expression of a minority and extremist view that would have been sadly all too familiar to most of the refugees from their experiences in Nazi Germany. Quite frankly, as his piece suggested, if nobody had thus far 'protested loudly against those Jews', the sentiment clearly wasn't widely shared.

The reality was that few bought into such unfounded and ludicrous ideas and there was no serious questioning of the Jewish community at Gwrych Castle, even after their second breach of the blackout regulations in May 1940. The reoffending must have caused some tutting or the shaking of heads in the town but the castle community hardly stood out as unique amongst offenders. On the same day that Erwin Seligmann faced the police court and received the second sanction, eleven other locals were also fined for similar offences, with six of them all coming from the same street (Peel Street).[373] In fact, and perhaps bizarrely, the only known complaint made to the local police relating to the suspected presence of an enemy spy in the area did not come from the local community at all – it was made by someone from inside the castle itself.

On occasions, the services of small groups of children were offered to locals who wanted their gardens tidying up for free. Henry Glanz and four other boys were working in the garden of a woman and were chatting away quite happily in German as they worked. The owner had been watching them for some time, as if intrigued. After a while she joined in their conversation, speaking to them in fluent German with a clear hint of an Austrian accent. The stunned teenagers fell silent. Reading their looks of surprise, the woman explained to them that her late husband had been Austrian, and that was how she had become so proficient in German. That evening, back at the castle, the five boys began arguing over what all this could have meant. One of them had become absolutely convinced that the woman's explanation was a risible cover story and that she must therefore be a Nazi spy. The others dismissed his claim and argued that such a conclusion was madness – what on earth, one of them asked, was there in Abergele that Hitler would have even remotely thought to be worth spying upon? Undeterred by the derision of his peers, the youngster took himself off to the Abergele police station to report his concerns. The woman was subsequently spoken to by the police who quickly established that her supposed 'cover story' was, in fact, completely true. Several days later, the group of five were due to return to the same property to continue working on the garden. Shamed and embarrassed by what had happened, and expecting a severe tongue-lashing, three of the group got cold feet and refused to go, leaving just two of them to pluck up enough courage to face the woman. To their surprise, and great relief, they did not receive the frosty reception they had expected. Instead they were praised by the woman for their vigilance and good citizenship.[374]

However, Abergele Urban District Councillor John Hargreaves was absolutely convinced that there was enemy fifth-column activity in North Wales and he was determined to be the man that would lead the crusade to root it out. During April 1940, Hargreaves had set up his own vigilante agitation group, with the aim of stamping out unpatriotic activities as well as weeding out dangerous and treacherous individuals within Denbighshire. By May 1940, he was claiming to have received 'fan mail' over his stance[375] and spoke of 'a fifth column in our midst'.[376] So vocal was he, and so powerful and convincing were his claims, that they even appeared in press reports well beyond the region. Given the beliefs of Hargreaves and his followers, the largely German community at Gwrych Castle should have stood out like a sore thumb as by far the most obvious target for suspicion to be found anywhere in North Wales. And yet, Hargreaves ignored them. Just a few weeks earlier, he had been a guest at the inaugural dinner of the local special constabulary along with Dr Julius Handler. Following toasts to both the King and the Queen, it was John Hargreaves himself that had looked Julius in the eye whilst proposing a toast to 'our guests'.[377]

Instead of the castle community, both he and his small band of 'fans' concentrated their fire on two teachers employed near Wrexham by the Denbighshire Local Authority who had declared themselves to be conscientious objectors. His verbal bile, no doubt appealing to those who wrote and sent him his 'fan mail', included him stating that teachers 'should be sent to work on the land and do real hard work, and preach their slimy peace propaganda stuff to the pigs.'[378] Hargreaves was not content to just hound the local teaching profession; he also turned on non-conformist ministers in the area as 'the prime movers behind the conchie [conscientious objector] classes'.[379] The Denbighshire Education Committee rejected his claims against the teachers as completely groundless, and local ministers simply ignored him rather than being drawn into a debate.

The most important point to note, however, is that even those who believed in and were actively seeking fifth-column activities across North Wales failed to find any reason to focus any energy on the large group of non-Christian, Germanic 'aliens' living within their midst at Gwrych Castle. And this was at a time when Churchill's rhetoric was giving them the perfect excuse to do so *and* the castle community had just catapulted itself back into the local headlines with a second breach of the blackout regulations. If there is any evidence to confirm that the foreign Jews at Gwrych Castle had been accepted by the local community then this must surely be the most convincing.[380]

His views were venomous but Councillor John Hargreaves was nevertheless symbolic of a significant mood change across the nation that was triggered by the German invasion of France in May 1940. On 14 May, the Local Defence Volunteers, often known simply as the LDV, the Home Guard or more colloquially as 'Dad's Army', was set up and volunteers were called for. Germany's invasion of France was rapid and Churchill ordered the evacuation of the British army from Dunkirk on 26 May. The night beforehand, given the growing tension and their recent blackout infringement, the castle community had decided to scale down their *Lag BaOmer* celebration, the central element of which would have been the lighting of a large bonfire that they had been constructing for several days.

Fears of a German invasion grew. Despite being a highly unlikely location for a German landing, Abergele was nevertheless by the sea and the locals realised their potential vulnerability. Just a few days after the call for volunteers for the LDV, a boy of the same age as the Gwrych refugees witnessed the first group of Abergele's 'Dads Army' volunteers in action. He saw 'a group of about a dozen men of all ages, carrying shotguns, long poles and pitchforks walking over the railway bridge at Pensarn. They appeared to be in a buoyant mood and were going to patrol the beach.'[381] By the end of the month over a hundred men from the town had volunteered for the Abergele unit of the LDV.

The military also took the possibility of an invasion along the North Wales coastline quite seriously. Whilst the Dunkirk evacuation was still going on, work began on the beach to dig a deep, concrete-lined trench stretching from Abergele and Pensarn railway station to Ty Crwn, around a half a mile to the west, and to a point on the shoreline directly north of Gwrych Castle. Dotted on the beach in front of the trench system were deposited a number of large concrete blocks designed to hinder landing craft and tanks and, at the centre of the line, a brick and concrete pillbox for machine-gunners to fire from was constructed. Some of those from the castle who were being given work by the Ministry of Labour found themselves involved in the construction work.

By 4 June 1940, at the conclusion of the evacuation from Dunkirk,

Churchill's thoughts on enemy aliens had hardened and in a statement to the House of Commons he said that, 'I feel not the slightest sympathy. Parliament has given us the powers to put down fifth-column activities with a strong hand, and we shall use those powers, subject to the supervision and correction of the House, without the slightest hesitation until we are satisfied, and more than satisfied, that this malignancy in our midst has been effectively stamped out.'

The way to stamp out the 'malignancy' most effectively was to take no chances and resort to the mass internment of all 'enemy aliens' all across Britain. This threat, if carried out, spelled potential disaster for the *Hachshara* project at Gwrych. Dr Julius Handler was extremely fearful of the developing public mood even though the Gwrych *Hachshara* had escaped the attention of Councillor Hargreaves and his fifth-column hunters. In correspondence he wrote, 'The events of the Battle of Dunkirk and its consequences gave rise to a deep feeling of anxiety to all at Gwrych Castle. Rumour had reached us that German and Austrian nationals were rounded up in London, especially in the Hampstead area and sent to internment camps on the Isle of Man, Canada and Australia.'[382]

The refugees knew the consequences of round-ups better than most; one of them, sixteen-year-old Eli Freier of Breslau, had spent some time in the Buchenwald concentration camp after *Kristallnacht*. There was a resigned expectation amongst many at Gwrych that before too long they would join their fellow Jews in internment camps such as the one on the Isle of Man. 'Refugee boys at Gwrych Castle in Wales were close enough to see the island through binoculars and, in full knowledge that they probably were to be interned there within a few days, wryly regarded newspaper advertisements offering "a peaceful holiday on the Isle of Man".'[383]

The absurdity of the situation that was developing was also not lost on many Jews, including Wolfgang Billig: 'Because I came with a Polish passport and had a different sticker on the back of my alien's registration book I was classed as a friendly alien and not interned. It was ironic that the colour of the passport determined our status and fate and not the fact that we were Jewish refugee children from the Nazis. In Germany we were hounded as Jews and as enemies of the state and when we thought we were free from fear, most were again treated like enemies.'[384]

On 18 June 1940, Churchill spoke to the nation, stating that, 'The Battle of France is over: the Battle of Britain is about to begin.' Britain now faced the very real possibility of invasion and the simple fact was that the country would be better served by utilising rather than interning those who had as much, if not more, reason to fight against Germany. In addition to this, the vast majority of those interned, or threatened with imminent internment, had been judged as category C just a few weeks or months earlier. Nevertheless, orders for the mass internment of enemy aliens were issued on Friday, 21 June 1940.

On that day, Wolfgang Billig, Bill Braun and the rest of their work team were harvesting turnips in the market gardens at Hen Wrych when they heard multiple vehicles pass by on the main road nearby. Several minutes later, one of them pointed to a fleet of black Humber police cars making their way up the main driveway to the castle several hundred yards away. PC Williams and his colleagues had repeatedly told them, on their occasional visits, that they had nothing to fear from the British police, but this time something was very different. Still, they returned to the turnips, speculating on what could be happening.

On the castle forecourt, the Chief Constable of Police from Colwyn Bay, accompanied by a phalanx of constables, climbed out of their cars. Erwin Seligmann and Dr Julius Handler invited the chief constable inside and the three disappeared into a room. Several of the *chaverim* mingled nearby, attempting to overhear the conversation. After some time, the three emerged and several of the *chaverim* who had not managed to scuttle away quickly enough were summoned over and given instructions to find and gather certain individuals.[385] One of them was Bill Braun.

Over the next hour or two a small group of those presently on site, all aged sixteen years or over, and all with either German or Austrian passports, was assembled. The chief constable stepped forward and told them that they were being detained immediately.[386] They were to be interned as enemy aliens and should pack their belongings and meet at the cars on the forecourt as swiftly as possible.

Because so many of the castle's inhabitants were minors, the chief constable acquiesced to a plea from Erwin and Julius for him to grant an exemption, at least temporarily, to the leadership group and a small number of teachers and *chaverim* over the age of eighteen. However, he told them that they were to operate under a strict curfew and were not to leave the estate without seeking permission from the authorities until further notice.

Erwin also argued that the 'employers' of the large number of young people working at local farms and businesses would need a day or two to make necessary adjustments for the loss of such crucial workers. In return for assurances that those individuals would be handed over, the chief constable accepted the compromise and left with Bill Braun and a small number of the castle's residents.

A few days later, final arrangements had been completed and Julius, in his brother's absence, chose to accompany a group of over a dozen German and Austrian boys and *chaverim* to Abergele police station on Llanfair Road. Once the names had been checked against lists provided by the chief constable, Julius handed the care of his group to a small police guard of the same local 'Bobbies' who had gone out of their way to befriend them. They were then marched away down the road past the Mynydd Seion chapel, through the heart of the town that had welcomed them and then on to the Abergele and Pensarn railway station. After a short wait on the platform, they were put on board a train to Liverpool where they were to be sorted according to their final internment destinations.[387] Julius found the whole thing 'a very traumatic experience'.[388]

The internees from Gwrych were held in Liverpool for several days before discovering their fate. Some of them, as they had fearfully predicted, ended up on the Isle of Man. Most of them, however, were sent overseas. A number were destined for a camp in Canada and they were boarded onto the SS *Ettrick* or the SS *Sobiecki* on 3 July 1940, which would have to run the Atlantic gauntlet in fear of U-boat predators. Amongst those aboard was the Gwrych FC footballer Edmund Schnitzer. It was his eighteenth birthday.[389] The *Ettrick* was filled with hundreds of internees, many of whom were Italian aliens.

> They were treated badly, being herded like cattle into the lower decks and kept mainly below deck in overcrowded, squalid and inhuman conditions, receiving only meagre rations of food and water. Some of the prisoners nicknamed it 'torpedo class'. They suffered a wretched ten-day voyage across the Atlantic before finally docking in the city of Quebec. Here they were met by a hostile and strongly armed guard, as Canada had been forewarned to take extra precaution as these prisoners were of a 'highly dangerous nature'.[390]

Eight of the youngsters who had been marched to the Abergele police station by Julius Handler and then through the town under police guard had come to Britain under the auspices of Youth *Aliyah* and most of them managed to stay together. One of their number, seventeen-year-old Eli Freier, later stated that they 'volunteered, together with the others, to be sent overseas'[391] rather than be held in Britain. Freier's time in the Buchenwald concentration camp meant he knew better than most that, if Britain really was facing the imminent threat of invasion, the last thing he and his friends would want was to be already under lock and key for the Nazis if they arrived.

Freier and the Gwrych group were placed aboard the HMT (Hired Military Transport) *Dunera* on 10 July 1940, bound for internment in Australia. Among them was Eli's older brother, nineteen-year-old Fritz, as well as Isidor Zelmanowicz, Hans Brandt, Siegfried (Sigi) Kahan, Moses Loewy and Abraham Samt who were all sixteen-year-olds originally from Germany. Wilhelm Landberger, aged eighteen, who hailed from Mattersdorf in Austria was with them, too.

Like those who had been transported on the SS *Ettrick* to Canada, the HMT *Dunera* internees suffered a horrific voyage to Australia. The ship was loaded at Liverpool to around double its designed capacity with just over 2,500 on board. The journey was long and perilous and like the *Ettrick* they faced the threat of being stalked by U-boats throughout their fifty-seven-day voyage. In fact, they encountered a U-boat almost immediately whilst heading south between Wales and Ireland. The U-boat fired two torpedoes, one of which missed, and the other fortunately failed to detonate on contact and harmlessly bounced off the hull of the ship. The 300 or so British guards on board included many men deemed too unreliable for the army or released from prison on condition that they serve in the forces. Under their hands some of the refugees suffered intimidation and beatings or had their personal possessions rifled through and items stolen. And then there were the terrible conditions on board:

> The ship was an overcrowded Hell-hole ... many men had to sleep on the floor or on tables. There was only one piece of soap for twenty men, and one towel for ten men, water was rationed ... Toilet facilities were far from adequate, even with makeshift latrines erected on the deck, and sewage flooded the decks. Dysentery ran through the ship. Blows with rifle butts and beatings from the soldiers were daily occurrences. One refugee tried to go to the latrines on deck during the night – which was out-of-bounds. He was bayoneted in the stomach by one of the guards and spent the rest of the voyage in the hospital. Food was bad, maggots in the bread and the butter and margarine was rancid.[392]

The *Dunera* refugees arrived at the Hay Internment Camp in New South Wales on 7 September 1940. The Gwrych internees all served time there 'in the middle of the desert'[393] until 29 December 1940 when they were moved to Malabar (otherwise known as Long Bay Gaol) near Sydney until 9 March 1941. During November 1941, through intervention driven by Youth *Aliyah*, they had each received approval from the Australian High Commission in London for onwards travel to Palestine, and all of them managed to get there in either 1941 or 1942.

Precisely how many of the German and Austrian boys from the Gwrych *Hachshara* were ordered to be interned is unclear, though it was at least seventeen and probably more like twenty – about one in five of all the males at the centre, or ten per cent of the castle's population, all of them from the ranks of the *chaverim* or the older *Aleph* group. It severely damaged the morale of all of those that remained at the castle. During that spring, the *Hachshara* had finally become a united community – what it was always intended to be – but in the days following 21 June 1940, many of the remaining refugees struggled to make sense of what had just happened and what it meant. Those that had been taken away were all enemies of the Nazis and no threat at all to their new host nation. They had all been cleared by the tribunals in Caernarfon. Many were ready to volunteer for the British army when they came of age, but they could not do so from within an internment camp. Most damaging of all, the experience of seeing their friends face internment made many of the youngsters and *chaverim* at Gwrych question other things. And, for some, those questions boiled down to something quite simple: just what was the point of all this?

Although nobody could have known it at the time, the internments of June 1940 were one of the key factors that would seal the fate of the Gwrych Castle *Hachshara*.

CHAPTER 10

———

'I couldn't see any purpose to it'

July–September 1940
Departures, arrivals and divisions

The absence of David Smith after his accident in April and the internments in June wounded the *Hachshara* deeply. However, something more fundamental had already begun to eat away at its long-term future. Though it may have gone largely unnoticed at the time, little by little, people were starting to leave.

The *chaverim*, by their very nature as a group of volunteers, had never been a constant group. Several of the original team from September 1939 had left during the following months, though there had been arrivals to replace them, such as Martin Steinberger who took over from the original carpenter, Alfred Kallner. Steinberger had arrived on a Kindertransport in early 1939 and been fostered by relatives who lived in London. He turned eighteen shortly afterwards and found work as a cabinetmaker in Wembley but, in order to continue his own preparations for *Aliyah*, he sought out a role as a *chaver* and was the perfect fit for voluntary work at Gwrych. Many of the new arrivals, like the new chef Leo Silbermann, shared the same basic story as Steinberger: they were eighteen or older and they were trying to find useful things to do that would also enhance the prospects for their own futures.

However, whilst that attracted people to Gwrych, it also lured them away. *Madricha* Hanna Zuntz, whose connections to some wealthy families had been instrumental in helping the *Hachshara* receive generous and practical donations, found a way to emigrate to Palestine on 9 March 1940. Many others left simply because they wanted to earn some money and move on with their own lives. Alfred Benjamin, who was exempted from internment as a class C alien on 13 February 1940, had left Gwrych almost immediately afterwards for Manchester and had since got married in London. Milli Koenigshoefer, from Breslau, who had appeared before the Caernarfon alien assessment tribunal in December 1939, left not long afterwards to find paid work and was registered as an alien by the police in Salford in June 1940 where she was working as a domestic servant.[394] Rolf 'Rudi' Grab departed in early 1940 and enlisted in the British Army a year later. One anonymous *chavera* posted her availability for work in the local press of North Wales, advertising her skills as either a cook or general domestic and describing herself as a 'nice, clean Jewish girl'.[395] Finding replacement *chaverim* was not easy and these losses were not balanced by gains.

Then, during the spring of 1940, *Bachad* was forced into some overall cost-cutting exercises, including reducing its financial support to the training centres – a situation the organisation's journal described as 'critical'.[396] Although the *chaverim* were not paid, *Bachad* was effectively subsidising their living costs by providing them with food and a roof over their heads, so reducing their numbers would therefore leave a little more in the kitty to spend on the *noar*. Consequently, 'large numbers'[397] of *chaverim* from across all of the *Hachsharot* centres were encouraged to leave and find paid work to support themselves. Many, in reality, did not really need much persuasion. This, combined with the internments, meant that the usual number of between forty and fifty *chaverim* at Gwrych fell to no more than thirty by the summer of 1940.

Not only had the overall numbers of *chaverim* declined but so had their collective quality. The original group had been dedicated to the *Hachshara's* cause. Some of the replacements shared those values, but they also included a growing number who were looking to become a *chaver* because of their own decreasing alternative options as much as any dedication to the Zionist cause. The problems caused by the lack of any financial support for the *chaverim*, as pointed out by the *Pegisha* in October 1939, were not only the reasons for the departure of some, including people like Milli Koenigshoefer, but it also made it more difficult to recruit quality replacements. Thus, each departure of a *chaver* had a minor, but at the same time very real, impact on the *Hachshara* as a whole. The sudden internment of several more of those original members of the team in one fell swoop in June 1940 therefore caused irreparable damage. Replacing them all would be impossible.

There had also been departures from amongst the *noar*. A fifth or more of the original cohort had been aged seventeen when the *Hachshara* opened and most had now turned eighteen. All were members of either Youth *Aliyah* or *Bachad*, and both Zionist organisations saw *Aliyah* to *Eretz Yisrael* as the main aim. Their place at Gwrych had been predicated upon them developing the necessary skills to pursue that ambition; therefore, once they attained the age of eighteen, they would be able to pursue this dream independently, and they were fully expected to do so.

However, the *Hachshara* had been set up before the war had begun. Now, the chances of getting to Palestine, which had been difficult enough in the first place, had been reduced still further. The course of the war thus far also suggested that those difficulties would remain for some considerable time into the future and even make the dream of *Aliyah* impossible. Immediately after the evacuation of Dunkirk, a small, somewhat bedraggled group of soldiers from a Scottish regiment arrived in the Abergele area for a brief period of recuperation. Their presence was a startling and very visible confirmation of the danger that Britain now faced. This, and the beginning of the Battle of Britain shortly afterwards, raised the terrifying prospect that the war could even end in victory for Germany and possibly in the not-too-far-distant future. Hanna Zuntz had successfully made *Aliyah*, but she was very much the exception and, over time, the youthful idealism of so many members of the castle community had been slowly, almost imperceptibly, eroding. The internment of a large group from the castle brought many more to a realisation that the cherished ambition of finding a way to Palestine was increasingly becoming nothing but a pipe dream.

The mood of the *Hachshara* was noticeably different after June 1940. A gloom and a sense of pointlessness began to emerge amongst some of those who had arrived with such optimism for a new life just the previous September. This was especially true for those who were approaching the age of eighteen and were having to face up to the reality that they really only had two options to choose from in the near future: become a *chaver*, either at Gwrych or another centre, or leave and find paid work.

David Smith's assistant, Ossi Findling, was one such disillusioned young man. His eighteenth birthday was just a few months away, in October 1940, and for some time he had been pondering what he would do next. The recent loss of his boss was undoubtedly very upsetting for Ossi, but it also perhaps acted as a catalyst that prompted him to reconsider his purpose and evaluate the wider issues that were concerning him. He concluded that, for him at least, the *Hachshara* dream was slowly dying: 'After *Pesach* 1940, I found that I was wasting my time to some extent. I wasn't learning anything ... I couldn't see any purpose to it and I was getting older and I thought it's time to earn some money.'[398]

Ossi was still in correspondence with his mother in Leipzig and, after expressing his increasing dismay about his own future, she wrote back pointing out that a rabbi they knew was in Britain – maybe he could help? After making enquiries, Ossi discovered that the rabbi in question was in Manchester. After some digging to find out more details of how to contact the rabbi, in late May 1940 – shortly before the internments happened – he walked into Abergele with some loose change in his pocket to make a phone call. The rabbi invited him to come over to Manchester. Ossi then hitch-hiked to Liverpool before getting lucky with a lift from a lorry driver who took him all the way to Manchester. The next day he arranged for a parcel service to collect his things from the castle. He found paid work as a furrier in Manchester before moving to London in 1942, and in 1944 he joined the British Army. Ossi never returned to the *Hachshara*.

Many others considering their options were now fairly experienced agricultural workers, making this a potential line of future employment. Prior to the internments, in April 1940, ten of the older boys had moved on to attend the University College of North Wales Agricultural Department where they were being paid agricultural minimum rates. Some of the girls, such as Fanni Flohr from Vienna, found domestic work.

Some of those further away from their eighteenth birthday were also considering their own futures and coming to the realisation that the *Hachshara* dream was not for them. Each child had their own reasons for reaching their conclusions – from the harsh life and poor living conditions they had endured at the castle to the wider issues of disruption and chaos in their young lives. They found their dreams of *Aliyah* crumbling into dust. Bill Braun said he thought that his time at Gwrych had brought things into a stark contrast for him and, as a result, 'destroyed a great deal of the convictions [and] Zionistic aspirations that I had at the time.'[399]

Salli Edelnand was also finding that he was 'not particularly interested in the lifestyle of a kibbutz',[400] and Manfred Alweiss 'later became disillusioned with the prospect'[401] of working towards his expected future. Both went on to become British citizens in later years and neither made *Aliyah*.

Although some of the *noar* had moved on before the internments of June 1940, that event significantly added to the sense of disillusionment and, as a consequence, the rate of departures rose.[402] The losses from both the *chaverim* and the *noar* were a major concern for Gwrych's leadership team and for Arieh Handler personally because, if the numbers fell too low, the viability of the entire enterprise would be compromised.

Arieh was aware that the overall number of residents at the Gwrych *Hachshara* had declined, but until now the losses had not been hugely significant, especially amongst the *chaverim* where replacements could be found, albeit with difficulty. However, the decreasing numbers of *noar* who could not be easily replaced was a more serious concern. A *Hachshara* without *noar* would cease to be a *Hachshara*. This accelerated after the sudden loss of the group who were interned. One new arrival at the castle, in late July 1940, estimated that the number of children at the *Hachshara* was somewhere between 100 and 150, which would suggest that the *noar* had lost somewhere between twenty-five to fifty per cent of its original composition in the ten months since September 1939.[403] That may have been a slight exaggeration, and the estimate was quite wide-ranging, but it does confirm that a serious problem was brewing.

Without intervention, it was quite possible that the numbers of children at the Gwrych Castle *Hachshara* could slip into a terminal decline. Arieh knew that injecting large numbers of newcomers who held less committed Zionist views into a centre that had succeeded in establishing the correct spirit of a *Hachshara* – and that was also now starting to prove itself as an example to others – could potentially derail it, but he had little choice.

However, finding new children would not be easy. When the Gwrych *Hachshara* had been created at the end of August 1939, reception camps for young Jews were full and being topped up daily by new arrivals via Kindertransport, but that had ended at the same time as the Gwrych *Hachshara* was opening its doors. With no new arrivals from Europe, the Gwrych *Hachshara* had no option but to look for replacement numbers from within the existing *Hachsharot* around the country.

Arieh therefore happily offered places at Gwrych to a group of Jewish refugees that were about to be evacuated from the Youth *Aliyah* centre at Llandough Castle near Cowbridge. After nearby Cardiff had been bombed for the first time on 3 July 1940, the decision was taken that the youngsters there were no longer safe and that they needed relocating to a more rural setting.[404]

Fifteen-year-old Gerhard Friedenfeld from Vienna, Austria, was amongst the group of somewhere between thirty and fifty youngsters that arrived at Gwrych in late July or early August 1940. Gerhard had grown up in a Jewish family that was not especially orthodox and that had assimilated into Viennese society to such an extent that the young man had attended the same local school that his father had attended rather than a Jewish school. His friends were not Jewish. He recalled, 'I went skating with them and swimming, and their fathers were my father's school friends.'[405] However, his father's faith in friendship proved to be misplaced. Gerhard remembered that he 'couldn't have been more wrong. And he was wrong, absolutely. They [his father's friends] switched instantly. When the Germans marched in [March 1938], they put on their brown uniforms ... and they put my father in jail.'[406]

In October 1938 his mother was given twenty-four hours' notice to hand over their property: 'So we had to scurry and rent a horse and a cart, and load it with whatever we could, and leave. Into no-man's-land, outside town ... and that's where we lived for three weeks, out under the open sky.'[407] A few weeks later they had to move again, to a refugee camp, where they were reunited with his father. In April 1939 the Nazis turned up at the camp. Gerhard recalled what happened:

> They selected some of us for what they called *turnen*. *Turnen* in German means to do gymnastics. And what they meant was beating and torture. And one of these torture methods consisted of forcing us to climb up high ladders, I mean twenty-five feet maybe, and to jump from the ladder onto cobblestones, just for fun. That's the way they amused themselves. And I don't know how many times I climbed up and jumped, and I broke my leg ... And that was the end of gymnastics for me. And a few days later, they allowed me to be taken to a hospital.[408]

Shortly afterwards, a man and a woman he had never met before came to the hospital 'and they asked me if I would like to go to England. And I said, "Well, I cannot make this decision. You would have to ask my parents." So evidently they went to see my parents in the camp, because four weeks later I was on a train to England. How they found me, how this was arranged, to this day I don't know.'[409] With his plaster cast removed early, and supplied with crutches, Gerhard found himself at a train station, having not seen his parents once since being hospitalised. Reflecting on this over fifty years later, he would remember that, 'I interpreted this as being neglected, pushed away. And this led to enormous anger on my side. Enormous. And not so many years ago, I was still a very angry man.'[410] In all likelihood, his parents were prevented from seeing him.

Gerhard arrived in Britain on 2 June 1939 and was initially fostered by the editor of the *New Statesman* magazine, who arranged for a new cast to be fitted to his broken leg at a nearby hospital. Several weeks later, once his leg had properly healed, he was sent to Great Engeham Farm and then, in the winter of 1939–40 he was relocated to Llandough Castle.

In June 1940, Gerhard – having anglicised his name to Gerard, and known as Gerry – found himself at the Gwrych *Hachshara* and he was immediately as unimpressed as his new colleagues who had arrived ten months earlier, declaring it to be 'A monstrosity. Cold! Couldn't heat it. Impossible. We had cold showers … no hot water.'[411]

Another of the new arrivals from Llandough was fourteen-year-old Mimi Schleissner from Marienbad, Czechoslovakia. Mimi also quickly saw behind the impressive facade of the castle and later recalled that life at Gwrych was 'quite an experience because that castle was an old Welsh castle. It was just like a fairy tale castle. It was all towers rising up from the sea. But to live there! They had no bathrooms, they had no heat. The only heat we had was fire … and the place was dark and [full of] stairs, being built on a hill.'[412]

Despite being a new arrival, Mimi also quickly picked up on the growing feeling that the *Hachshara* dream of *Aliyah* was in decline: 'Everyone thought by then that really, truly, I don't think we'll ever get to Palestine and the war was in full swing then.'[413]

The new arrivals from Llandough were an essential part of ensuring that the flagship *Hachshara* at Gwrych had a viable short-term future, but this would come at a price.

Materially speaking, the community at Gwrych had never been well off and it had been heavily reliant on the donations it received. Those donations had been significant and without them the project would have floundered very early on, but they had only covered the cost of the basics. A visitor to the castle in September 1940, a year after it had first opened, noted that 'the contrast between all this architectural and scenic grandeur and the primitive nature of the accommodation within its framework is very striking. It suffices only for a very spartan life.'[414] The installation of a second shower and bath in September was the only thing to celebrate in an otherwise increasingly bleak picture.

The slow decline in numbers at the castle in the first half of 1940 had the inadvertent effect of allowing the limited resources to be less thinly spread and thus the residents may have started to develop an illusion of improvement by the summer of 1940. However, the arrival of the Llandough children put the *Hachshara* back at its original capacity and the current residents could not have failed to notice the impact the new residents had on the food available to them. Since his arrival a few months earlier, the new chef, Leo Silbermann, had revolutionised the kitchen, where he was now assisted by two *chaverim*, Rivka Alterman and Lotte Milgrom, who was 'an expert in home economics'.[415] The quality of food had improved but, more importantly, despite national food rationing, the quantity per person had also increased as the number of mouths to feed had declined. The arrival of the new group changed this dramatically and, regardless of Silbermann's creativity, the impact was felt immediately. By September 1940, the pantry was stocked with food for only 100 people to maintain the 200 or so who now lived in the castle.

Not only did the physical presence of the new group of children create tensions within the community, but so did their different way of thinking. The newcomers from South Wales were generally a little less religious, a little less orthodox and a little less Zionist than those already at Gwrych. Mimi Schleissner did not really warm to her new colleagues and later described the *Hachshara* community she had now joined as 'a *Mizrachi* group. A left-wing, Zionist group … and being as the *Mizrachi* group was there first they thought they owned it and we weren't as religious as they were.'[416]

That Arieh Handler was willing to allow the strength of Zionism within the group to be diluted in order to maintain viable numbers at the castle was even more evident with the arrival of two new *chaverim* who joined at about the same time as the Llandough group. James Burke and his wife were the only people from outside of the Jewish faith to ever reside at the *Hachshara* and were, with both having just turned thirty, amongst its oldest residents. James, originally from St Helens, had been something of a nomad over the previous five years, travelling between Wales, England, Switzerland and Austria as a member of the International Volunteer Service for Peace (IVSP). He had declared himself to be a conscientious objector upon the outbreak of war but his stance was not pursued by the authorities as Parliament had accepted membership of the IVSP as a form of national service due to its focus on assisting communities through natural or economic disasters. During war time its members did such things as helping people caught up in the Blitz, assisting the more vulnerable inside community air raid shelters, clearing bombed sites, aiding those made homeless and caring for refugees fleeing from Nazism. As a landscape gardener by trade, James had found himself a role assisting with the agricultural training of a Jewish refugee group at Barham House, a small *Hachshara* in Suffolk, and it was from there that he and his wife moved to Gwrych.

One contemporary account states that James Burke was appointed to be in charge of the group at Gwrych but this is not true.[417] He arrived in the guise of a typical *chaver* and a teacher of English and he may have been appointed to, at least partially, fill the role of being the castle's natural Briton in the absence of David Smith. In that regard he might have become a de facto member of the leadership team. Whether he was or was not, he was certainly more than happy for people to have that impression of him. When he faced a military service tribunal in Colwyn Bay in August 1940, who were assessing him for conscription following his claims to be a conscientious objector, he most definitely exaggerated his importance at Gwrych castle. He even went as far as hinting that he was actually in charge of the whole enterprise and then made no attempt to dissuade the panel when they arrived at that erroneous conclusion. He also made sure that they noted that 'he was doing work of national importance as the children under his care were finding they were not being hated like they were in Germany ... he and his wife were the only Christians in the camp and were teaching them English and all about English life.'[418] Nobody on the panel apparently questioned whether the Englishman before them should really have been teaching children in Wales about 'Welsh life', but the tribunal's 'chairman told Burke that they had been impressed by his evidence' and that his appeal against his conscription was granted, 'so long as he remains in his present employment.'[419]

That James Burke was so willing to project himself as a leader at the *Hachshara* may also have unintentionally added to another problem: the fragmentation of the leadership team. There is no doubt that the unity of the leadership group at the Gwrych *Hachshara* was slowly starting to fracture during 1940. David Smith was in a hospital in London and showing no imminent signs of a recovery from his injuries, let alone a return to the castle. Despite the fact that the Gwrych Castle *Hachshara* was so close to his heart, Arieh Handler was a busy man and often elsewhere establishing, developing and monitoring other projects and he had become just an occasional visitor. His guiding hand was severely missed, especially by Erwin Seligmann. There was no doubt that Arieh had the utmost faith in Erwin as the head of the project, but whether Erwin had faith in himself is less clear, and whether he had the right aptitude for the 'top job' might also be questioned. Despite his enormous success as the leader of the *Hachshara* project at Gwrych, Erwin had never been entirely happy at the castle. Privately, he had believed from the beginning that his efforts at Gwrych were unappreciated and that his influence was limited by others. He had written to friends at Great Engeham: 'How I should love to be back at the camp. Not to waste my strength uselessly. To find more trust and confidence and to have a sense of responsibility. For responsibility gives strength.'[420]

And now he had James Burke to contend with, a man with strong convictions, great experience, an abundance of self-confidence and clear abilities in self-promotion. But Burke was also a man that lacked any of the Zionist principles that guided Erwin and a man that would, by encouraging the belief that he was in charge, unknowingly add to Erwin's concerns that his authority was not being taken seriously. From the summer of 1940, it seems that Erwin slowly began to disappear into the background.[421]

The final member of the leadership team, Rabbi Sperber, was distracted by his own issues. There had been complaints from the *noar* about his educational provision from the very beginning, and during the summer of 1940 he finally relented to making some limited changes. He had been open to the demands for providing a slightly wider curriculum but only as long as the core subjects were in no way diminished. In September 1940, he stated that 'we are a *Bachad Hachshara*, and thus our conception of life is fixed … All that is done here … should be consciously directed towards the educational aim'[422] – that aim being the goal of establishing a Jewish homeland. However, he was now willing to establish a broader curriculum as long as this was carefully selected to complement their central Zionist vision. The changes he was willing to make were thus somewhat minimal and fell far short of those demanded through the *Assefah*.

Rabbi Sperber also amended the existing timetable of two blocks of around three hours so that teaching now took place from 8 a.m. until 10.15 a.m. for the afternoon workers, and from 3.30 p.m. until 7 p.m. for the morning workers. As most of David Granek's work rosters rotated every month, the imbalance between educational hours for the morning and the afternoon workers was expected to even itself out over time.

The clear influence of Rabbi Sperber's views can be seen in the slightly revised curriculum that he established. The afternoon workers learned English, Hebrew and about the Old Testament, while morning workers learned English, Hebrew, general geography and the geography of Palestine. Some of these classes were divided into their three *plugoth* while others were taught all together.

Part of the reason that Rabbi Sperber finally relented to making changes was the constantly changing personnel amongst the *chaverim*. New arrivals were generally a little less committed or passionate towards the Zionist cause and he had reluctantly come to accept that his small teaching staff did not all subscribe themselves as fully to his vision as he would have liked, or indeed have the knowledge and abilities he required.

Miriam Sperber summed up the problem her husband faced: 'The instructors who had arrived from Germany were cultured and had a good secular education ... but they were not ... completely immersed in Torah study ... while all were Zionists, they could not speak Hebrew.'[423]

However, the new *chaverim* had other skills to offer and, recognising this, Rabbi Sperber also gave his consent to them offering voluntary classes in subjects they felt more comfortable in at the end of the 'compulsory' day. From 8 p.m. to 9 p.m. the refugees could opt to study either drawing or physics, and between 9 p.m. and 10 p.m. they could learn first aid with Dr Handler or join the debating group. On other occasions, handicraft was also an option and a *chaver* who had arrived from Belgium also offered to teach some French. Miriam also showed her support for her husband's new initiative by offering to teach psychology to some of the older girls.

The evening classes proved to be quite popular, though in truth this was probably aided by a desire to avoid roster duties in the evening. Herman Rothman, always on the lookout for ways to play the system to his own advantage, somewhat regretted his decision to join the debating group, which looked to him to be the easiest option available, when he discovered that it was mainly attended by the older members and that they had debates about things he could not understand.

Despite Rabbi Sperber's willingness to adapt the curriculum, the simple fact was that the children at Gwrych received learning that was of a very limited scope. There was also a question over the quality of education that was on offer. Some of the *chaverim* were referred to as teachers but, in reality, none of them were actually qualified and virtually all of them were only a few years, and often just a few months, older than the students arrayed before them. Therefore, inevitably, the teaching was enthusiastic but not always very effective.

Part of the reason Ossi Findling gave for walking away was that he wasn't learning anything and many others had similar complaints. Herman Rothman remembered that, 'We talked about Zionism, we talked about religion and many, many subjects. We did not receive any formal education.'[424] Henry Steinberg's recollection of his education at the *Hachshara* was similar: 'We had – I wouldn't call it classes – but we had some ways of learning whatever it was that we wanted to learn. But formal education, there was none.'[425] The only thing that had lodged in the mind of Baruch Spergel when interviewed over sixty years later was that, 'at Gwrych Castle we were taught some Hebrew, we were taught to work – to labour.'[426] Ruth Kessel, a little harshly, simply recalled that 'there was no education' at all.[427] Mimi Schleissner arrived at Gwrych in the summer of 1940, at the same time as Rabbi Sperber's revamp of the curriculum, and was extremely concerned by the state of education at the castle. 'I was getting older,' she remembered. 'By then I was fifteen. I was getting classes in English, classes in Hebrew ... but I didn't really have any education.'[428]

From the point of view of the *noar*, the thing they felt the most let down by was the teaching of English. Many had come to Britain with a smattering of knowledge of the language but only a few could speak English well. It had also very quickly become apparent on the farms that the English they were hearing bore little resemblance to what they had been taught at home and what they were now being taught at the castle. Isi Peterseil, who had arrived with no knowledge at all of English, decided after six months that he would be better off teaching himself and, armed with a dictionary, he got to work. Bill Braun – who was resident at the castle before Rabbi Sperber's revamp of the curriculum – had thought the English teaching to be so bad that he had also felt the need 'to teach myself English. I tried to read the British papers as often as I could. Then I tried reading literature. I started with plays. To this day I have trouble with prepositions!'[429] Herman Rothman was one of the few who could speak English very well before he had arrived but he also found the quality of the teaching so poor that, 'My English went to sleep and became marred by a German accent.'[430] Henry Glanz thought exactly the same thing and, at the age of ninety-six, a trace of a German accent is still audible in his speech despite having lived in Britain for over eighty years.[431]

Immediately prior to moving to the Gwrych *Hachshara*, Rabbi Sperber had been teaching in a *Yeshiva* school in London and he had hoped to create one at the castle shortly after his arrival. It had not yet materialised but now he deemed it to be an essential step to take. For its location, he chose the folly known as Lady Emily's Tower that sat high up in the woods of the Gwrych estate and well off the beaten track – meaning there would be little chance of being disturbed. It also had a tranquil air, with a magnificent view out to sea that inspired reflection. Above the door were inscribed words that helped convince the Rabbi in his choice: 'The Sea is His, and He made it.' (Psalms 95:5).

Here, Rabbi Sperber offered education for up to fifteen boys at a time, concentrating on religious texts, primarily the Talmud and the Torah. The *Yeshiva* students would be freed from all work roster duties so that lessons could take place at those times. With the limited floor space of the tower it must have been a little cramped but the Rabbi did not mind and many of the boys enthusiastically signed up. A few weeks later, with the Rabbi's assistance, Youth *Aliyah* members set up a rival group just for the girls, focusing on the Old Testament, Hebrew, the Torah and Jewish Law.

As August 1940 rolled into September, one of the Rabbi's *Yeshiva* students, Erich Roper, was busy making plans to produce a bumper-sized newsletter, or yearbook, to mark the first anniversary of the Gwrych *Hachshara*. Unfortunately, Bill Braun was one of his original co-editors and Bill had been interned. Although other youngsters such as Mary Auskerin, Eli Freier (also later interned) and Roper's friend Carl Schäfler had volunteered to assist him on several editions, the task of preparing the special issue would now fall mainly on Erich's shoulders. Erich was a driven and thoughtful young man. Aside from work on local farms, his castle duties saw him working with Schäfler on routine castle maintenance and also as one of the forestry workers. In the evenings, apart from checking that the castle satisfied the demands of the blackout, he attended the new night classes and happily got involved in the sort of highbrow debates that Herman Rothman found difficult to follow. He was interested in politics, and had formed the 'party' that had won the *Kongress* earlier in the year with the support of Rabbi Sperber, with whom he was particularly close. The pair would spend much time discussing doctrine and theology together, as well as contemplating the world that they now found themselves in.

Erich was a staunch believer in Zionism and the *Hachshara* project but even he had begun to waver during recent months as a result of events in the war and the impact of the internment of many friends. He realised that the entire community needed hauling back to its feet after the knocks it had taken during the summer and that everyone needed reminding of their original purpose and to be given a new focus for moving things forward. He was determined to use *Sefer ha-shanah*, the planned Gwrych Castle yearbook, as a vehicle to achieve both those things. Therefore, he invited all members of the community to submit articles describing any positive aspects of life that they had experienced over the last twelve months, and got to work preparing his editorial piece. But before he had completed it, the already ailing *Hachshara* received two more significant body blows.

Several weeks earlier, one of the *noar*, David Kowalski, had fallen ill. Kowalski had arrived at Gwrych as one of the original Kindertransport refugees selected from Great Engeham, along with two classmates, including Salli Edelnand, from his hometown of Halberstadt in Germany. Aged thirteen at the time, Kowalski was the youngest refugee at the castle. It is possible that Erwin Seligmann had deliberately overlooked his age so as not to separate him from two familiar faces: he was, after all, *nearly* fourteen. There is no record of the details of the illness, but Dr Handler was so worried about David that he had him sent to a hospital in Liverpool. In the first week of September, the young refugee died. A promising life, dedicated towards *Eretz Yisrael* was tragically over far too soon. And all dreams were dashed. It was almost a metaphor for all of the children at Gwrych Castle.

As Erich sat contemplating the yearbook, he took the time to write an obituary:

> David Kowalski was … young and promising … He came here with us to find his way to *Eretz Yisrael*. Serious-minded, he applied himself to his training work, and took an active part in the *Chevra* [group] life. He was the hope and pride of his parents, who were looking forward to living and working together with him once again. An insidious disease took him from us in the prime of his life, but we shall not forget him.[432]

On 16 September, the *Hachshara* received news of the second blow. The previous day, David Smith had died in a hospital in London as a result of the injuries received during his car crash near Holywell five months earlier. *Habonim*, the organisation he represented, said that they had lost one 'of its outstanding leaders',[433] and so had the Gwrych *Hachshara*.

Although a relatively remote figure to many of the refugees, Smith had been the legal and financial mind behind the whole project and, far more importantly, he had been the moderator between the *Bachad* and Youth *Aliyah* factions at the castle. He had been the glue that had bound the leadership team together, especially in the periods when Arieh Handler was elsewhere. His absence since the accident had probably been a catalyst for Erwin Seligmann's slow withdrawal into insecurity and Rabbi Sperber's increasing distraction towards religious matters, and now there was nothing to stop that process from continuing.

It therefore fell to Erich to pen a second obituary:

> David Smith, whose death is mourned by all of us, played a decisive part in the life of our castle. Only those acquainted with the difficulties we had to contend with here, in the first period, can appreciate the value of his work. Into the dark and gloomy castle life, full of misery, he brought some happiness and comfort. He worked untiringly to improve conditions in his capacity as manager, but far more than by his official work, he helped us with his personal interest, with his friendliness and cheerfulness. We all looked upon him as a dear *chaver*. His door was open to all, and his heart was responsive to the great and little troubles of every individual *chaver*, young or old. His memory will always remain with us.[434]

To add to the bleakness of late summer 1940, the prospects for *Aliyah* had also taken another turn for the worse. Travel to Palestine was already a difficult option, but the upper age limit for emigration visas was now set at seventeen, meaning that many members of the community were no longer eligible anyway. So what was the point in staying in or maintaining a *Hachshara*? It was all well and good working hard for the Zionist dream with no pay but, if the Zionist dream was turning sour, then working hard for nothing had very little appeal. Many left to find paid work or to join the armed forces when their age permitted, and others were considering those options. Consequently, the numbers of young people at the *Hachshara* continued to decline.

Logic dictated that, without a constant new supply of fourteen-year-olds, the community at the castle had a maximum lifespan of four years, and probably much less unless something urgent was done. The new arrivals from Llandough had stabilised the immediate future for the Gwrych *Hachshara* but, at the same time, they had fundamentally altered it. A quarter or more of all the residents had not been involved in establishing and developing the ethos of the place. Many of the older ones, the *chaverim* who had been instrumental in leading the *Hachshara* to its high point in the spring of 1940, had left or been interned. It was almost as if the old *Hachshara* had come to an end and a new *Hachshara* was being born – one with a different outlook and a revised educational input. And this was causing some friction between the original cohort and the new blood.

Solving frictions at the castle was one of the key reasons that Arieh Handler had appointed David Smith to the leadership team, but Smith was no longer around. With Rabbi Sperber increasingly distracted by his own work in the *Yeshiva*, the increasingly isolated Erwin Seligmann was left to run the show in the face of his own self-doubt and a growing belief that he was being undermined.

Not for the first time, the future of the Gwrych *Hachshara* hung in the balance. It desperately needed to reinvent itself and find a new vision; if it could not, its days would be numbered.

CHAPTER 11

'Not quite the haven they anticipated'

October 1940–September 1941
Bombs, weddings and the closing down of the Gwrych *Hachshara*

Erich Roper worked hard on the refugee community's celebratory first anniversary yearbook. There would not be a second. The Gwrych *Hachshara* had been damaged severely in recent months and although nobody, including Arieh Handler, could be certain, the reality was that the centre was in terminal decline.

Yet Erich viewed the yearbook as an opportunity to rekindle the spirit of the *Hachshara*. He wanted to remind everyone of the vision that the founders had fought so hard to attain and to introduce that vision to the new cohort from Llandough. In his editorial he wrote, 'A year has passed since the moment we took our first step, a step in the direction of life … We want to run before us again all the events of the past year so we can learn from them for next year!'[435] He went on to remind everyone of their incredible achievements in creating an agricultural training centre to be proud of: 'When comrades from Youth *Aliyah* come here, when we all meet youngsters from the town

Above: The north elevation of Gwrych Castle from a tower viewpoint in the north-west, looking down on part of the forecourt. The gardens to the east of the castle and the access road heading out through the gatehouse towards Nant-y-Bella lodge are both visible towards the top of the picture. Photograph taken during the freezing winter of 1939–1940. *(From the collection of Henry Steinberg, courtesy of Alan Steinberg.)*

Below: The forecourt and main entrance to Gwrych Castle. *(© Sabena Jane Blackbird / Alamy Stock Photo.)*

Above: Gwrych Castle in later years, when allowed to fall into decay.
(© Simon Baylis / Alamy Stock Photo.)

REGENCY ROOM AND BANQUETING HALL, GWRYCH CASTLE, ABERGELE.   59187.

Above: The two adjacent rooms used for dining. *(With permission of Gwrych Castle.)*

Below: The entrance hall. *(With permission of Gwrych Castle.)*

ENTRANCE HALL, GWRYCH CASTLE   59179

Above: The top of the marble staircase, which Mr and Mrs Handler descended as part of their wedding celebrations in December 1940. *(With permission of Gwrych Castle)*

Below: Dr Julius Handler. *(Courtesy of Debbie Nead and Jacqui Press.)*

Above: Arieh Handler (standing, left), directing colleagues.
(Courtesy of the Handler family.)

Right: Erwin Seligmann.
(Courtesy of Hanna Seligmann-Prokocimer via Verity Steele.)

Above left: The 12th Earl of Dundonald. *(Credit: An Encyclopedia of Canadian Biography. 1904. Image in the public domain via Wikipedia.)*

Above right: Rabbi Sperber, Passover at the castle, 1940.
(From the collection of Henry Steinberg, courtesy of Alan Steinberg.)

Below: Gerhard (Gerry) Friedenfeld with his parents, c.1938.
(Molly Friedenfeld.)

Above: Erwin Seligmann (tall man, front row, left of centre), leaning on the shoulder of David Granek to his immediate right. Henry Glanz is on the front row, fifth person to Seligmann's left. Gwrych Castle, April 1940. *(From the collection of Henry Steinberg, courtesy of Alan Steinberg.)*

Left: Josef Altberg at Gwrych Castle. *(Courtesy of Helen Levy.)*

Above: Tosca Sussmann (right), with her sister in Berlin, just before her Kindertransport journey. *(United States Holocaust Memorial Museum, courtesy of Tosca Kempler.)*

Opposite top: Erich Roper (bottom right, kneeling) and friends at Gwrych. *(Courtesy of the Roper family.)*

Opposite bottom: Adi Better (kneeling left) and Henry Steinberg (kneeling centre) with a group of friends in the castle forecourt area. The boy on the right is victim of the oldest trick in the book – someone waving fingers behind your head as the photograph is taken. *(Credit: From the collection of Henry Steinberg, courtesy of Alan Steinberg.)*

Above: Henry Glanz (left) and a friend take a walk into Abergele.
(Courtesy of Henry Glanz.)

Opposite: Six of the Gwrych boys.
(Credit: From the collection of Henry Steinberg, courtesy of Alan Steinberg.)

Top left: Henry Steinberg (right), with his brother David, 1940. *(From the collection of Henry Steinberg, courtesy of Alan Steinberg.)*

Top right: Roll call on the castle forecourt by the main entrance. Although not proven, this shaky photograph is reputed to have captured the moment when Arieh Handler assembled the children to announce the news that Britain had declared war on 3 September 1939. *(From the collection of Henry Steinberg, courtesy of Alan Steinberg.)*

Above: Christmas party at the Church House, Abergele, held for evacuees from Merseyside in 1939, and attended by Dr Julius Handler. *(Liverpool Evening Express, 1 January 1940.)*

Above: Forestry workers digging a drainage ditch on the Gwrych estate. Henry Glanz is in the centre, fourth from the left. *(Courtesy of Henry Glanz.)*

Below: Education: a group of girls in the dining room. *(Credits: From the collection of Henry Steinberg, courtesy of Alan Steinberg.)*

Above: The 'Haifa gang' from *pluga Aleph*, Henry Steinberg (right), Adi Better (kneeling), Isi Gewurtz and Froyum (nickname for Ephraim). *(From the collection of Henry Steinberg, courtesy of Alan Steinberg.)*

Below: The Seder meal in the dining room, *Pesach*, April 1940. Tosca Kempler's notes to the photograph read: 'Standing is Eva Carlebach. To her left is Erwin Seligmann. Girl next to boy (which looks like Herman Rothman) is Bertel Karmiol. Bottom left in glasses is Esther Graudenz. Bottom centre is Betti Einhorn and bottom right are Edith Perlmutter, Bertel Rosenberg and Ruth Kessel. In centre, far right is Hersh Lerner.' *(United States Holocaust Memorial Museum Photo Archives #49971, courtesy of Tosca Kempler.)*

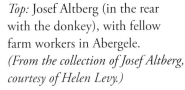

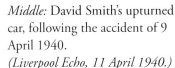

Top: Josef Altberg (in the rear with the donkey), with fellow farm workers in Abergele.
(From the collection of Josef Altberg, courtesy of Helen Levy.)

Middle: David Smith's upturned car, following the accident of 9 April 1940.
(Liverpool Echo, 11 April 1940.)

Bottom: Henry Steinberg and friends on a day out with friends from Wolf Gottlieb's hostel in St Asaph. The man on the right is in miltary uniform and may be a former chaver who had left to join the forces.
(From the collection of Henry Steinberg, courtesy of Alan Steinberg.)

Top: Residents of the Gwrych *Hachshara* gather on 22 April 1940, before the first day of *Pesach* to hear the *Hamotzi* blessing from Rabbi Sperber. *(From the collection of Henry Steinberg, courtesy of Alan Steinberg.)*

Middle: Fun in the forest. *(From the collection of Henry Steinberg, courtesy of Alan Steinberg.)*

Bottom: The wedding celebrations of Arieh Handler and Henny Prilutsky, held at the castle, December 1940. *(Courtesy of the Handler family.)*

... what do we talk about? What do we show them? The farm.'[436]

Erich acknowledged the idea that the vision for the future was in danger, mainly because some had begun to waver in their idealistic resolve. He implied that two colleagues had begun writing for the yearbook but that they had not completed their contribution as they had not been brave enough to envision the future clearly enough. He also considered that many others had become far too comfortable with being looked after by others and that an 'apathy and passiveness'[437] now pervaded the community. He recognised that the course of the war had dampened their enthusiasm to stick to the dream, but if the community could hold true to their Jewish beliefs, the answers would present themselves eventually. Whilst they waited patiently for answers, Erich reminded his readers of what they *did* know: that they were the builders of the future, one *Hachshara* amongst many, with the purpose to create *Eretz Yisrael* and that 'with the help of God we will succeed.'[438]

How effective Erich's words were is unknown, but every member of the community was given a copy of the yearbook. His mentor, Rabbi Sperber, no doubt preached the same or similar arguments at every available opportunity. Their message was quite simple: things were tough, but they always had been tough. The aim was *Eretz Yisrael*, and nothing could or should be allowed to shake them from that path. Therefore, for members of the Gwrych *Hachshara*, even though wider events had encroached upon the community and dampened its spirit, it was to be business as usual. And business as usual it was. The surviving, though now much changed, community at the Gwrych Castle *Hachshara* quietly continued with their well-established routines of daily work on local farms, duties on the estate and education.

However, reversing the rot that was creating the 'apathy and passiveness' that Erich had spoken of was not a simple thing to achieve. The Battle of Britain was nearing its end but the German aerial campaign was transitioning into the Blitz. Although the threat of invasion had eased a little, it had most definitely not gone away. And there still remained no realistic possibility of making *Aliyah* to Palestine in the near future. Thus, for many, Erich Roper's vision, and his suggestion that they should just 'stick at it', sounded increasingly hollow and the steady loss of those nearing the age of eighteen continued unabated.

Another of the original residents, Henry Steinberg, had begun seriously considering whether it was time for him to move on. His older brother was at a different *Hachshara* and his younger brother was at a school in Bedford. The three had finally agreed for each of them to throw in the towel at whatever venture each was currently pursuing and to unite in Manchester, where they would collectively figure out their next steps. Steinberg came to the realisation that 'since *Aliyah* seemed remote [and] the war [made] the journey to Israel too perilous, this seemed like a good idea.'[439] He left the Gwrych *Hachshara* in October 1940.

Confidence in Roper's vision was also being eroded for another reason. The war, which until now had been relatively distant from everyone in Abergele, had arrived on their doorstep. During and following the Battle of Britain, the occasional enemy plane had been spotted in the skies of North Wales. In August, one had dropped some leaflets, a few of which had been snapped up eagerly by Abergele natives. The four-page booklet, purporting to have been written by Hitler himself, had the title of 'A Last Appeal to Reason'. Locals commented that it would at least be a useful thing to wipe their backsides on. In September 1940, a lone Dornier Do 17 German bomber, separated from its formation somewhere over northern England, was chased along the North Wales coastline by an RAF fighter plane. Over Towyn, two miles from Abergele, the bomber was hit and it crashed into the sea off Rhyl. This spillover from the German Blitz attacks on the big cities was to repeat itself a couple of weeks later in Abergele, with tragic consequences.

At dusk in the early evening of Thursday, 3 October 1940, a lone German Junkers Ju 88 bomber, considerably lost and separated from its squadron, was looking for landmarks to help inform its navigation. As the cloud was low that day, the bomber's pilot dropped altitude and had picked up the railway line running from Rhyl to Abergele. At the tennis courts at Pensarn, it suddenly changed course, possibly because the pilot saw the hill upon which Gwrych Castle sits looming out of the cloud and semi-darkness. At the speed they were going they would have flown straight into it in seconds so the pilot banked steeply upwards and to the left, turning almost full circle to avoid the hill. Either to quickly gain altitude, or panicking that he might crash-land with his three large bombs on board, he jettisoned the devices and then the bomber vanished into the night, its final fate unknown. It had all happened so quickly and unexpectedly that the local Air Raid Control Room at Pentre Mawr park had been caught unaware and was unable to sound the air raid siren in time.

One of the bombs dropped was a *flammenbombe*, known in Britain as an oil bomb, designed to ignite and spread fire across a large area. It hit a concrete yard by a bungalow near the High Street and burnt the structure to the ground. The other two bombs were both high explosive (HE). One landed in a garden along the High Street, injuring five people when it exploded. The third bomb landed on a bungalow in Highfield Park at the top end of the High Street, destroying it and damaging a number of other buildings nearby. The bungalow was home to three sisters. Two of them, fifty-nine-year-old Catherine (Katie) Roberts and sixty-six-year-old Mary (Minnie) Roberts, were both killed. The third sister was unaccounted for and it was not until around midnight that fire and rescue services, accompanied by a small army of local helpers who inadvertently hampered the speed of the operation, finally found her buried in the rubble. She was badly injured but alive.

Due to censorship, very little of the bombing was recorded at the time. The subsequent edition of the *Abergele Visitor* gave a brief but sufficiently vague account of the affair, even referring to the incident as having happened in 'a North Wales coastal town'.[440] The *North Wales Weekly News*, in its weekly roundup of events in Abergele, made absolutely no mention at all of the deaths or the damage, leading instead on the story of a snooker handicap match and breaking the news that a giant potato weighing over two pounds had been dug up on a local allotment. The only contemporary reference to the death of the two sisters appeared in the *Liverpool Echo* of 5 October 1940, where it was simply stated, very ambiguously, that they had both died 'suddenly'. Nevertheless, the bombing *had* happened.[441] A twelve-year-old Abergele boy 'witnessed the bombs being dropped by a German aircraft and which destroyed properties at Highfield Park'[442] and damaged around forty others. Many locals visited the huge crater on Highfield Park over the following days, including a young ARP helper from Abergele who noted that 'from its dimensions, the bomb must have been a large one.'[443]

There was considerable local gossip over whether the attack had been deliberate and, if so, what the target could have been. Could it have been the gasworks at the Old Mill? The market hall? Or the castle and its Jewish refugees?

Seven days later, almost certainly as a consequence of lessons learned from the event, the Abergele Urban District Fire Brigade, along with several other units in the district, ran training exercises 'to study methods of conveying water to blazing buildings.'[444] Almost immediately, the same thing nearly happened again when another lone German bomber raced along the North Wales coastal railway track from the east at just over roof height. On this occasion the bomber dropped its bomb load on the beach near the Abergele and Pensarn train station where the shingle absorbed most of the energy from three large explosions. Two days later, on Saturday, 12 October 1940, a Spitfire on a training exercise crashed near Bryngwenallt Hall on Llanfair Road, killing the pilot. The town council, at a meeting on 15 October, stood in silence 'as a token of sympathy for the two ladies who had unfortunately been killed ... and also for the young man who was killed in a flying accident over the weekend.'[445]

The following night, two more lost Ju 88 bombers appeared in the skies over Abergele. They were engaged by a British fighter which pursued one, forcing it down into fields about ten miles south-east of the town. All four German crew members were killed. The other bomber turned away and jettisoned its payload over a farm near Abergele, damaging an outbuilding and killing two sheep. All of these events, in such a short space of time, were shocking and distressing to the entire Abergele community – but they were particularly poignant for the refugees at Gwrych Castle, who reflected fearfully that the long arm of the Nazis could finally reach out for them once more.

Despite all the gloom, there were still things to bring joy to the residents of the Gwrych *Hachshara* during this period. On 12 October 1940, the castle's inhabitants observed Yom Kippur, which provided an ideal opportunity for Rabbi Sperber to attempt to refocus the *noar* on their purpose. Then, on 4 November, to everyone's delight, Miriam Sperber gave birth to her third child, Daniel, at the castle. Back in the spring of 1940, the unborn Daniel had somehow embodied the hope of a new life for everyone, and his arrival, if only briefly, reminded the community of their former optimism.

Adding to the celebratory tone, Robert Weitsch from Vienna, who had just turned sixteen and was working at Hafodunos Hall, passed his tribunal in Caernarfon on 15 November and subsequently avoided internment. That month also saw the arrival of a small group of young Jews at Rose Hill in nearby St Asaph, providing the opportunity for easy day trips to mingle with different but like-minded young people. And there was a new regular visitor to Gwrych in the form of the founder of the Rose Hill centre, Rabbi Wolf Gottlieb.

Gottlieb was a pre-war associate and friend of Arieh Handler. Both men had been watched closely by Adolf Eichmann and the SS. As Director of the Youth *Aliyah* school in Vienna, he had assisted in helping Jews get out of Austria but was arrested by a branch of the Gestapo as part of the *Polenaktion*, a campaign directed specifically against 'foreign' Polish Jews in the country. He was detained briefly and, after his release, the Rabbi assisted in organising a Kindertransport of over 600 children to Palestine and a few more to Britain. He himself arrived in Britain in March 1939.

Gottlieb was soon appointed Superintendent of Jewish education within Britain, a role that led him to encounter David Smith of *Habonim* who held a similar passion for education. He also worked with Rabbi Sperber whilst he was running his *Yeshiva* school in London. The two had already established a firm friendship which dated back to their days in Vienna and it is highly likely that it was upon Gottlieb's recommendation that Sperber had been appointed by Arieh Handler to be the rabbi for Gwrych Castle in September 1939.

At that time, Gottlieb was working with young Jews at the Talmud Torah school in Liverpool and, just over a year later, he had followed the example of his friend Arieh Handler in setting up a home for Jewish youth in North Wales, albeit it on a much smaller scale than the Gwrych Castle *Hachshara*, at Rose Hill in St Asaph.[446]

On 2 December, and to the amazement of all, a former regular visitor, Gunter Heilbrunn, turned up at the castle. He had been released from his internment on the Isle of Man. The most amazed and delighted resident was Lies Teppich. The pair had planned to marry back in June but Heilbrunn had been detained the day before their intended wedding. On 5 December, their long-awaited marriage finally took place at the Abergele Registry Office followed by a Jewish ceremony at the castle which was conducted by Rabbi Sperber.

A birth, a wedding, the arrival of new colleagues in the area and signs of internment being relaxed were all significant boosts to the wavering morale of the members of the Gwrych *Hachshara* but, just as things were starting to look a little brighter, the German bombers returned.

This time it was not just a lone, lost aircraft but a multitude of bombers passing over the North Wales coast. As the Republic of Ireland was neutral and thus not under blackout rules, some enemy bomber formations used it as a navigational jumping-off point before bombing targets in Northern Ireland or turning towards the rich industrial areas of the English north-west.[447] Over the three nights of 20, 21 and 22 December 1940, the *Luftwaffe* came in waves to deliver huge raids on Liverpool.

The terror unleashed on the city is almost impossible to describe.

One young factory worker, Phyllis Kaye of Anfield, witnessed a river of water flowing through a city street from a burst water main, carrying with it multiple corpses, scattered from a nearby mortuary that had received a direct hit.[448]

The first of those three terrible nights of the Liverpool Blitz once more brought the war uncomfortably close to the doorstep of the Gwrych *Hachshara* when a German Heinkel bomber released two huge parachute mines over the neighbouring village of Llanddulas. Designed to land in water and remain inert until a magnetic detector was triggered by a passing metal ship, they could also be used on land where they would explode after a short delay. One, by pure chance, fell into a pond and caused little damage other than to spray mud all over a number of nearby properties. The other hit dry land and exploded, creating a huge crater adjacent to what is now junction 23 of the A55. Luckily, nobody was injured.

On the third night, 22 December, Gwrych Castle itself became, unintentionally, the target of another lost German bomber. It released a string of small bombs, at least six of which came down randomly in the woods and fields of the Gwrych estate. Mercifully, all landed some way away from the building and exploded without harm to any member of the castle community. One bomb landed on a garage in the town in which two of the Gwrych youngsters, including Henry Glanz, worked voluntarily during the day.[449] Fortunately the bomb didn't detonate but it left a hole in the roof of a workshop and debris scattered widely around. The next day, the garage remained closed as the explosive was made safe by the armed services. The following day, when Henry and his friend turned up for work, the owner, very angry at all things German, shouted at them, 'You buggers did it! You buggers clear it up!'[450] This level of anger was temporary and rare; most of the local community had great sympathy with the refugees and what the bombing must have meant for them. One young Abergele man, helping out with ARP duties, later commented that, 'It must have come as a shock to the refugees located at the castle. They had come to our country for refuge and safety, only to find that the quiet locality was not quite the haven they anticipated.'[451]

In the darkness of those three cold winter nights, quiet groups of young Jews assembled on the castle forecourt as the planes hummed high overhead – the same courtyard which they had milled about in fifteen months earlier, having been told by Arieh Handler that war had broken out.[452] The children stood in silence, watching the sky redden and glow as Liverpool burned in the distance and 365 people lost their lives. Many of them spent those three December nights not just thinking of those in Liverpool, but of their relatives at home.

Despite the sombre mood brought on by the bombing of Liverpool, there was one thing that was energising the beleaguered community – the prospect of the return of Arieh Handler and his impending marriage to Henny Prilutsky. Although their actual wedding was in London, they were due to return to the castle quickly so that their marriage ceremony could be celebrated in the traditional Jewish way. It would be conducted by a special guest, Rabbi Unterman (who would later become the Chief Rabbi of Israel), assisted by Rabbi Sperber as well Arieh's old friend Rabbi Gottlieb.

There was also the news that Arieh had called the first ever truly national meeting of *Bachad*, a *Pegisha*, which was due to be held at the castle to coincide with his return. Some eighty or more highly important delegates from the movement were due to arrive both for the meeting and to be guests at the wedding. As they would be staying overnight, the housekeeping team worked frantically to spruce up a number of bedrooms, directed as best she could by Miriam Sperber carrying her small baby in her arms. A number of youngsters were told that they would have to be 'evicted' from their usual rooms and cram into somebody else's room, but it was widely considered a small price to pay. To add to the excitement, all of this was due to fall during Chanukah, which would begin on 24 December. Those not involved in preparations for the wedding or the *Pegisha* threw themselves heart and soul into preparations for that.

Thus, by 29 December 1940, the date chosen for the ceremony to solemnise the marriage of Mr and Mrs Handler, the castle was in pristine condition. Everything had been done to make the castle as grand as possible for the event. The main hall 'was festively decorated'[453] and the sweeping marble staircase, the showpiece of the castle interior, had received specific attention from Miriam Sperber's housekeeping girls (for once not trying to dodge their duties) so it could play a central part in the occasion.

The children, all placed in specific locations around the castle with something akin to military planning, were excited about the arrival of the bride and groom. The couple would make a grand entrance by sweeping down the magnificent staircase, and lining it on either side would be all the girls, each holding a candle which would be lit immediately before the pair began their descent. The girls were dressed in the best clothes they could muster and many, at last, had found a use for all the fancy but impractical donations, especially the hats and high-heeled shoes.

Then, with everything ready and the moment the happy couple were supposed to arrive upon them… nothing happened. Few were surprised. Both Arieh and Erwin had a reputation for turning up late for things, to the extent that many of the castle's residents had developed a humorous term for their tardiness: it was referred to as 'Jewish punctuality'. The youngsters stood around as their mood slowly changed from excited chatter to tongue-in-cheek comments about Arieh's timekeeping, and then to bored silences accompanied by much shuffling of feet and staring off into the distance. Time ticked on. Arieh's eventual arrival was three hours later than intended, 'because he wanted to pop into the movement's conference which was taking place on the same day.'[454] There was actually more to it than that. He had not just 'popped in'. Although nobody outside of the *Pegisha* knew it on the day, something important enough to delay him for that length of time had been under discussion.

Following the lengthy hold-up in proceedings, the newly married couple met at the south entrance of the castle's main building to make their formal entry, arm-in-arm, down the full length of the marble staircase. As planned, their route was lined on either side by the refugee girls as a guard of honour, each holding a lit candle – the only lights in the room. Young Gerry Friedenfeld recalled that, 'I fell in love with her, with Henny Prilutsky. She was just gorgeous. I still remember that. She was just a beauty.'[455]

Arieh, wearing a dark suit, and Henny, in a wedding gown of white lace with a long train, and carrying a bouquet of white chrysanthemums, were greeted at the foot of the staircase by the Rabbis Unterman, Sperber and Gottlieb, as well as Arieh's best man, his brother Julius. Also there to greet them was the castle's very own youth orchestra, organised for the day by Herman Rothman.[456]

The wedding reception was held in the dining room with around 220 invited guests. Many of them were attending the *Bachad Pegisha,* but there were also friends of the couple and a few members of the Abergele community who had shown support for the *Hachshara* project. The reception was followed by photographs in the castle's grounds and, when all was done, the bride and groom waved their goodbyes and set off for a brief honeymoon in Llandudno.

The event would become etched into the memories of all who were there as one of the greatest moments to happen during their entire time at the castle, despite the fact that on the day 'the castle was bare and cold. In fact, it was freezing … there was very little food, but nobody cared about such small things.'[457] Henry Glanz, nearly eighty years later, instantly and proudly recalled that 'I was one of the pole-bearers for the *chuppah* [the canopy under which the bride and groom stand during a Jewish wedding ceremony].'[458]

But this event would be the final high point in the history of the Gwrych *Hachshara.* As Arieh Handler proudly accompanied his new wife down the marble staircase to the music of the orchestra his brother had initiated, surrounded by the children he had assembled, flanked by the colleagues from *Bachad* and *Bnei Akiva* that he led, he knew that the centre was living on borrowed time. That very afternoon, in the important meeting that had made him three hours late for his own wedding celebrations, it had just been agreed that the Gwrych *Hachshara* was to be closed down.

———————

The *Bachad Pegisha* of 29 December 1940 had a number of important things to discuss. The Gwrych *Hachshara* faced a number of mounting problems that appeared to be increasingly impossible to resolve. The Nazis, to all intents and purposes, controlled Europe, and the dream of achieving *Aliyah* in any practical sense was further away than it ever had been. Some of the *chaverim* had moved on and were proving difficult to replace. Many of the *noar*, when they reached the age of eighteen, were also departing. And many of the original cohort were now hundreds, and in some cases thousands, of miles away, locked up in internment camps. However, these problems were shared across the entire *Hachsharot* movement and not unique to Gwrych, so why did the *Bachad Pegisha* take the decision to begin winding the Gwrych *Hachshara* down? The records of the discussions at that meeting do not exist, which has allowed for several explanations to be put forward.

The official explanation from *Bachad*'s youth wing, *Bnei Akiva*, is that, for one reason or another, the Earl of Dundonald was responsible for closing the *Hachshara* down. They stated that 'the Gwrych oasis for refugees ended abruptly with the Earl of Dundonald being forced to sell the estate for death duties, and the War Office who had requisitioned the castle ordered their expulsion.'[459] This is, however, incorrect. At the time, the castle was effectively government property and they were paying the Earl the sum of £200 per annum to keep it as a requisitioned site. There is no record of any government expulsion order which, in any case, would only have been issued if the government had decided that the estate could be better utilised towards the war effort. They had developed no plans for it before the idea of the *Hachshara* was floated, and once the refugee group departed later in

1941 they still apparently had no plans for it as the castle remained empty and unused for any government or military purpose for the remainder of the war. The government would have been shooting itself in the foot by expelling the inhabitants, as the community was actively contributing to the local agricultural economy and a number of youngsters at the castle were also being employed locally by the Ministry of Labour. As the castle was requisitioned, it would have been difficult for the Earl to put the property up for sale and he did not do so until after the war when it sold for a huge loss; he received just £12,000, a deficit of £66,000 on the price his father had purchased it for just eighteen years earlier. In fact, the eventual sale in 1946 was temporarily held up because of a delay in the issuing of the derequisitioning order by the government.

One of the delegates at the *Bachad Pegisha* of December 1940 had a different take on the Earl's motives. Jack Sklan, one of the founders of *Bnei Akiva* in Britain, later stated that, 'after eighteen months in Gwrych, the Earl of Dundonald had been walking past with his agent and asked what the sound of singing was (it was *zemirot* which are Jewish hymns). When he found out they were Jews, he said "Get them out of here! I didn't know they were Jews."'[460] This is total nonsense, given that the Earl had been consulted on and consented to the plans for the *Hachshara* and had even contributed towards basic and essential repairs. Also, if this is to be believed, the land agent who continued to run the wider estate finances must have been unaware to the point of sheer incompetence (or deliberately hiding it from the Earl in a conspiratorial fashion) of the fact that 200 Jews were living in the castle. It's equally unlikely that the Earl didn't speak with his land agent for eighteen months, or to his younger brother who was living in one of the estate's lodges.[461] In fact, even *Bachad*'s own news journal a year earlier had referred to the fact that their use of the castle had only been 'made possible by the magnanimity of Lord Dundonald'.[462] It is also quite likely that he had 'put in a good word' with the government during the requisitioning handover on behalf of *Bachad*.

Another reason to dismiss this claim is that the Earl wasn't at all local: he was in Scotland and came nowhere near the castle at any time. He would certainly not have been wandering merrily past in 1941 with his land agent. It should also be noted that there is absolutely nothing to suggest that the Earl held any antisemitic views. Indeed, he had grown up cosseted by his mother, the countess, who had a number of Jewish friends within her circle.

Another common suggestion is that the *Hachshara* was closed down as a result of local farming work drying up,[463] but this, too, cannot be correct. Denbighshire's agricultural quotas had been significantly increased during the war, causing local farmers to fret about the labour implications. This was a problem exacerbated by the fact that many of their indigenous labourers, both male and female, were joining the forces or finding other war-related work. By May 1940, the Abergele Farmer's Union had commented that they faced 'the greatest crisis in our industry for our farms have been denuded of their labour',[464] and noted three farms of over 150 acres where only one man was employed. Yet local and regional newspapers consistently reported on the regular horse, cattle and poultry markets in Abergele and observed no notable change in trading between 1939 and 1941. This was due to the existence of the Gwrych *Hachshara*, and the refugees – free labour – who were in increasing demand. By way of just one example, Gwyneth Griffiths of Abergele, who worked in the dairy at Tan-y-dderwen Farm alongside one of the Jewish boys from the castle, joined the RAF, forcing the farmer to request a second boy from the castle to fill the gap.

The labour force provided by the Gwrych *Hachshara* remained in demand until its very end and local farms began to struggle to fill the gaps being caused by its demise. In August 1941, Tan-y-dderwen Farm had to advertise as far away as Liverpool for 'two young girls, willing to learn, to undertake all duties of small farmhouse'.[465] As final proof of just how important the *Hachshara* had been for the area, a mere nine months after the centre's closure a Land Army unit of thirty-nine women had to be stationed in the town to provide replacement workers to the district's farms.

It is therefore quite clear that there were no external pressures on *Bachad* to close the Gwrych Castle *Hachshara*. The decision must have come from within. However, as the Gwrych *Hachshara* had been opened as a flagship for the *Hachsharot* movement, it would 'politically' have been far more convenient for *Bachad* to suggest that they were forced to close the centre rather than them having to admit to some kind of failure. This may go some way towards explaining their official line of blaming Lord Dundonald. Generally speaking, the *Bnei Akiva* mindset at the time was broadly socialist, and thus blaming a downturn of fortune on the aristocracy would have been par for the course. Additionally, Jack Sklan was not directly connected with the Gwrych *Hachshara* and only ever visited it twice, once in its first few weeks of existence and again in December 1940 to attend the *Pegisha* and Arieh Handler's wedding whilst he had a weekend leave from service in the British army. It's possible that he had either made up the story of Lord Dundonald suddenly taking against a community of Jews, or heard it second-hand. Sklan had certainly changed his tune significantly since the centre's inception in 1939 when he had written that the castle 'had been obtained through the goodwill of the Earl Dundonald'.[466] All this adds some weight to the idea that *Bachad* deliberately spread, or at least allowed to circulate, misinformation over their own decision to close the *Hachshara*.

In reality, the problem that was bringing things to a head was financial. The regular running costs of the Gwrych *Hachshara* are not known but they must have been huge. Estimates for the funding required for the *Hachshara* at Whittingehame Farm, when it was established in 1939 with around fifty residents, was £10,000 per annum.[467] The Gwrych *Hachshara* was opened with four times that number of people and was thus significantly more expensive to run. It would be reasonable to extrapolate that costs may therefore have been in the region of £40,000 per year.[468] By the spring of 1940, with budgets dwindling rapidly now that a war was on, *Bachad* could only earmark £10,000 'for the maintenance and extension'[469] of its entire portfolio of *Hachsharot*. Whatever portion of that ended up at Gwrych is also unclear, but it would almost certainly have been the proverbial drop in the ocean. It has already been noted that, during the spring of 1940, *Bachad* had been forced to cut back on the number of *chaverim* it could afford to accommodate in its centres, and that situation was to get worse as the year went on.

The running costs did not include very significant additional overheads caused by the castle building itself. Despite all the best efforts of those at Gwrych, by the end of 1940 it was still pretty much the same cold, dark and damp shell that it had been when the Handler brothers had first arrived on their scouting mission in August 1939. The budget left little money for spending on improvements. Jack Sklan had noted during the freezing first winter of 1939–40 that attention to a number of 'essential' items 'was put off until funds should permit their being attended to'.[470] However, little was actually done. Nine months later this was acknowledged in the September 1940 yearbook: 'The progress made in one year serves to throw into somewhat sharp relief what still requires to be done and achieved. On the material side many improvements are essential: in sanitation, eating arrangements, heating and water facilities, rest, recreation and class rooms.'[471]

On top of this, further expensive repairs to the building were required. The 13th Earl had contributed to some of the recent roof repairs though possibly reluctantly, and he was unlikely to help further given that he had no intention of ever living there again and was probably already considering selling the property when the war was over. Therefore, most of the money would have to come from other sources, such as those distributed by *Habonim*, and the charitable donations that had been behind so much of what had happened in the early months. The latter were, unfortunately, also starting to dry up. More regular income was also being squeezed. All of these mounting financial problems were compounded at Gwrych by the fact that they were no longer able to call upon David Smith and his uncanny ability to find funds from various sources.

Therefore, at the December 1940 *Pegisha,* Arieh Handler and fellow members of the *Bachad* executive had to confront the difficult question as to whether they should, or indeed could, continue to throw vast sums of money at Gwrych at the expense of smaller and more economical *Hachsharot*, many of which were in more modern premises that required much less maintenance and development.

To be factored into the financial argument was the reality that the whole project had been dying a slow and inevitable death for several months as the numbers of *noar* and *chaverim* had begun to dwindle away, coupled with a lack of new arrivals to replace them. Several thousand Jewish children below the age of fourteen had arrived via Kindertransport but most of those were in foster care and the minority who were not under such arrangements were already in the more economical and smaller *Bachad Hachsharot*, and they would have to be closed if their youngsters were transferred to Gwrych. In fact, the general lack of new 'recruits' resulted in *Bachad* also having to close several other centres over the next twelve months.

Even if a source of youngsters for Gwrych could be found within Britain, they would not be a hand-picked 'elite' as around half of the original Gwrych cohort were. The arrival of the 'less Zionist' Llandough group had proved tricky. Wouldn't this diminish the *Hachshara's* status as some sort of flagship for the movement? Was it worth committing significant expenditure to a centre that was no longer any more special than the others? Retaining the Gwrych *Hachshara* was clearly not a viable option.

There was one final factor that may have been in the back of the minds of Arieh Handler and the *Bachad* executives during that meeting. The concept of *Bachad* having a high-class training centre, led by first-rate instructors such as Erwin Seligmann, and with religious instruction at its core, still made as much sense as it had back in the summer of 1939. There was no desire to lose any of that. Gwrych was clearly not financially sustainable but if an alternative, cheaper location could be found then the Gwrych concept could be replicated elsewhere. It is perhaps not a coincidence that, in the very same month that Gwrych did finally close its doors, in September 1941, *Bachad* unveiled a new centre that they had been working on for some time, in a building donated by the Cadbury family: Avoncroft Agricultural College at Bromsgrove in Worcestershire.

Avoncroft College was announced by the *Bachad* movement as a 'well equipped, modern building, where it will be possible to concentrate a fairly large group … it is situated in good farming country and offers favourable prospects … the house contains a fine library and … it is intended to increase the scope of the cultural work.'[472] To all intents and purposes, Avoncroft offered *Bachad* the opportunity of replicating Gwrych, but far more cheaply. A member of the *chaverim* there later commented that 'at last the *Bachad* has found a home worthy of its great aims.'[473]

Creating a mark-two version of Arieh Handler's original vision of a 'super-centre' also allowed the rectification of any mistakes that may have been made the first time round. One of them, in truth, was the location in Abergele. The relationship that had been forged between town and castle was quite exceptional but, contrary to the fantasy of William Gruffydd, the Jewish people were not 'massing' in North Wales. Consequently, the Gwrych centre was somewhat isolated and cut off from the wider Jewish community. A *chaver* at Avoncroft later noted that a distinct benefit of the new location in Bromsgrove was that it allowed the youngsters there to have 'established connections with the Zionist youth of Birmingham'.[474]

Another significant error at Gwrych had been the creation of a leadership team with shared responsibilities. Although, on paper, the leader was the talented and experienced Erwin Seligmann, in reality he quickly felt undermined and somewhat powerless. Erwin was installed as the clear head of the new Bromsgrove project and, crucially, without anybody to potentially challenge his authority.

A lot of time, effort and money, not to mention a great deal of *Bachad*'s 'political capital' had gone into the Gwrych *Hachshara* and thus, despite having good reasons to shut it down, a major announcement could have been perceived as a public admittance of a very expensive failure. Therefore, Gwrych would be allowed to wind down slowly, almost imperceptibly, over several months. It was to be seen as being replaced rather than closed, and Avoncroft could be seen as an upgrade. To add to this illusion, the children at Gwrych were never given a clear explanation of what was happening and they were left to develop their own conclusions over the years that followed. Henry Glanz, for example always assumed that the closure had something to do with the *Bnei Akiva* explanation that the Earl of Dundonald had simply wanted his castle back. Allowing that untruth to take hold was also a handy way for *Bachad* to side-step their own responsibility for the decision.

The plan for the children at Gwrych was to slowly disperse them to other *Hachsharot*, handily filling gaps developing in other centres as their own eighteen-year-olds moved on. Through January and February 1941 the Gwrych *Hachshara* continued to function in its normal way and follow its well-established routines of education and work. The steady trickle of departures from the ranks of both the *noar* and *chaverim* continued but without intervention, as they eased pressure on plans being drawn up to relocate those that remained. In fact, youngsters were now being 'encouraged'[475] to look to move on. When Mary Auskerin and several others, including Adi Better and Sonia Marder (who would marry three years later), applied to join the Organisation for Rehabilitation and Training (ORT) School in Leeds, which was driven by Jewish values, nobody attempted to dissuade them.

The first organised departures took place during March 1941 when a number of the children were relocated to other Youth *Aliyah* or *Bachad* centres including those at Buckingham, Donnington near Shrewsbury, Sealand near Chester and Handsworth in Birmingham. During that same month, *madricha* Fanny Redner left Gwrych to join Rabbi Gottlieb in his hostel in St Asaph.

The most important departure in March 1941 was that of Dr Julius Handler. Julius would have been of great benefit to any other *Hachshara*, but whilst loyally supportive of his younger brother, and committed to the Gwrych experiment, he was not a zealous Zionist and he had little desire to experience the hardships of another centre. Also, his personal prospects had improved significantly. He was now officially a 'friendly' rather than 'enemy' alien and, with a war on, he was allowed to practise his true profession of medicine. He therefore decided to leave Gwrych in order to take up a new, and properly paid, position at Wrexham Memorial Hospital, which had been arranged for him by Sir Henry Jones, a Denbighshire MP and a patron of the Gwrych community. No attempt was made to find a new medical supervisor to replace him.

On Sunday, 6 April, two members of the *chaverim*, David Granek and Selly Neufeld, married at the local registry office. This was followed by a traditional Jewish marriage ceremony, conducted by Rabbi Sperber, at Gwrych Castle.[476] Shortly afterwards however, the newly married couple moved away to join a small Jewish refugee centre near Hawarden. Martin Steinberger, the castle's carpenter, also moved on during April.

That same month, a further ten of the *noar* were transferred to other centres. Several moved to join a small Jewish community centre that had been developed nearby, at Nantclwyd Lodge in Ruthin. The group included Herman Rothman.

The gradual departures through March and April 1941 did not go unnoticed by those that remained. Even without any particular announcement having been made, a sense of inevitability about leaving Gwrych in the near future began to take root. The only real question was when – rather than why – their turn to move would come.

It may therefore be no coincidence that, at this time, Rabbi Sperber declared that the Gwrych *Hachshara* had adopted a new prophet as its guiding hand. Of the twelve minor Jewish prophets, Amos had been selected as the generic symbol of the wider *Hachsharot* movement: a humble shepherd unafraid to deliver his message of social justice to the rich and powerful who favoured materialism above spirituality. As apt as Amos was in terms of representation, Gwrych now turned to Job. Job was a man whose faith was tested to destruction by repeated disasters and who lost everything important to him. Despite this, he had remained loyal and did not question higher authority or the purpose that his God had for him.

Henry Glanz was not swayed by the clear hint that lay behind the adoption of Job as the guiding prophet. He had little interest in being transferred to another *Hachshara* and chose to pre-empt the inevitable. In May 1941, he left Gwrych and began to make his way to London, where he intended to reunite with his sister, Gisela. His savings from the *kupa* combined with backhanders from farmers only managed to get him as far as Birmingham. There he found a hostel and for the next three months he helped to clear bomb sites as a way of earning enough money to fund the next leg of his journey towards the capital. On one occasion, he was given a gun and asked to keep a watch on a captured German airman. Much to the young airman's surprise, Henry began a conversation with him in German. When Glanz told the prisoner that he was Jewish and from Kiel, the German seemed genuinely confused as to why he did not have devil's horns protruding from his head.[477]

Further transfers were made during May and by the end of the month only a handful of youngsters remained at Gwrych. Most of the original cohort had, by now, moved on and those that remained were mainly from the Llandough group that had arrived during the previous summer. Both Erwin Seligmann and Rabbi Sperber remained on site but, to all intents and purposes, the Gwrych *Hachshara* had ceased to exist and had done so without any particular announcement to mark its demise. The May 1941 edition of *Bachad*'s own journal listed the addresses for all of its centres which, due to the general financial difficulties, had now been reduced to just thirteen.[478] Despite still being open, it is very telling that Gwrych was not included on the list.

The only comment of any kind made in relation to Gwrych appeared in a letter written to the people of Abergele and printed in the *Abergele Visitor* on 24 May 1941.

THANKS

The British Council for Agricultural Training of Refugee Youth take this opportunity of expressing their sincere thanks and appreciation to all those who have shown friendship to, and who have cooperated in the welfare of this group up till now resident at Gwrych Castle. All those who have been interested in these young people will be pleased to learn that they are now assisting in the national effort in these days of emergency, and are working on the land in various parts of the country. The British Council also desires to thank all the tradesfolk who have helped so much in the running of the establishment which is now closed.

Maurice Mitzman, Hon. Secretary
Bloomsbury House, London, WC1

Although officially closed, the centre still had a few residents but, between June and August, most of those that remained were also slowly filtered out. This was seemingly done in batches of similar age groups according to Celia Kreisel. She turned eighteen in July 1941 and, along with several other older children, lingered on until they had secured paid work. Having got a job with a men's shirt manufacturer in Leeds, Kreisel rented a room there and departed Gwrych in August. The following year in Leeds, she bumped into Mondek Winczelberg, who had left Gwrych to become a Hebrew teacher. Neither had developed a particular interest in each other in Wales, but once reunited they fell in love and married in 1943. In 1946, the pair emigrated to the USA.

The final departures, including that of Mimi Schleissner, took place in September 1941. From the final group, some went to Bydown Farm in Devon (which was also closed, a month later, in October 1941) and a few to Wolf Gottlieb's *Bachad* hostel in St Asaph which was possibly a case of Gottlieb doing his old friend, Arieh Handler, a favour.

Closing the Gwrych *Hachshara* was a slow and relatively uneventful process, and the folk of Abergele, with the exception of the farmers, barely noticed its decline. Bit by bit the community at the castle faded from view and then it just simply wasn't there any more. Besides the letter of May 1941, there was nothing in the local press and nothing to mark its ending. All of this allowed for the slow erosion of memory that made it possible for a local historian to later write about the community, 'How could one have possibly lived in Abergele since 1946 and not heard one word about them?'[479]

We have no idea who the final youngster to leave Gwrych in September 1941 was. We have no idea how they felt about it. Possibly they were just relieved to move on or possibly they were excited to be going somewhere else. They may have been one of the original cohort that had arrived lonely, scared and confused almost exactly two years earlier. Whoever they were, had they taken a last glance over their shoulder at the castellated mansion on the wooded hillside, they would have caught one final glimpse of a building that had changed their lives and where something truly incredible had been attempted. For two years, Gwrych Castle had housed some quite remarkable people, traumatised and threatened by cataclysmic events that were outside of their control. It had played its part in helping them to escape the horrors of the Holocaust that claimed the lives of so many of their families and friends. If Gwrych Castle had done nothing else, at the very least it had given them a respite from a horrific wider reality. As Henry Glanz simply put it, it had given them the opportunity to have 'a happy time within a sad time'.[480]

EPILOGUE

'This place gave us a new life'

From 1941–46 Gwrych Castle sat empty and idle. It was derequisitioned in 1946 and Lord Dundonald put it up for sale at auction. It was bought for just £12,000 by a Wrexham businessman who intended for it to become his home.[481] The new owner sold it three years later and until 1968 the castle was open to the public in the hope of it becoming the 'showplace of Wales'. It was then sold again, to an entertainment company who, for the next twenty years offered mock medieval banquets, markets and jousts to the paying public until it closed in 1987. In 1990 it was purchased by an absentee American businessman with lofty ambitions of turning it into a hotel but little happened other than the site being used as a location for a Hollywood film. Unprotected and uncared for, the building rapidly deteriorated and fell prey to asset-stripping and vandalism. The ceilings and floors collapsed. The fabric of the building rotted. There was a fire and the roofs fell in. By the turn of the century, it was little more than a wrecked husk. It was sold again, in 2007, to a hotel chain who planned to renovate the building but, shortly afterwards, the company went into administration. Purchased by the Gwrych Castle Preservation Trust in 2018, its decay has been halted and the slow process of returning it to its former glory is under way. In 2020 and 2021 the castle came to national attention when it played host to the popular TV show *I'm a Celebrity, Get Me Out of Here!* Henry Glanz, aged ninety-six, watched the show, but briefly and with little interest. The place bore little resemblance to how he remembered it.

The collective enterprise known as the Gwrych *Hachshara* is an important aspect of the story of refugees who fled from Nazism to Britain, and an aspect that is not well known. There is extensive literature on the experiences of Kindertransport refugees, most of which is focused on those who went into some form of foster care. However very little is known about the *Hachsharot*. As one historian put it, 'In refugee history, the wartime *Hachsharot* are perhaps best seen as transient phenomena: footprints made by refugees … They have left few traces on the ground of the English countryside.'[482] Despite the reference to English *Hachsharot*, the same point would be equally true of those in Wales and, until now, it was certainly true of Gwrych Castle.

The ambition behind the Gwrych *Hachshara* was huge and it succeeded in becoming, albeit briefly, the flagship for the *Hachsharot* movement that it was always intended to be. However, given that it lasted just two years and faded away into nothingness with barely a whimper or even any real recognition of its end, it would be easy to regard the whole enterprise as a failure. In some ways, of course, it could have been seen to fail but, if it did, that was due to a series of insurmountable problems that were largely beyond its own control.

When it was first mooted in the summer of 1939, it had seemed like a practical idea to set up training centres for children in the hope and expectation that family reunifications would take place in Palestine in the not-too-far-distant future. Arieh Handler's idea of establishing a large centre was also a sensible one as it would act as a model for other centres as well helping to ease the burdens in overcrowded reception centres.

However, the outbreak of war put an end to the Kindertransport and the hundreds or thousands of young Jewish children who would otherwise have made it to Britain – from which Gwrych would have recruited to replace natural departures – were now trapped inside a Nazi-controlled Europe from which they could not escape. To a large extent therefore, the root of the Gwrych *Hachshara*'s ultimate demise lay in its timing; it was set up to fulfil a function in a world that had altered fundamentally within a week of its creation. That alteration also significantly reduced the short-term prospects of *Aliyah* for all at Gwrych and thus, for some, their long-term commitment to it. The *Hachshara*'s fate, once the basic foundations upon which it was predicated had been knocked from under it, was accelerated by other factors beyond its control such as the loss of David Smith. The day that the chief constable of Colwyn Bay arrived at the castle to intern some of the community can also be seen as a pivotal point. From that day onwards, the *Hachshara* declined rapidly and by December it was recognised by those responsible for it that it had no future. The final factor in the *Hachshara*'s failure was the building itself. Gwrych Castle was extremely attractive to *Bachad* as it was in a rural area but the building itself was deceptive in its grandeur. Money poured in, especially in the early days as wealthy individuals donated generously, but once that was exhausted the basic sources of income were insufficient to maintain it, let alone make any improvements. To put it simply, by choosing Gwrych Castle, *Bachad* had bitten off more than it could chew.

However, the Gwrych *Hachshara* should not be remembered for its end, but for what it tried to achieve and for the example it set. In that regard, it was an enormous success. After the chaotic opening days, and almost against the odds, the children at the castle established a bond and a community that was remarkable. Together, they developed and came to agree upon a vision for a better future. Visitors from other *Hachsharot* commented on the spirit and ambition that the *noar* of Gwrych displayed. The fact that the centre was chosen as the place to host them all at a *Pegisha* in October 1939 showed how much the project impressed people. It was chosen again for a meeting of the leaders of *Bachad* and *Bnei Akiva* in December 1940, the first ever to be held on British soil. Arieh Handler appointed a permanent rabbi at the castle and chose it as the venue for his own wedding. All this speaks volumes for its status within Zionist youth circles. The importance of Gwrych and what it had tried to achieve should therefore not be underestimated.

What happened at Gwrych Castle between 1939 and 1941 was significant for the local community, too. In Abergele and the surrounding area, the children became a visible and essential part of the landscape for nearly two years. As refugees, they contributed massively to the local agricultural economy and, in many ways, personified the 'Dig for Victory' mentality. Their presence was a subject of great interest for many in the local community and there were moments of friendship, mutual respect, tension, high drama and comedy as Jew and Gentile tried to get the measure of each other. Although the refugees' time in Abergele was only of a short duration, it resulted in the creation of several unique bonds, and some of the relationships forged with the locals led to actual friendships being formed.

Salli Edelnand struck up a good relationship with Albert Appleby, the head gamekeeper of the Gwrych estate. Albert lived at Nant-y-Bella Lodge, near to where Salli had encountered his first local, the welly-wearing Wil Davies back on 1 September 1939. When Salli (now John) returned to Abergele for a visit in 1987, he made a point of calling in to see the family. 'I … stopped at Nant-y-Bella Lodge which again had happy memories. Mr and Mrs Appleby with four daughters and one son resided in this lodge. I had tea with the family many times, without the knowledge of the castle management because this was strictly forbidden as only kosher food was allowed. I accompanied Mr Appleby on many occasions when he was on duty in his capacity as gamekeeper for the Gwrych Castle Estate. Rabbit-shooting with his priceless ferrets was one of his particular interests.'[483]

Ossi Findling, on a visit to the castle, forty years after hitch-hiking his way from Abergele all the way to Manchester, commented that 'this place gave us a new life and we really felt what it meant to be free. We will be eternally grateful to the Welsh people for that.'

That the Jews of Gwrych contributed to the local community, albeit briefly, is beyond question, and that they benefitted in return, and were enormously grateful, is also unquestionable. In a speech at the castle in 1940, Arieh Handler listed many contributors, but acknowledged that 'last not least' was 'the friendliness and kindness we have always received from the citizens of Abergele who deserve our utmost appreciation.'[484]

But the most important aspect of Gwrych was the group of individuals within it. Most of those 200 or so souls, had Kindertransport not existed, would have been lost in the Holocaust along with all the contributions to the world that they had yet to make. Julius Handler recalled that many of the boys at Gwrych went on to serve in Allied forces and that they 'distinguished themselves in various theatres of war … it was indeed with a great feeling of satisfaction to see some of them again in London with medals pinned to their chests.'[485] Away from the military, another child from the castle went on to become a Hollywood movie producer and worked with Julie Andrews. Hanna Zuntz became an internationally recognised ceramicist. Alfred Benjamin returned to scientific photography and, from his home in Los Angeles, wrote articles on the subject that appeared in professional journals.

Most, of course, went on to live more quiet lives. Several went on to study at university. They moved to London, the USA and other places. They worked in commerce and manufacturing. They became confectioners, furniture makers, tailors, teachers, child care assistants and nurses. One became a customs and excise officer. Jesse Zierler stayed in Britain and became a graphic designer. None ended up choosing a career in agriculture.

Many of the youngsters grew to make a difference in the lives of others or in their own fields, and a number also, of course, finally achieved the Zionist dream and made their home in Palestine, or Israel (from 1948). One group of Gwrych youngsters went on to set up Kibbutz *Lavi*, which still operates to this day and where the final ripples of the Gwrych *Hachshara* legacy linger on.

Unfortunately, the promise of a long life proved not to be the case for some of the Gwrych *chaverim*. David Granek had married Selly Neufeld at the castle in the final days of the *Hachshara* before moving to a centre in Hawarden. Unfortunately, Granek died there in the autumn of 1942, aged just thirty. *Chaver* Rolf 'Rudi' Grab was born in Breslau in 1919, and had left Gwrych in the spring or early summer of 1940 to find work as a trainee gown maker and machinist in Cheetham, Manchester. He was interned on the Isle of Man between 21 June 1940 and 6 March 1941. Upon release, he enlisted into the British Army, serving as a private in the Royal Army Ordnance Corps. At the conclusion of the war, he was posted to Palestine to serve with the RAOC as part of general peacekeeping operations. He died on 28 April 1946, the day before his twenty-seventh birthday, after being involved in an unspecified accident. He was buried in Ramleh War Cemetery, near Tel Aviv.

Many others lived long lives, though. Salli Edelnand had arrived at Gwrych on 31 August 1939 with two schoolmates from Halberstadt in Germany. One of them, David Kowalski, had died in 1940. By 1941, when Gwrych was being wound down and Salli was approaching the age of seventeen, he had lost the desire to continue to work towards *Aliyah*. 'I rather think that I was not particularly interested in the lifestyle of a kibbutz, hence the reason when Gwrych Castle closed we were offered positions in other kibbutzim I decided to join an aunt who lived in Leicester.'[486] It was there that he anglicised his name to John. He chose to stay in Britain after the war, got married and settled down. His parents and his younger sister died in the Warsaw Ghetto in 1942 or 1943. One of the things that Salli had carried with him to the castle was a silver watch made by his father and, in a roundabout way, the family watchmaking tradition would survive. John Edelnand would later gift that watch to a great-nephew who had showed an interest in it. This nephew was Itay Noy, who is now a renowned watchmaker in Israel.

Henry Steinberg left Gwrych for Rossett, possibly via Rabbi Wolf Gottlieb's hostel at Rose Hill in St Asaph. He shortly afterwards moved to Manchester to reunite with his siblings. There, he found work in a clothing factory making military uniforms and emigrated after the war. He remained in touch with two of the 'Haifa Gang' from Gwrych Castle for the rest of his life.

Mimi Schleissner, who had arrived at Gwrych in 1940 from Llandough Castle, was one of the last to depart from Gwrych in September

1941, when she was transferred to Bydown Farm, Barnstaple, Devon. That centre closed shortly afterwards and she then attended Cheltenham Technical College until early 1944. She then found work in a day-care nursery and quickly became head nurse. There she met an American GI, Edward Ormond, and they married in November 1944. Fortunately, both of Mimi's parents survived the war, having managed to get to Palestine from Czechoslovakia via illegal routes in January 1940, and the family reunited in Palestine in 1946. Mimi emigrated to the USA with her new husband and later attended Washington University before settling in Ohio. She published her memoir *Kindertransport: A Rescued Child*, in 2016.

Gerry Friedenfeld, who had been transferred to Gwrych with Mimi Schleissner after arriving in Britain with a broken leg thanks to the Nazis, ended up in the USA by a more circuitous route. In 1943, aged eighteen, Friedenfeld volunteered to join the 1st Czechoslovak Independent Armoured Brigade Group, a unit of expatriate Czechs organised and equipped by the British Army. Serving as the driver of a Cromwell tank, his unit landed in Normandy in 1944 before receiving orders to contain German forces around Dunkirk until it surrendered in May 1945. From there, the brigade moved to Czechoslovakia and combined with the reformed Czech Army. There, he recalls that he 'made the enormous mistake of staying in Czechoslovakia. I should have taken out British citizenship.'[487] Some time later, he managed to emigrate to the USA, where he died in 2015.

Austrian Wilhelm Braun, mostly known as Willy or Bill whilst at Gwrych, had been one of the instigators of the castle newsletter and was working in the market garden at Hen Wrych when the police arrived to detain him and others as 'enemy aliens' in June 1940. He was interned in Canada and decided to stay there after his release. He attended the University of Toronto, where he gained a PhD, before becoming Professor of German Literature and Jewish Studies at the University of Rochester in New York, USA. During that time, he married and went on to have two children. He died in Rochester in 2014, aged ninety-three. In later life he reflected on what he learned from the dark days of his childhood: 'From generation to generation, people must be taught. Since it happened once, I do not think there is any way we can say it won't happen again. All I can teach my children is, you're not safe. Whether this will work, I cannot tell.'[488]

David Smith's assistant Ossi Findling had been one of the first of the *noar* to arrive at Gwrych, accompanying the suitcases loaded at Great Engeham. After leaving Gwrych he lived briefly in Manchester under the auspices of the Jewish Refugee Committee, before moving to Salford to be with Dr Koppenheim's Manchester Refugee Committee. There, he found work as a machinist in a garment factory making uniforms for the army. He joined the Local Defence Volunteers (the Home Guard) before joining the British Army in 1944. He served three years, firstly with the Royal Army Ordnance Corps and then with the Intelligence Corps. Between September and October 1946, he acted as an army interpreter and interrogator at the war crimes trials of the commanders of the Bergen-Belsen concentration camp. Eleven were sentenced to death and hanged in December 1946. From October 1946 to the spring of 1947 he was based at Flossenburg near Hanover as part of a team interrogating 20,000 German prisoners of war. He became a British citizen in 1947 and left the army at Christmas that year having attained the rank of sergeant. He married a fellow Jewish refugee in London in 1950 and settled in Britain. Findling received his last letter from home, via the Red Cross, in January 1942. His family were deported to a ghetto in Rzeszow in south-east Poland and, although their exact fate is not known, they did not survive the war. The Rzeszow ghetto was largely liquidated during July 1942 with many thousands being sent to the Belzec death camp in cattle trains, where they were gassed upon arrival. Hundreds more were taken out and shot in nearby woods.

Herman Rothman was relocated to Nantclwyd Lodge, near Ruthin, during the closure of Gwrych. Aged twenty, he joined the British Army in 1944 and served as a private with the Royal West Kent Regiment and then as an interpreter with 4th Battalion, King's Own Scottish Borderers in north-west Europe between 1944 and 1945. In early 1945 he was posted to the Intelligence Corps in Germany and promoted to sergeant. He was stationed at the Westertimke and Fallingbostel prisoner of war camps and given the job of interrogating high-ranking Nazi war criminals. When papers were discovered in the clothing of a man who had been Joseph Goebbels's press secretary, he and a team of four others were given the task of translating them. The documents turned out to be the originals of Hitler's personal and political wills, and included Goebbels's addendum. Later, he interrogated Hermann Karnau, a police guard in Hitler's bunker, to establish further information into the investigation over Hitler's death. Herman became a British citizen in 1947, married in 1949 and went on to become a lawyer. In 2009 he published his book, *Hitler's Will*. His father, who had been sent to Sachsenhausen concentration camp but had been released due to the efforts of a friendly policeman, survived the war and managed to emigrate to Palestine. His mother also managed to join him there.

Erich Roper was also amongst the original editors of the castle newsletter, *Der Daat Hachshara*, as well as producer of the yearbook and responsible for the castle's (often lax) blackout procedures. Despite being Austrian, he avoided internment due to his Polish ancestry. At Gwrych Castle, Erich saw Rabbi Sperber as his mentor and stayed in touch and even visited him on occasion in later years. His father had managed to emigrate early in the war to Tel Aviv but his mother and brother were separated from him. They tried to escape to Palestine via Yugoslavia on the November 1939 Kladovo Transport, an illegal refugee transport that had set off from Vienna. The transport got stuck in Yugoslavia and, following the German invasion of Yugoslavia in April 1941, the group were recaptured and held in the Sabac labour camp before being moved to the Sajmiste concentration camp in January 1942. His mother, Ernestine, was murdered between March and May 1942 at Zasavica near Sabac along with many others, probably in mobile gas vans. A small number of the original transport did survive and were moved elsewhere. The fate of Erich's much younger brother,

Oswald Roper, is officially unknown, but someone of the same name and age died at the Theresienstadt concentration camp shortly after its liberation by Soviet forces in May 1945, when a typhus epidemic swept through the emaciated inmates, killing nearly 1,000 of them. After leaving Gwrych, Erich moved to Glasgow where he enrolled in a *Yeshiva* and served in the Glasgow Volunteer Fire Service until the end of the war. He then moved to London where he met his wife and became a businessman. Erich remained very active within *Bnei Akiva* for the remainder of his life and he finally emigrated to Israel in 1981, where he died in 1988, aged sixty-four.

Wolfgang Billig was 'relocated to a smaller *Bnei Akiva* centre, a house called Glengower at St Asaph, in North Wales. There I was together with some *chaverim* who were previously at a *Hachshara* establishment in Millisle, Northern Ireland. While at St Asaph, I worked at the car repair shop of John Glyn Jones. Well, it was mostly Fordson Tractors that I helped to recondition. At Glengower there were only about ten or twelve of us and several made *Aliyah* after the war and subsequently established Kibbutz *Lavi*.'[489] After St Asaph he joined the British army, enlisting into the Royal Army Service Corps. Shortly before D-Day in 1944, Billig decided to change his name, as a precaution just in case he was to ever taken prisoner:

> My name was Wolfgang Billig. The first name was very
> German and the last name wasn't German at all – it was
> Polish-Galician and was sometimes spelled Villig. It would
> surely raise questions. I went to a village near where we
> were stationed, walked into a phone booth and looked at
> the phone book. All I knew was that I wanted to keep my
> initials. I saw a name like William but thought it was too
> common. Then I saw Walter – it was a good name because
> I didn't know where I'd end up and it could fit in many
> cultures. I still needed a last name. I saw ones like Baker,
> Butcher, Bailey, Brown – too common. Then I saw the

Right Honourable Bingham. That sounded good. That evening I did what perhaps a newly married woman does – I tried my new signature. But next morning, during roll call, when the sergeant major called out 'Driver Bingham', there was no reply. Everyone looked around – there was no one new there. The sergeant major pointed to me with a smirk and said, 'Isn't your new name Bingham?'[490]

On D-Day, 6 June 1944, Driver Walter Bingham drove a DUKW amphibious vehicle onto a beach in Normandy. Shortly afterwards, as Operation Overlord pushed inland from the beaches, and with the DUKWs now effectively irrelevant to the battle, Bingham volunteered himself as an ambulance driver and was attached to 130 field ambulances. In this new role, he found himself being sent 'right to the front lines, with bombs, missiles and bullets going off all around us.'[491] During what became known as the Battle for Hill 122, fought between 3 and 5 July 1944, Bingham's ambulance was hit. 'The officer helping load the ambulance was blown to pieces, the medic was injured, I managed to get away.'[492] Bingham returned to base, immediately jumped into another ambulance and went back out under heavy fire to collect more wounded men. For this act of bravery, he was awarded the Military Medal on 19 October 1944, including a citation from Field Marshal Bernard Montgomery and a letter from King George VI. As an ambulance driver, often close to the front line, Bingham also inevitably encountered the enemy. 'I also took wounded Germans. I had been issued cigarettes and bars of chocolate to give to the wounded. I also gave them to the Germans. But I did a bit of psychological torture, too. I would say: "You know, the driver who is driving you is a Jew, and the doctor who will treat you is also a Jew." This scared them more than anything. Most of them had never even seen a Jew.'[493]

Bingham was then transferred to General Eisenhower's Supreme Headquarters Allied Expeditionary Force and sent back to a secret office in London to become a documents specialist. He ended up in

Hamburg at the end of the war, examining local documents to identify Nazis. 'I expanded my work to counter-intelligence. I could wear civilian clothing. I was entitled to speak to Germans, though the army prohibited fraternising with the enemy. I had permission to carry a pistol of enemy origin – a Luger. I could literally do whatever I liked. I went to different areas, investigated, looked for Nazis.' Amongst those he encountered was Joachim von Ribbentrop, the former Nazi foreign minister. 'They had taken away his civilian clothing in case he had any poison hidden there. He was brought into my office to be interrogated and I was only interested in asking about the extermination of the Jews. He said he "didn't know anything about that", that it was "all the Führer". He was the first to hang in Nuremberg.'[494]

Following this, Bingham was given compassionate leave to visit his mother, who had survived the Holocaust, in Sweden. He was demobilised from the army in 1947. He was invited to be one of the founders of Kibbutz *Lavi*, which several of the Gwrych children were involved in, but turned it down. He gained a degree in Politics and Philosophy from Birkbeck College, University of London. In a varied later life he worked as a manufacturer of children's clothing, did a stint as the Harrods Santa Claus, and worked as a journalist and in radio. He also acted in numerous TV shows and movies, including playing a wizard in *Harry Potter and the Philosopher's Stone* and *Harry Potter and the Chamber of Secrets*. His wife died in 1990 and he moved to Israel in 2004 where he hosted a popular radio show, *Walter's World*, for many years. In February of 2018 he was awarded France's highest honour, the *Legion d'Honneur*, for his role in the Normandy landings of 1944.

Dr Julius Handler chose to pursue a quiet life after Gwrych. Having secured work as a doctor in Wrexham, he later moved to London, where he married in 1945. He remained a medical practitioner until his retirement. He died, aged eighty, in 1990. As a mark of how respected this quiet, unassuming, musical man was, hundreds gathered at his funeral in order to pay their respects.

Rabbi Shmuel Sperber became a welfare worker with the Refugee

Children's Movement in Manchester after Gwrych and remained there until February 1945. He and his wife, Miriam, later emigrated to Israel and lived in Jerusalem. Rabbi Sperber passed away in 1984, aged eighty, and Miriam in 1992, aged ninety. Their third child, Daniel, who was born at Gwrych Castle in November 1940, is a Professor of Talmud at Bar-Ilan University in Jerusalem.

Erwin Seligmann briefly became an instructor at the Rose Hill centre in St Asaph after Gwrych Castle was vacated but, after that, was sent to Bromsgrove, where he was put in charge of Kibbutz *Shivat Tzion*, at Avoncroft College, as the most senior *Bachad* member there. At long last, he got the opportunity to run things the way he felt was best and, as it proved, successfully. At Avoncroft, Erwin was referred to by Arieh Handler as 'the brains behind the operation'. His eldest brother, Avraham, who had also worked for *Bachad*, was murdered at Auschwitz during the war. Erwin emigrated shortly after the conclusion of the war and arrived in *Eretz Yisrael* in June 1946. He renewed his art education, and taught drawing, writing and graphics at the Bezalel School of Art in Jerusalem. He was among the first art teachers in the country to teach at religious further education colleges. In later life he was awarded the Life's Work Prize of the Ministry of Education and Culture for his work in this field. He passed away in 1990, on the sixty-first anniversary of the opening of the Gwrych Castle *Hachshara*.

Arieh Handler continued his work with *Bachad* and the *Hachsharot* movement. Although Avoncroft College was in some ways a replacement for Gwrych, what Arieh really wanted was for *Bachad* to own their own fully functioning farm that could be run entirely by their own principles and with no interference. After a further two years of fundraising he succeeded in raising sufficient capital to buy a run-down farm at Thaxted in Essex in 1944. Learning from prior experience, including that gained at Gwrych, Thaxted became the final, and ultimately the most successful, flagship for the *Hachsharot* movement.

After the war, Arieh was involved with the emigration of survivors of the Holocaust and refugees to Palestine, before emigrating himself in 1947. He was personally invited by David Ben-Gurion to attend the Israeli Independence Declaration ceremony in Tel Aviv in 1948. In 1956 he returned to Britain at the behest of the Israeli government to help develop an insurance company. He continued to be involved with the rescue of Jews, particularly from the Soviet Union and Ethiopia. He became a friend of Prime Minister Harold Wilson and was a supporter of the Labour Party. He went on to meet other prime ministers such as Margaret Thatcher and Tony Blair. He became president of the *Mizrachi* Federation within Britain and was a member of the Jewish Board of Deputies. Arieh Handler returned to Israel in 2006 and he died in Jerusalem in 2011. Wolfgang Billig, now Walter Bingham, had become good friends with him after the war and wrote that, 'Arieh Handler was an amazing person who achieved so much as a young man in his early twenties. Hundreds of us really owe our lives to his efforts. May his memory be forever a blessing.'[495]

May the memories of all of the refugees at Gwrych Castle be forever a blessing.

APPENDIX I

Nominal Roll of those known to have been at Gwrych Castle between 1939 and 1941

Surname	Forename(s)	Nationality
Adler	Jacob (Jack)	
Alt	Sigmund	
Altberg	Josef	
Alterman	Rivka	
Alweiss	Manfred	German
Aranowicz	Lotte	
Auskerin	Mary	
Bauch	Erich	Czech
Becker	Osias	
Behrend	Norbert [unclear]	
Benjamin	Alfred	German
Better	Avraham (Adi)	German
Bieder	Malli	
Billig	Wolfgang	German
Blum	Hermann	German
Blum	Margot	
Blum	Rachel	German
Brandt	Hans	German
Braun	Wilhelm	German

Breitel	Berta	
Burke	James	British
Carlebach	Eva	German
Chajes	Leopold	Polish
Diamant	Max Israel	German
Donner	Caecilie	Austrian
Drukarz	Gerhard	German
Duhl	Uscher	
Dürst	Uscher	
Edelnand	Salli	German
Einhorn	Betti	
Elert	Adolf	German
Ellern	Aron	
F	Anni	
F	Edith	
Ferber	Salomon	
Findling	Osias	German
Fink	Regine	
Fisch	Ruth	
Flaschmann	Benno	
Flaschmann	Hertha/Herthel	German
Flohr	Fanni	Austrian
Fraenkel	Ephraim	
Freier	Eli	German
Freier	Fritz Israel	German
Friedenfeld	Gerhard	Austrian
Friedler	Moritz	Austrian
Friedmann	Leo	

Appendix I

Geller	Samuelis	German
Gerson	Pauline (Karo)	German
Getta	Anna Debora	
Gewurtz	Chaia	
Gewurtz	Isi	
Glanz	Henry	Polish
Glatt	Josef	
Grab	Rolf Rudi	German
Granek	David	Polish
Graudenz	Esther	
Gruenbaum	Isi	
Handler	Arieh	German
Handler	Julius	German
Hausner	Lotti	Austrian
Heisler-Lieberman	Erika	German
Herzka	Erich	
Hirsch	Julius	German
Hochberg	Julius	
Horn	Charlotte	
Horovitz	Selma	German
Intrator	Alma	
Irsiak	Ignaty	
Issler	Mordecai	
Kahan	Siegfried	German
Kahn	Alfred	German
Kalcheim	Ruth	
Kallner	Alfred	German
Karmiol	Bertel	German

Katz	Hanni	Polish
Kessel	Ruth	German
Khan	Meta	German
Koenigshoefer	Milli	German
Kollmann	Felix	German
Kowalski	David	
Kreisel	Celia	German
Kreisel	Gertrude	German
Lachs		
Landberger	Wilhelm	Austrian
Leidert	Margarete	German
Lerner	Bernhard	
Lerner	Hersh	
Levin	Annie	
Levin	Erica	
Liwerant	Bernhard	
Loewy	Moses	German
M	Edith	
Mahr	Hermann	
Manela	Leon	Spanish
Marder	Sonia	German
Mehrl	Charlotte	
Mehrl	Moses	
Metzger	Edith	
Metzger	Esther	
Milgrom	Lotte	
Muller	Ruth Sara	German
Natawovicz	Gitta	Polish

Neufeld	Selly	
P	Franz	
Perl	Siegfried	German
Perlmutter	Edith	German
Peterseil	Isaak (Isi)	German
R	Erich	
R	Hanni	
Rechtschaffen	Hermann	
Redner	Fanny	Polish
Reich	Fanni	
Reisz	Alice	
Rembacz	Malli	
Ring	Ruth	
Roper	Erich J	
Rosen	Edward	
Rosen	Eli	
Rosenberg	Bertel	
Rosenblum		
Rothman	Herman	German
Samt	Abraham	German
Sandberg	Ernst	German
Schäfler	Chaim (Carl)	
Schiff	Elisabeth S.	
Schindel	Suzy	
Schleissner	Mimi	Czech
Schneider	Arisch	
Schnitzer	Edmund	German
Seligmann	Eliezer Israel (Erwin)	German

Silbermann	Leo	German
Smith	David	
Sperber	Miriam	Russian
Sperber	Samuel (Shmuel)	Romanian
Spergel	Baruch	Czech
Steinberg	Heinrich (Henry)	German
Steinberger	Martin	German
Sternheim	Benno	
Storch	Saul	
Sussmann	Tosca	German
Szydlow	Sigmund	German
Tempel	Schimon	German
Teppich	Lies	Polish
Urbach	Richard	
Urmann	Oskar	Stateless
W	Abraham	
Wagner	Bernhard	
Wallenfels	Kurt	
Weisner	Esther	German
Weissmann	Inge	German
Weissmann	Senta	
Weitsch	Robert	Austrian
Wildstein	Ruth	Stateless
Winczelberg	Josef	
Winczelberg	Mondek	Polish
Wolf	Leo	
Zelmanowicz	Isidor	Polish
Zierler	Jesse	German

Zollmann	Anni	German
Zolmanotz	Isi	
Zuntz	Hanna	German
	Alize	
	Berni	
	Drori	
	Gidi	
	Irszak	
	Joel	
	Margot	
	Marian	
	Moli	
	Monni	
	Mulli	
	Nathan	
	Rebecca	
	Regine	
	Tommi	
	Tutti	
	Ulli	
	Vera	
	Wolf	

(Gaps in the above indicate that information is unknown or uncertain, or are deliberate to preserve anonymity.)

APPENDIX II

Glossary

Aliyah   To achieve emigration to *Eretz Yisrael*, the land
                    of Israel.

Assefah   The name given to the general council, run by
                    and for the youngsters at the castle.

Bachad   The adult organisation of which *Bnei Akiva* is
                    the youth wing.

Bnei Akiva   Religious Zionist youth movement, the youth
                    wing of *Bachad*.

Chanukah   Winter festival. Also known as Hanukkah.

chaver,   Male and female singular of *chaverim*.
chavera   A volunteer/worker/friend.

chaverim   Collective noun for volunteers/workers/
                    friends, used in the main text for those at
                    Gwrych aged eighteen and above, in order to
                    differentiate them from the *noar*.

Eretz Yisrael   Traditional Jewish name for the land of Israel.

Habonim   A Zionist youth movement with an emphasis
                    on education. Culturally socialist.

Hachshara   Literally 'preparation', used as a name for an
                    agricultural training centre. Plural *Hachsharot*.

kibbutz	A Jewish collective community. Plural kibbutzim.
Kinder-transport	The collective name for the transport of groups of Jewish children to Britain from Nazi Germany in 1938 and 1939.
Kristallnacht	Also known as 'Crystal Night' or 'Night of the Broken Glass'. A Nazi organised pogrom against German Jews in November 1938.
kupa	A kitty for spending money.
madrich, madricha	Male and female singular of the plural *madrichim*, a collective term used within Zionist youth movements for a group leader/guide /head counsellor/supervisor. The title often ascribed to Erwin Seligmann.
matzah	A thin, cracker-like bread eaten during *Pesach*.
Mizrachi	International religious Zionist movement.
noar	Generic term for those at the castle under the age of eighteen and not working as a *chaver/chavera*.
Pegisha	A meeting or get-together of different Jewish groups, usually held over a weekend.
Pesach	Festival also known as Passover. Commemorates the story of the Exodus, and is celebrated for seven or eight days. It is one of the most widely observed Jewish holidays. *Pesach* is observed by avoiding leavened bread, and highlighted by the *Seder* meals that include four cups of wine, eating *matzah* and bitter herbs, and retelling the story of the Exodus.

Purim Festival. Commemorates the salvation of the Jewish people in ancient Persia from Haman's plot 'to destroy, kill and annihilate all the Jews, young and old, infants and women, in a single day.' Often celebrated as a day of fun, and involving fancy dress.

Rosh Hashanah Festival. Marks the day God created Adam and Eve, and celebrated as the Jewish New Year. Includes candle-lighting in the evenings, festive meals with sweet delicacies during the night and day, prayer services that include the sounding of the ram's horn (*shofar*) on both mornings, and desisting from creative work.

Sukkot Festival. *Sukkot* celebrates the gathering of the harvest. Work is forbidden, candles are lit in the evening, and festive meals are prepared.

Torah The five books of Moses that form the foundation for Jewish instruction and guidance.

Yeshiva A Jewish school focused on traditional religious texts, primarily the Talmud and the Torah.

Yom Kippur Festival. Yom Kippur is the holiest day of the year, the 'Day of Atonement'. Marked by a day of prayer and abstinence from food and drink, amongst other things.

Youth *Aliyah* Jewish youth organisation dedicated to progressing Jewish youth towards *Aliyah*. (In Hebrew, *Aliyat Hanoar*.)

Zionism A movement for the establishment of a Jewish nation (*Eretz Yisrael*) in Palestine.

ACKNOWLEDGEMENTS

I am hugely grateful to the following:

Professor Nathan Abrams of Bangor University for his interest and sharing information on the Jewish community within Llandudno. The Association of Jewish Refugees (AJR) and associated *Kindertransport Newsletter*. Dr Mark Baker of the Gwrych Castle Preservation Trust. Hilary Bennett. Carol Bunyan, researcher of the HMT *Dunera*. Peter Collins of the Luton Rotary Club. John (Salli) Edelnand and Henry Glanz, both child refugees at Gwrych Castle, for sharing their memories and experiences of that time with me. Lyn Glanz for photographic colourisation. Howard Falksohn, archivist at The Wiener Library, London. Molly Friedenfeld for permission to use information relating to her father, Gerry Friedenfeld. Heidi Goldsmith, who arrived in Abergele as an evacuee in 1940 for sharing the story of her uncle as well as her own memories. Freema Gottlieb for information relating to her father, Wolf Gottlieb. Dr Andrea Hammel at Aberystwyth University for her encouragement as well as corrections and comments regarding Kindertransport. Danny Handler and Aviv Handler for sharing memories related to their father and grandfather, Arieh Handler. Laura Henley for sharing her research into the Youth *Aliyah* centre at Llandough Castle. Cheryl Hesketh at Conwy Library Service. Derrick and Elaine Hesketh. Helen Levy for information and photographs relating to her father, Josef Altberg. Megan Lewis at The United States Holocaust Memorial Museum in Washington DC. Deryl Ann Mahon, granddaughter of PC Sam Williams. Alison Maloney. Debbie Nead and Jacqui Press, for discussions and information relating to their father and grandfather, Dr Julius Handler. Dr Cai Parry-Jones of Bangor University for helpful suggestions regarding the wider Jewish communities within North Wales around the time of World War Two. Marcus Roberts, Director of JTrails. Ariel and Daniel Roper, sons of Erich Roper, for information concerning their father's time at the castle, for Hebrew translations, and advice relating to Jewish customs. Anthony Royle. The staff of the British Library at Boston Spa, especially Brian Sherwood. Emily Smith. Professor Daniel Sperber, Bar-Ilan University, Israel, son of Rabbi Shmuel and Miriam Sperber, for information about the *Hachshara* passed to him by his parents, and for sending me a copy of his mother's autobiography. I am particularly indebted to Verity Steele, researching a PhD at Southampton University relating to *Bachad* and the Thaxted training centre, for her research suggestions, support and valuable additional information, especially in relation to Erwin Seligmann. Alan Steinberg, for information relating to his father, Henry Steinberg, and for the opportunity to see his father's collection of photographs and his unpublished autobiography. Anne Vaccari at JewishGen.org.

I would like to offer my thanks to staff at the University of Wales Press and in particular to Clare Grist Taylor (without whose honest views the story would have been told very differently and very badly), and my editors – Amy Feldman, Abbie Headon and Caroline Goldsmith – for their amazing attention to detail.

NOTES

1   Glanz, Henry – quotations taken from interviews with the author, 2020 and 2021.

2   Due to changes in local authorities, Abergele is now in Conwy.

3   *Liverpool Echo*, 25 July 1939.

4   By October 1939 the council was facing severe financial problems and a subcommittee was set up to investigate. It did not take long for them to observe that one reason might have been their own profligacy: 'the finance committee had passed 72 bills amounting in all to £1,370 in 15 minutes' (*Manchester Evening News*, 19 October 1939). The investigation changed little as, with laudable but hopelessly naive optimism, they continued to pour money into a publicity campaign for the summer 1940 holiday season.

5   *Manchester Evening News*, 11 July 1939.

6   *Flintshire County Herald*, 7 July 1939.

7   British Listed Buildings, *www.britishlistedbuildings.co.uk*.

8   *Rhyl Journal*, 9 October 1909.

9   Baker, Mark, *Gwrych Castle: An Official Guide*, Gwrych Castle Preservation Trust, 2018.

10   *Western Mail*, 25 July 1939.

11   *Birmingham Daily Post*, 9 August 1939.

12   Equivalent to about £13,000 at the time of writing using the Bank of England Inflation Calculator, *www.bankofengland.co.uk/monetary-policy/inflation/inflation-calculator*.

13   German annexation of Austria in March 1938.

14   Emigration to *Eretz Yisrael*, the land of Israel.

15   Agricultural collectives.

16   There were a number of these centres: one near Frankfurt; Schniebinchen in what is now Poland; Landwerk Neuendorf in Steinhöfel, near Berlin; Fraustadt in Posen; and Altona-Blankenese near Hamburg. Several of the youngsters who would finally arrive

at Gwrych Castle had experience of the Alton-Blankenese *Vorbereitungslager*.

17 'Arieh Handler', *The Jewish Chronicle*, 8 July 2011 at *pressreader. com*.

18 Lipczer, Jonny, 'Tributes to Arieh Handler', *The Jewish Chronicle*, 23 May 2011.

19 Lipczer, Jonny, 'Tributes to Arieh Handler', *The Jewish Chronicle*, 23 May 2011.

20 Handler, Julius, letter to Mrs Williams, 16 January 1981, author's collection.

21 Eichmann was a key instigator of the 'Final Solution' known as the Holocaust. He escaped Germany in 1945 but was hunted down by Mossad, Israel's intelligence agency, in Argentina in 1960. He was taken to Israel to stand charges of crimes against humanity, found guilty and executed by hanging on 1 June 1962.

22 'This Day in Jewish History. 2011: Leader of Religious Zionism in UK Dies', *Haaretz*, 19 May 2014.

23 *Nottingham Journal*, 11 November 1938.

24 A maximum age of seventeen was stipulated.

25 The equivalent of over £2,000 today.

26 No suggestion of limits to the numbers was made by the British government. Youth *Aliyah* hoped to move 1,000, but many Jewish refugee agencies thought that around 5,000 might be a realistic goal. As testament to their combined efforts, the final number would be double that.

27 The following day, the Nazis held a nationwide 'day of solidarity'. Jews were ordered to stay off the streets between noon and 8 p.m. because, according to Himmler, Head of the SS, they had 'no share in the solidarity of the German nation'.

28 A number of additional children were picked up from Hamburg along the way.

29 The Nazis did not object to the Kindertransport, but refused to assist. The Hook of Holland was used as the Nazis would not allow German ports to be used.

30 The equivalent of over £20 million today at the time of writing (Bank of England Inflation Calculator).

31 Frazer, Jenni, 'On the Brink', article from *The Jewish Chronicle*,

issue and date unknown, quoting Sam Goldsmith, a British-based correspondent for *Haboker*, the most widely circulated Hebrew newspaper in Palestine at the time.

32 *Chayenu*, Organ of the *Torah Va'Avodah* Movement and *Brit Chalutzim Dati'im* of Western Europe, Vol. II, No. 2, February–March 1940.

33 By the end of 1939, *Bachad* had 570 of its members resident in a training centre. A third of them would be at Gwrych Castle.

34 *Chayenu*, Organ of the *Torah Va'Avodah* Movement and *Brit Chalutzim Dati'im* of Western Europe, Vol. I, No. 2, November–December 1939.

35 Golan, Ester, *Auf Wiedersehen in unserem Land*, Econ, 1995.

36 Sperber, Miriam, *Grandmother's Tales: An Autobiography*, Imrei Shefer Publications, 1990.

37 Sperber, Miriam, *Grandmother's Tales: An Autobiography*, Imrei Shefer Publications, 1990.

38 Handler, Julius, letter to Mrs Williams, 16 January 1981, author's collection.

39 It is not known which three rooms they were, but the chapel was likely to have been one of them. Three outbuildings had also been earmarked for storage and were thus also inaccessible.

40 His name is also given in several sources as Granck, Gornich or Garnick, but his real name, as it appears in the civil registration of marriages and deaths, was Granek.

41 *Flintshire County Herald*, 31 March 1939. Work stopped shortly afterwards when it was realised that the caves were too far away, and too difficult to get to in the event of a genuine raid.

42 Handler, Arieh, Imperial War Museum oral history sound files, interview recorded with Lyn E. Smith, September 2002, catalogue number 23830.

43 According to the testimony of James Burke, who later volunteered for work at Gwrych Castle, quoted in Roper, Erich, in Various authors, *Sefer ha-shanah, Gwrych Castle Yearbook*, Jewish Agency for Israel, Youth *Aliyah* Department, September 1940.

44 Various authors, *Sefer ha-shanah, Gwrych Castle Yearbook*, Jewish Agency for Israel, Youth *Aliyah* Department, September 1940.

45 Leverton, Bertha and Lowensohn, Shmuel, *I Came Alone: The*

Stories of the Kindertransports, The Book Guild Ltd, 1990.

46 Leverton, Bertha and Lowensohn, Shmuel, *I Came Alone: The Stories of the Kindertransports*, The Book Guild Ltd, 1990.

47 Rothman, Herman, Imperial War Museum oral history sound file, interview recorded with Peter Hart, February 2008, catalogue number 30627.

48 He was arrested and sent to Sachsenhausen concentration camp in October 1939.

49 Rothman, Herman, Imperial War Museum oral history sound file, interview recorded with Peter Hart, February 2008, catalogue number 30627.

50 Rothman, Herman, Imperial War Museum oral history sound file, interview recorded with Peter Hart, February 2008, catalogue number 30627.

51 Rothman, Herman, Imperial War Museum oral history sound file, interview recorded with Peter Hart, February 2008, catalogue number 30627.

52 Family anecdote related to the author by Ariel Roper, son of Erich Roper.

53 Bingham, Walter, *www.bauk.org/1936-1939/*.

54 'Walter Bingham at 91', *The Jerusalem Post*, 22 January 2015.

55 Bingham, Walter, formerly Wolfgang Billig, interview with Cross Rhythms Radio, 28 July 2018.

56 Walter Bingham, formerly Wolfgang Billig, interview with Cross Rhythms Radio, 28 July 2018.

57 Bingham, Walter, *www.bauk.org/1936-1939/*.

58 As he would later be called; he was Isi Gewurtz at the time.

59 Steinberg, Henry, unpublished autobiography.

60 Steinberg, Henry, Shoah Project, interview, August 1996.

61 Steinberg, Henry, unpublished autobiography.

62 Steinberg, Henry, unpublished autobiography.

63 Steinberg, Henry, unpublished autobiography.

64 Edelnand, John, 'There's a Welcome in the Hillside', *Abergele Field Club and Historical Society Review* No. 6, 1987.

65 Edelnand, John, 'There's a Welcome in the Hillside', *Abergele Field Club and Historical Society Review* No. 6, 1987.

66 Findling, Osias, Holocaust Survivors Centre Interviews, Jewish

survivors of the Holocaust, interview recorded with Gillian van Gelder, British Library, July 2000.

67 'Survivors Recall Fleeing Nazis in Holocaust', *www.cbsnews.com/news/ survivors-recall-kindertransport-flight-from-nazis*, 2 December 2013.

68 'Survivors Recall Fleeing Nazis in Holocaust', *www.cbsnews.com/news/ survivors-recall-kindertransport-flight-from-nazis*, 2 December 2013.

69 Findling, Osias, Holocaust Survivors Centre Interviews, Jewish survivors of the Holocaust, interview recorded with Gillian van Gelder, British Library, July 2000.

70 Glanz, Henry, 'The Kindertransport with Herman Rothman and Henry Glanz', *Dan Snow's History Hit Podcast*, BBC, January 2019.

71 Alweiss, Manfred, *Kindertransport Newsletter*, April 2006. Alweiss later anglicised his name to Manfred Wildman and joined the British Army. He became a British citizen in 1947 and lived in Purley, Surrey.

72 Alweiss, Manfred, *Kindertransport Newsletter*, April 2006.

73 Alweiss, Manfred, *Kindertransport Newsletter*, April 2006.

74 Alweiss, Manfred, *Kindertransport Newsletter*, April 2006.

75 Alweiss, Manfred, *Kindertransport Newsletter*, April 2006.

76 Findling, Osias, Holocaust Survivors Centre Interviews, Jewish survivors of the Holocaust, interview recorded with Gillian van Gelder, British Library, July 2000.

77 Alweiss, Manfred, *Kindertransport Newsletter*, April 2006.

78 Duchinsky, Erich, quoted in Turner, Barry, ... *And the Policeman Smiled: 10,000 Children Escape from Nazi Europe*, Bloomsbury Publishing plc, new edition, 1991. The caretaker at Gwrych was Bill Price. As the castle was empty at the time, this was something of a 'non-job' and his main work was being a forester on the estate.

79 Seligmann, Erwin, letter, Wiener Library, document 1372/1/53.

80 Alweiss, Manfred, *Kindertransport Newsletter*, April 2006.

81 Alweiss, Manfred, *Kindertransport Newsletter*, April 2006.

82 *Abergele Visitor*, 9 September 1939.

83 'Good morning, little boy. How are you today?'

84 Edelnand, John, 'There's a Welcome in the Hillside', *Abergele Field Club and Historical Society Review* No. 6, 1987.

85 Rothman, Herman, *Imperial War Museum oral history sound file*,

interview recorded with Peter Hart, February 2008, catalogue number 30627.

86 Leverton, Bertha and Lowensohn, Shmuel, *I Came Alone: The Stories of the Kindertransports*, The Book Guild Ltd, 1990. The castle was actually only just over 100 years old at the time, but Zierler was not to know that.

87 Bingham, Walter, 'Walter Bingham, formerly Wolfgang Billig', interview with Cross Rhythms Radio, 28 July 2018.

88 Bingham, Walter, *www.bauk.org/1936-1939/*.

89 Wincelburg (née Kreisel), Celia, USC Shoah Project, interview, October 1999.

90 Kessel, Ruth, in Kon, Helen, *The Book of Ruth: The Journey of a Kindertransport Teenager*, Helemy, 2014.

91 Better (née Marder), Sonia, USC Shoah Project, interview, August 1996.

92 Bingham, Walter, *www.bauk.org/1936-1939/*.

93 Roper, Erich (Yis'akhar Roper), Braun, Willy (Ze'ev Hayim Broyn), Liwerant, Bernhard (Binyamin Liverant), editors, *Da'at ha-hevrah,* 2 February 1940. Translation from the Hebrew by Ariel Roper, translation from the German by the author.

94 Kessel, Ruth, in Kon, Helen, *The Book of Ruth: The Journey of a Kindertransport Teenager*, Helemy, 2014.

95 *Abergele Visitor*, 9 September 1939.

96 Rothman, Herman, Imperial War Museum oral history sound file, interview recorded with Peter Hart, February 2008, catalogue number 30627.

97 Seligmann, Erwin, letter, Wiener Library, document 1372/1/53.

98 Glasser, Ruth, quoted in Wynne Williams, E., 'Jewish Refugees at Gwrych Castle', *Abergele Field Club and Historical Society Review* No. 1, 1982.

99 Seligmann, Erwin, in Various authors, *Sefer ha-shanah, Gwrych Castle Yearbook*, Jewish Agency for Israel, Youth *Aliyah* Department, 1940.

100 Bingham, Walter, *www.bauk.org/1936-1939/*.

101 Seligmann, Erwin, Wiener Library, document 1372/1/53.

102 Alweiss, Manfred, *Kindertransport Newsletter*, April 2006.

103 Steinberg, Henry, Shoah Project, interview, August 1996.

104 Today known as *Habonim Dror*. This is their own definition: *www. habodror.org.uk/about-us/*.

105 Sperber, Miriam, *Grandmother's Tales: An Autobiography*, Imrei Shefer Publications, 1990.

106 *The Jewish Chronicle*, 27 September 1940.

107 For example, in December 1939, Smith would attend a conference of leading Zionist educators concerned about the paucity of Jewish education for young Jews in Britain. When the discussion moved on to the 2–3,000 young Jews who would spend the winter in camps across Britain such as those at Gwrych Castle, Smith proposed the need for Zionist youth groups to act together in union, arguing that the various movements 'should lay aside the many and important differences of function which divide them and concentrate on building a solid foundation for future work.' His proposals were agreed upon.

108 *The Jewish Chronicle*, 27 September 1940.

109 Glanz, Henry, interview with the author, December 2020.

110 Glanz, Henry, interview with the author, December 2020.

111 Steinberg, Henry, Shoah Project, interview, August 1996.

112 Kessel, Ruth, in Kon, Helen, *The Book of Ruth: The Journey of a Kindertransport Teenager*, Helemy, 2014.

113 Sperber, Miriam, *Grandmother's Tales: An Autobiography*, Imrei Shefer Publications, 1990.

114 Findling, Osias, Holocaust Survivors Centre Interviews, Jewish survivors of the Holocaust, interview recorded with Gillian van Gelder, July 2000, British Library.

115 Sperber, Miriam, *Grandmother's Tales: An Autobiography*, Imrei Shefer Publications, 1990.

116 That part of Ukraine had been incorporated into the Russian Empire in 1793, before gaining independence in 1991.

117 Sperber, Miriam, *Grandmother's Tales: An Autobiography*, Imrei Shefer Publications, 1990.

118 Nead, Debbie, daughter of Julius Handler, in conversation with the author.

119 The term *chaverim* is a rather loose one, meaning friend, member or helper. In that regard, all members of the Gwrych *Hachshara* were *chaverim*, though it will be used here as a term specifically

for the adult volunteers as a way of distinguishing them from the children, the *noar*, under the age of eighteen.

120 Findling, Osias, Holocaust Survivors Centre Interviews, Jewish survivors of the Holocaust, interview recorded with Gillian van Gelder, British Library, July 2000.

121 Ferber married Rebekka Igelfeld in Hackney in the spring of 1944 and the pair emigrated 26 October 1947. He became a naturalised US citizen in May 1953 whilst living on Broadway, New York, and changed his name from Salomon to Solomon. He died in New York, 23 November 1994.

122 Glanz, Henry, interview with the author, December 2020.

123 Glanz, Henry, interview with the author, December 2020.

124 *Liverpool Daily Post*, 18 September 1939.

125 Handler, Julius, letter to Mrs Williams, 16 January 1981, author's collection.

126 *Daily Mirror*, 12 October 1939.

127 Edelnand, John, 'There's a Welcome in the Hillside', *Abergele Field Club and Historical Society Review* No. 6, 1987.

128 Spergel, Baruch, Voice/Vision Holocaust Survivor Oral History Archive, University of Michigan, interview with Zivla Fischler and Baruch Spergel, February 2008.

129 Seligmann, Erwin, letter, Wiener Library, document 1372/1/53.

130 Various authors, *Sefer ha-shanah, Gwrych Castle Yearbook*, Jewish Agency for Israel, Youth *Aliyah* Department, 1940.

131 Rothman, Herman, Imperial War Museum oral history sound file, interview recorded with Peter Hart, February 2008, catalogue number 30627.

132 Lovenheim, Barbara, *Perilous Journeys: Personal Stories of German and Austrian Jews Who Escaped the Nazis*, Center for Holocaust Awareness and Information, 2001.

133 Lovenheim, Barbara, *Perilous Journeys: Personal Stories of German and Austrian Jews Who Escaped the Nazis*, Center for Holocaust Awareness and Information, 2001.

134 Lovenheim, Barbara, *Perilous Journeys: Personal Stories of German and Austrian Jews Who Escaped the Nazis*, Center for Holocaust Awareness and Information, 2001.

135 Lovenheim, Barbara, *Perilous Journeys: Personal Stories of German*

and Austrian Jews Who Escaped the Nazis, Center for Holocaust Awareness and Information, 2001.

136 Seligmann, Erwin, letter, Wiener Library, document 1372/1/53.

137 Both terms appear in the 1939 Register, though as a reflection of the prevailing views on gender some of the boys were called 'students'. The girls were always called 'trainees'.

138 Benjamin, Alfred, *Journey to Self: A True Story*, XLibris Corporation, 2005.

139 *Chayenu*, Organ of the *Torah Va'Avodah* Movement and *Brit Chalutzim Dati'im* of Western Europe, Vol. I, No. 2, November–December 1939.

140 Roper, Erich, and Various authors, *Sefer ha-shanah, Gwrych Castle Yearbook*, Jewish Agency for Israel, Youth *Aliyah* Department, September 1940.

141 Roper, Erich, and Various authors, *Sefer ha-shanah, Gwrych Castle Yearbook*, Jewish Agency for Israel, Youth *Aliyah* Department, September 1940.

142 Handler, Julius, letter to Mrs Williams, 16 January 1981, author's collection.

143 *Pluga* (or sometimes *kvutzot*) is the singular form, *plugoth* when plural.

144 Rothman, Herman, Imperial War Museum oral history sound file, interview recorded with Peter Hart, February 2008, catalogue number 30627.

145 Bingham, Walter, *www.bauk.org/1936-1939/*.

146 Various authors, *Sefer ha-shanah, Gwrych Castle Yearbook*, Jewish Agency for Israel, Youth *Aliyah* Department, 1940.

147 Drellich (née Heisler-Lieberman), Erika, USC Shoah Project, interview, August 2000.

148 Sperber, Miriam, *Grandmother's Tales: An Autobiography*, Imrei Shefer Publications, 1990.

149 Sperber, Miriam, *Grandmother's Tales: An Autobiography*, Imrei Shefer Publications, 1990.

150 Seligmann, Erwin, letter, Wiener Library, document 1372/1/53.

151 Glanz, Henry, interview with the author, December 2020.

152 *North Wales Weekly News*, 2 May 1940.

153 Kessel, Ruth, in Kon, Helen, *The Book of Ruth: The Journey of a*

Kindertransport Teenager, Helemy, 2014.

154 Braun, Wilhelm, Oral History Project, Jewish Community of Rochester, New York, January 1977, interview with Dennis Klein (transcript).

155 Sperber, Miriam, *Grandmother's Tales: An Autobiography*, Imrei Shefer Publications, 1990.

156 Bingham, Walter, *www.bauk.org/1936-1939/*.

157 Erich Roper also spent much of his time on forestry work around the Gwrych estate.

158 Ormond, Mimi, United States Holocaust Memorial Museum Collection, Gift of the National Council of Jewish Women, Cleveland Section, interview with Minda Jaffe, 1985, Accession Number: 1993.A.0087.37.

159 Sperber, Miriam, *Grandmother's Tales: An Autobiography*, Imrei Shefer Publications, 1990. This account does raise the question as to why, according to Billig, the role of looking after the lamps was 'a sought-after job'.

160 Various authors, *Sefer ha-shanah, Gwrych Castle Yearbook*, Jewish Agency for Israel, Youth *Aliyah* Department, 1940.

161 Various authors, *Sefer ha-shanah, Gwrych Castle Yearbook*, Jewish Agency for Israel, Youth *Aliyah* Department, 1940.

162 Bingham, Walter, *www.bauk.org/1936-1939/*.

163 Bingham, Walter, *www.bauk.org/1936-1939/*.

164 He emigrated to the USA in February 1940, citing his occupation as carpenter.

165 Various authors, *Sefer ha-shanah, Gwrych Castle Yearbook*, Jewish Agency for Israel, Youth *Aliyah* Department, 1940.

166 Bingham, Walter, *www.bauk.org/1936-1939/*.

167 Various authors, *Sefer ha-shanah, Gwrych Castle Yearbook*, Jewish Agency for Israel, Youth *Aliyah* Department, 1940.

168 Various authors, *Sefer ha-shanah, Gwrych Castle Yearbook*, Jewish Agency for Israel, Youth *Aliyah* Department, 1940.

169 Wincelburg (née Kreisel), Celia, USC Shoah Project, interview, October 1999.

170 Better (née Marder), Sonia, USC Shoah Project, interview, August 1996.

171 Seligmann, Erwin, letter, Wiener Library, document 1372/1/53.

172   See later for a possible explanation of this conundrum many years later.

173   Ormond, Mimi, United States Holocaust Memorial Museum Collection, Gift of the National Council of Jewish Women, Cleveland Section, interview with Minda Jaffe, 1985, Accession Number: 1993.A.0087.37.

174   Sperber, Miriam, *Grandmother's Tales: An Autobiography*, Imrei Shefer Publications, 1990.

175   Dr Mark Baker of the Gwrych Preservation Trust has explained that the water pump, when installed, was an extremely efficient model.

176   Seligmann, Erwin, letter, Wiener Library, document 1372/1/53.

177   Various authors, *Sefer ha-shanah, Gwrych Castle Yearbook*, Jewish Agency for Israel, Youth *Aliyah* Department, 1940.

178   Sperber, Miriam, *Grandmother's Tales: An Autobiography*, Imrei Shefer Publications, 1990.

179   Sperber, Miriam, *Grandmother's Tales: An Autobiography*, Imrei Shefer Publications, 1990.

180   Bingham, Walter, quoted in *The Jewish Chronicle*, 'The *I'm a Celebrity* castle's secret role in the Kindertransport', 26 November 2020.

181   *North Wales Weekly News*, 2 May 1940.

182   Sperber, Miriam, *Grandmother's Tales: An Autobiography*, Imrei Shefer Publications, 1990.

183   Various authors, *Sefer ha-shanah, Gwrych Castle Yearbook*, Jewish Agency for Israel, Youth *Aliyah* Department, 1940.

184   Various authors, *Sefer ha-shanah, Gwrych Castle Yearbook*, Jewish Agency for Israel, Youth *Aliyah* Department, 1940.

185   Findling, Osias, Holocaust Survivors Centre Interviews, Jewish survivors of the Holocaust, interview recorded with Gillian van Gelder, July 2000, British Library. Note: David Gestetner invented the first effective duplicating machine, a forerunner of the photocopier. Findling had presumably confused David Gestetner with his son Sigmund, as David had died in March 1939. Sigmund Gestetner was noted for, amongst other things, his generosity towards Jewish refugees who had fled Nazi Germany.

186   Later Baron Sieff (1966) and chair of Marks and Spencer 1964–67.

187 Handler, Julius, letter to Mrs Williams, 16 January 1981, author's collection.

188 Roper, Erich, in Various authors, *Sefer ha-shanah, Gwrych Castle Yearbook*, Jewish Agency for Israel, Youth *Aliyah* Department, 1940.

189 Seligmann, Erwin, letter, Wiener Library, document 1372/1/53.

190 Seligmann, Erwin, letter, Wiener Library, document 1372/1/53.

191 Steinberg, Henry, Shoah Project, interview, August 1996.

192 Handler, Arieh, Imperial War Museum oral history sound files, interview recorded with Lyn E. Smith, September 2002, catalogue number 23830.

193 At the same tribunal that day were three other Jews from the Abergele area: Maria Frommer, a sixty-two-year-old journalist and Romanian by birth, who lived at Parc Bungalow, St George; Veronika Gottlieb, aged sixty-two, of Kinmel Hall, St George; Ruth Glasser, aged nineteen, a domestic servant at Hendre Bach, Abergele, and a regular visitor at the castle. All were categorised class C.

194 The category B decisions are hard to explain except by assuming that the Caernarfon tribunal was still 'finding its feet' in October 1939 and that it may have been a little trigger-happy at first. Sir John Anderson, the Home Secretary, was pressed on the issue of regional variations in Parliament in November 1939 and replied that 'it is difficult, if not impossible, to ensure an absolute uniformity of standard; but very careful instructions were issued to the tribunals in the first instance and steps are being taken as far as possible by personal contact to ensure that the practice will conform to a reasonable standard.' Hansard, 2 November 1939, vol. 352 cc2094–6.

195 Better (née Marder), Sonia, USC Shoah Project, interview, August 1996.

196 Rothman, Herman, Imperial War Museum oral history sound file, interview recorded with Peter Hart, February 2008, catalogue number 30627.

197 Glanz, Henry, interview with the author, January 2021.

198 Steinberg, Henry, unpublished autobiography.

199 Steinberg, Henry, unpublished autobiography.

200 Roper, Erich (Yis'akhar Roper), Braun, Willy (Ze'ev Hayim Broyn), Liwerant, Bernhard (Binyamin Liverant), editors, *Da'at ha-hevrah*, 2 February 1940.

201 Glanz, Henry. Interview with the author, January 2021. The attack, on German shipping in the Kiel Canal, had happened on 17 September 1939.

202 Glanz, Henry, interview with the author, December 2020.

203 Steinberg, Henry, Shoah Project, interview, August 1996.

204 Findling, Osias, Holocaust Survivors Centre Interviews, Jewish survivors of the Holocaust, interview recorded with Gillian van Gelder, July 2000, British Library.

205 Friedenfeld, Gerard, Kindertransport Association Oral History Project Interview, November 13, 1993.

206 Glanz, Henry, interview with the author, December 2020.

207 Wolfisz, Francine, '*The Children who found safety in the I'm a Celebrity… Castle*', *Jewish News*, 19 November 2020.

208 Moses Mendelssohn Akademie, Internationale Begegnungsstatte Halberstadt.

209 Emde, Constanze, *Ein Kieler Jude erinnert sich (A Kiel Jew remembers)*, shz.de 27 January 2014.

210 Rothman, Herman, Imperial War Museum oral history sound file, interview recorded with Peter Hart, February 2008, catalogue number 30627.

211 Friedenfeld, Gerard, Kindertransport Association Oral History Project Interview, November 13, 1993.

212 Glanz, Henry, interview with the author January 2021.

213 Drellich (née Heisler-Lieberman), Erika, USC Shoah Project, interview, August 2000.

214 Steinberg, Henry, unpublished autobiography.

215 Her name has not been included here, as requested by Henry Glanz, to preserve her anonymity.

216 *Konzenstrationslager*, which translates to concentration camp.

217 Glanz, Henry, email to the author, 2020.

218 Various authors, *Sefer ha-shanah, Gwrych Castle Yearbook*, Jewish Agency for Israel, Youth *Aliyah* Department, 1940.

219 Leverton, Bertha and Lowensohn, Shmuel, *I Came Alone: The Stories of the Kindertransports*, The Book Guild Ltd, 1990.

220 Glanz, Henry, interview with the author, December 2020.

221 Although this was some time later, Colwyn Bay Social Services donated items of sports equipment in May 1940, including tennis balls and some golf clubs.

222 Glanz, Henry, interview with the author, December 2020.

223 *Abergele Visitor*, 21 October 1939.

224 Roper, Erich (Yis'akhar Roper), Braun, Willy (Ze'ev Hayim Broyn), Liwerant, Bernhard (Binyamin Liverant), editors, *Da'at ha-hevrah*, 2 February 1940. In Hebrew, German and English. Translation from the Hebrew by Ariel Roper, translation from the German by the author.

225 Rothman, Herman, Imperial War Museum oral history sound file, interview recorded with Peter Hart, February 2008, catalogue number 30627.

226 Wynne Williams, E., 'Jewish Refugees at Gwrych Castle', *Abergele Field Club and Historical Society Review* No. 1, 1982.

227 Kessel, Ruth, in Kon, Helen, *The Book of Ruth: The Journey of a Kindertransport Teenager*, Helemy, 2014.

228 Rothman, Herman 'The Kindertransport with Herman Rothman and Henry Glanz', *Dan Snow's History Hit* podcast, BBC, January 2019.

229 Rose, Aubrey, *Arieh Handler: Modest Jewish Hero*, Lennard Publishing, 2010.

230 Rose, Aubrey, *Arieh Handler: Modest Jewish Hero*, Lennard Publishing, 2010.

231 Rose, Aubrey, *Arieh Handler: Modest Jewish Hero*, Lennard Publishing, 2010.

232 Rose, Aubrey, *Arieh Handler: Modest Jewish Hero*, Lennard Publishing, 2010.

233 Rose, Aubrey, *Arieh Handler: Modest Jewish Hero*, Lennard Publishing, 2010.

234 Glanz, Henry, interview with the author, December 2020.

235 Glanz, Henry, interview with the author, December 2020.

236 *Chayenu*, Organ of the *Torah Va'Avodah* Movement and *Brit Chalutzim Dati'im* of Western Europe, Vol. I, No. 2, November–December 1939.

237 Sperber, Miriam, *Grandmother's Tales: An Autobiography*, Imrei Shefer Publications, 1990.

238 Rothman, Herman, Imperial War Museum oral history sound file, interview recorded with Peter Hart, February 2008, catalogue number 30627.

239 Handler, Arieh, Imperial War Museum oral history sound files, interview recorded with Lyn E. Smith, September 2002, catalogue number 23830.

240 Sperber, Miriam, *Grandmother's Tales: An Autobiography*, Imrei Shefer Publications, 1990.

241 Handler, Julius, letter to Mrs Williams, 16 January 1981, author's collection.

242 Glanz, Henry, interview with the author, January 2021.

243 *Ein brief von seiner erwürden Herrn Dr J. H. Hertz, Oberrabbiner Gross Britanniens*, a leaflet given to all Kindertransport children upon arrival in Britain.

244 Handler, Julius, letter to Mrs Williams, 16 January 1981, author's collection.

245 *Chayenu*, Organ of the *Torah Va'Avodah* Movement and *Brit Chalutzim Dati'im* of Western Europe, Vol. I, No. 2, November–December 1939.

246 Part of the Gwrych estate.

247 Wynne Williams, E., 'Jewish Refugees at Gwrych Castle', *Abergele Field Club and Historical Society Review* No. 1, 1982.

248 The equivalent of £28,000 at the time of writing.

249 *North Wales Weekly News*, 11 January 1940.

250 *Liverpool Daily Post*, 8 January 1940.

251 *North Wales Weekly News*, 11 January 1940.

252 *Abergele Visitor*, 13 January 1940.

253 The equivalent of £280 at the time of writing.

254 Griffiths, Robert J., *The War Years, Personal Memories of Pensarn and the Abergele Area, 1939–45*, self-published, year unknown.

255 *Liverpool Daily Post*, 20 November 1939.

256 *Liverpool Daily Post*, 18 December 1939 and *Edinburgh Evening News*, 4 December 1939.

257 *Liverpool Daily Post*, 6 November 1939.

258 *Abergele Visitor*, 12 April 1941.

259 *Abergele Visitor*, 22 February 1941.

260 *Abergele Visitor*, 30 March 1940.

261 *Abergele Visitor*, 30 March 1940.

262 *Abergele Visitor*, 20 July 1940.

263 *Abergele Visitor*, 20 July 1940.

264 *Abergele Visitor*, 20 July 1940.

265 *Abergele Visitor*, 20 July 1940.

266 *Abergele Visitor*, 20 July 1940.

267 Roper, Erich (Yis'akhar Roper), Braun, Willy (Ze'ev Hayim Broyn), Liwerant, Bernhard (Binyamin Liverant), editors, *Da'at ha-hevrah*, 2 February 1940.

268 *Liverpool Daily Post*, 1 January 1940.

269 Handler, Julius, letter to Mrs Williams, 16 January 1981, author's collection.

270 Sperber, Miriam, *Grandmother's Tales: An Autobiography*, Imrei Shefer Publications, 1990.

271 Sperber, Miriam, *Grandmother's Tales: An Autobiography*, Imrei Shefer Publications, 1990.

272 Sperber, Miriam, *Grandmother's Tales: An Autobiography*, Imrei Shefer Publications, 1990.

273 *The Jewish Chronicle*, 3 May 1940.

274 Edelnand, John, 'There's a Welcome in the Hillside', *Abergele Field Club and Historical Society Review* No. 6, 1987.

275 *The Jewish Chronicle*, 5 January 1940. Solomon Eleazer Sklan was the father of Jack Sklan, the founder member of *Bnei Akiva* in Britain. To contextualise this and other donations, £100 in 1940 is roughly the equivalent of £5,600 in 2019.

276 Bank of England Inflation Calculator, *www.bankofengland.co.uk/ monetary-policy/inflation/inflation-calculator*.

277 Roper, Erich (Yis'akhar Roper), Braun, Willy (Ze'ev Hayim Broyn), Liwerant, Bernhard (Binyamin Liverant), editors, *Da'at ha-hevrah*, 2 February 1940.

278 The slogan had been introduced in 1935.

279 Kessel, Ruth, in Kon, Helen, *The Book of Ruth: The Journey of a Kindertransport Teenager*, Helemy, 2014.

280 Glanz, Henry, interview with the author, December 2020.

281 Edelnand, John, 'There's a Welcome in the Hillside', *Abergele Field Club and Historical Society Review* No. 6, 1987.

282 *North Wales Weekly News*, 1 February 1940.

283 *North Wales Weekly News*, 1 February 1940.

284 Better (née Marder), Sonia, USC Shoah Project, interview, August 1996.

285 Better (née Marder), Sonia, USC Shoah Project, interview, August 1996.

286 *North Wales Weekly News*, 2 May 1940.

287 Leverton, Bertha and Lowensohn, Shmuel, *I Came Alone: The Stories of the Kindertransports*, The Book Guild Ltd, 1990.

288 Roper, Erich (Yis'akhar Roper), Braun, Willy (Ze'ev Hayim Broyn), Liwerant, Bernhard (Binyamin Liverant), editors, *Da'at ha-ḥevrah*, 2 February 1940.

289 Roper, Erich (Yis'akhar Roper), Braun, Willy (Ze'ev Hayim Broyn), Liwerant, Bernhard (Binyamin Liverant), editors, *Da'at ha-ḥevrah*, 2 February 1940.

290 Many more games followed over the next twelve months though, sadly, no details survive other than a comment in the year book of September 1940 that the team began playing well beyond the town of Abergele.

291 Roper, Erich (Yis'akhar Roper), Braun, Willy (Ze'ev Ḥayim Broyn), Liwerant, Bernhard (Binyamin Liveraṇt), editors, *Da'at ha-ḥevrah*, 2 February 1940.

292 Roper, Erich (Yis'akhar Roper), Braun, Willy (Ze'ev Ḥayim Broyn), Liwerant, Bernhard (Binyamin Liveraṇt), editors, *Da'at ha-ḥevrah*, 2 February 1940.

293 Handler, Julius, letter to Mrs Williams, 16 January 1981, author's collection.

294 Roper, Erich (Yis'akhar Roper), Braun, Willy (Ze'ev Hayim Broyn), Liwerant, Bernhard (Binyamin Liverant), editors, *Da'at ha-ḥevrah*, 2 February 1940.

295 Roper, Erich (Yis'akhar Roper), Braun, Willy (Ze'ev Hayim Broyn), Liwerant, Bernhard (Binyamin Liverant), editors, *Da'at ha-ḥevrah*, 2 February 1940.

296 Roper, Erich (Yis'akhar Roper), Braun, Willy (Ze'ev Hayim Broyn), Liwerant, Bernhard (Binyamin Liverant), editors, *Da'at ha-ḥevrah*, 2 February 1940.

297 Roper, Erich (Yis'akhar Roper), Braun, Willy (Ze'ev Hayim Broyn), Liwerant, Bernhard (Binyamin Liverant), editors, *Da'at

ha-ḥevrah, 2 February 1940. Subsequent quotations relating to the Kongress are from the same source.

298 Roper, Erich (Yis'akhar Roper), Braun, Willy (Ze'ev Hayim Broyn), Liwerant, Bernhard (Binyamin Liverant), editors, *Da'at ha-ḥevrah*, 2 February 1940.

299 Roper, Erich (Yis'akhar Roper), Braun, Willy (Ze'ev Hayim Broyn), Liwerant, Bernhard (Binyamin Liverant), editors, *Da'at ha-ḥevrah*, 26 May 1940.

300 Herman Rothman, Imperial War Museum oral history sound file, interview recorded with Peter Hart, February 2008, catalogue number 30627.

301 *Chayenu*, Organ of the *Torah Va'Avodah* Movement and *Brit Chalutzim Dati'im* of Western Europe, Vol. II, No. 2, February–March 1940.

302 *Chayenu*, Organ of the *Torah Va'Avodah* Movement and *Brit Chalutzim Dati'im* of Western Europe, Vol. II, No. 2, February–March 1940.

303 *Chayenu*, Organ of the *Torah Va'Avodah* Movement and *Brit Chalutzim Dati'im* of Western Europe, Vol. II, No. 2, February–March 1940.

304 Roper, Erich (Yis'akhar Roper), Braun, Willy (Ze'ev Hayim Broyn), Liwerant, Bernhard (Binyamin Liverant), editors, *Da'at ha-ḥevrah*, 2 February 1940.

305 Baumel-Schwartz, J. T., *Never Look Back: The Jewish Refugee Children in Great Britain, 1938–1945*, Shofar Supplements in Jewish Studies, Purdue University Press, 2012.

306 Rothman, Herman, Imperial War Museum oral history sound file, interview recorded with Peter Hart, February 2008, catalogue number 30627.

307 Glanz, Henry, interview with the author, December 2020.

308 Pine, Fanny, AJR Refugee Voices Archive, Twitter feed 13 November 2020.

309 For example, see Turner, Barry, … *And the Policeman Smiled: 10,000 Children Escape from Nazi Europe*, Bloomsbury Publishing plc, new edition, 1991.

310 Dunstan, Fred, Wiener Library, 1372/1/ 8.

311 By later standards, a charge that this was child labour would be rel-

evant. However, in 1939, the school leaving age was fourteen. All Gwrych residents were fourteen or over, so the idea that they could or should work would have been perfectly normal at the time.

312 Rothman, Herman, Imperial War Museum oral history sound file, interview recorded with Peter Hart, February 2008, catalogue number 30627.

313 Henry Glanz, 'The Kindertransport with Herman Rothman and Henry Glanz', *Dan Snow's History Hit Podcast*, BBC, January 2019.

314 Edelnand, John, 'There's a Welcome in the Hillside', *Abergele Field Club and Historical Society Review* No. 6, 1987.

315 Glanz, Henry, interview with the author, January 2021.

316 Glanz, Henry, interview with the author, January 2021.

317 Bingham, Walter, *www.bauk.org/1936-1939/*.

318 Glanz, Henry, interview with the author, January 2021.

319 Glanz, Henry, interview with the author, January 2021.

320 Interview with Walter Bingham, *The Jerusalem Post*, 22 January 2015.

321 Edelnand, John, 'There's a Welcome in the Hillside', *Abergele Field Club and Historical Society Review* No. 6, 1987.

322 Handler, Julius, letter to Mrs Williams, 16 January 1981, author's collection.

323 *North Wales Weekly News*, 2 May 1940.

324 *North Wales Weekly News*, 2 May 1940.

325 Ruth Glasser would marry a local man and, as Mrs Ruth Jones, ended up living in Pentrefoelas.

326 *North Wales Weekly News*, 2 May 1940.

327 *North Wales Weekly News*, 2 May 1940.

328 *North Wales Weekly News*, 2 May 1940.

329 *North Wales Weekly News*, 2 May 1940.

330 Unfortunately, whether that offer was taken up, or what the youngsters made of such a totally alien sport, remains a mystery.

331 *North Wales Weekly News*, 23 May 1940, and *Abergele Visitor*, 25 May 1940.

332 Braun, Wilhelm, Oral History Project, Jewish Community of Rochester, New York, January 1977, interview with Dennis Klein (transcript).

333 Braun, Wilhelm, Oral History Project, Jewish Community of

Rochester, New York, January 1977, interview with Dennis Klein (transcript).

334 Glanz, Henry, interview with the author, December 2020.

335 Kessel, Ruth, in Kon, Helen, *The Book of Ruth: The Journey of a Kindertransport Teenager*, Helemy, 2014.

336 Edelnand, John, 'There's a Welcome in the Hillside', *Abergele Field Club and Historical Society Review* No. 6, 1987.

337 Glanz, Henry, interview with the author, January 2021.

338 Glanz, Henry, interview with the author, January 2021.

339 Glanz, Henry, interview with the author, December 2020.

340 Glanz, Henry, interview with the author, December 2020.

341 Hochberg (née Auskerin), Mary, USC Shoah Project, interview, May 1997.

342 Leverton, Bertha and Lowensohn, Shmuel, *I Came Alone: The Stories of the Kindertransports*, The Book Guild Ltd, 1990.

343 Glanz, Henry, interview with the author, January 2021.

344 Glanz, Henry, interview with the author, January 2021.

345 *Abergele Visitor*, 7 September 1940.

346 *Abergele Visitor*, 31 August 1940.

347 *Abergele Visitor*, 7 September 1940.

348 *Abergele Visitor*, 7 September 1940.

349 *Abergele Visitor*, 7 September 1940.

350 *Time May Change Me*, BBC, 2008.

351 Kessel, Ruth, in Kon, Helen, *The Book of Ruth: The Journey of a Kindertransport Teenager*, Helemy, 2014.

352 *Time May Change Me*, BBC, 2008.

353 Leverton, Bertha and Lowensohn, Shmuel, *I Came Alone: The Stories of the Kindertransports*, The Book Guild Ltd, 1990.

354 Leverton, Bertha and Lowensohn, Shmuel, *I Came Alone: The Stories of the Kindertransports*, The Book Guild Ltd, 1990.

355 *The Jewish Chronicle*, 1 March 1940.

356 *North Wales Weekly News*, 11 April 1940.

357 Karo Jael Pauline Gerson from Stuttgart, Germany. Often referred to as Caroline, though she preferred Pauline.

358 *Liverpool Evening Express*, 11 April 1940.

359 *Liverpool Daily Post*, 7 March 1940.

360 A group within a country who are sympathetic to, or working for,

its enemies.

361 *Abergele Visitor*, 8 June 1940.
362 *Abergele Visitor*, 8 June 1940.
363 Kessel, Ruth, in Kon, Helen, *The Book of Ruth: The Journey of a Kindertransport Teenager*, Helemy, 2014.
364 Glanz, Henry, interview with the author, January 2021.
365 Steinberg, Henry, Shoah Project, interview, August 1996.
366 Kessel, Ruth, in Kon, Helen, *The Book of Ruth: The Journey of a Kindertransport Teenager*, Helemy, 2014.
367 Edelnand, John, 'There's a Welcome in the Hillside', *Abergele Field Club and Historical Society Review* No. 6, 1987.
368 *Time May Change Me*, BBC, 2008.
369 Jones, Richard Wyn, *The Fascist Party in Wales? Plaid Cymru, Welsh Nationalism and the Accusation of Fascism*, University of Wales Press 2014.
370 It should be noted that the excellent study by Richard Wyn Jones puts such comments within a wider context. To varying degrees, antisemitism at the time was not unusual within certain sections of British society, and the views expressed by Gruffydd were certainly not ones held officially by Plaid Cymru.
371 Kessel, Ruth, in Kon, Helen, *The Book of Ruth: The Journey of a Kindertransport Teenager*, Helemy, 2014.
372 Estimated by Dr Cai Parry-Jones, email exchange with the author.
373 A further forty-four people from Abergele were fined for similar breaches during that same month.
374 Glanz, Henry, interview with the author, December 2020.
375 *Liverpool Daily Post*, 7 May 1940.
376 *Western Mail*, 7 May 1940.
377 *Abergele Visitor*, 16 March 1940.
378 *Western Mail*, 7 May 1940.
379 *Birmingham Daily Gazette*, 7 May 1940.
380 Regardless, Hargreaves and his group continued to agitate and several weeks later he got himself elected to the Education Selection Committee where he could 'vet' future employees to the teaching profession. He then turned on the Education Committee itself, accusing it of damaging the war effort by meeting in Ruthin rather than Colwyn Bay as 'it was a wicked waste of petrol … the petrol

could be better utilised in a tank or an aeroplane.' *North Wales Weekly News*, 30 May 1940.

381   Griffiths, Robert J., *The War Years, Personal Memories of Pensarn and the Abergele Area, 1939–45*, self-published, year unknown.

382   Handler, Julius, letter to Mrs Williams, 16 January 1981, author's collection.

383   Baumel-Schwartz, J. T., *Never Look Back: The Jewish Refugee Children in Great Britain, 1938–1945*, Shofar Supplements in Jewish Studies, Purdue University Press, 2012.

384   Bingham, Walter, *www.bauk.org/1936-1939/*.

385   Bingham, Walter, *www.bauk.org/1936-1939/*.

386   Handler, Julius, letter to Mrs Williams, 16 January 1981, author's collection.

387   It is curious to note that not a single local newspaper reported on the events of this time.

388   Handler, Julius, letter to Mrs Williams, 16 January 1981, author's collection.

389   Following his release from internment a year later, Schnitzer joined the Canadian Air Force and served in a bomber.

390   *The Internment of Italian Enemy Aliens, www.shapcott-family.com/mylittleitaly02/page10.html*.

391   Freier, Eli (née Dror), letter, Wiener Library 1368/2/2/29.

392   Parkinson, Alan, *From Marple to Hay and Back, www.marple-uk.com/misc/dunera.pdf*.

393   Dror, Eli (formerly Eli Freier), letter, Wiener Library 1368/2/2/29.

394   Salford Police Register of Aliens 1916–1965, Manchester Police Museum, Box 5 No 3/3063E.

395   *North Wales Weekly News*, 19 September 1940.

396   *Chayenu*, Organ of the *Torah Va'Avodah* Movement and *Brit Chalutzim Dati'im* of Western Europe, Vol. II, No. 2, February–March 1940.

397   *Chayenu*, Organ of the *Torah Va'Avodah* Movement and *Brit Chalutzim Dati'im* of Western Europe, Vol. II, No. 2, February–March 1940.

398   Findling, Osias, Holocaust Survivors Centre Interviews, Jewish survivors of the Holocaust, interview with Gillian van Gelder, July 2000, British Library.

399 Braun, Wilhelm, Oral History Project, Jewish Community of Rochester, New York, January 1977, interview with Dennis Klein (transcript).

400 Edelnand, John, letter to the author.

401 Alweiss, Manfred, *Kindertransport Newsletter*, April 2006. A *Chalutz* is a person who emigrates to Israel to work in agriculture or forestry.

402 According to the Kindertransport Survey 2007, by the Association of Jewish Refugees, a fifteen-year-old German boy left to join the Kinnersley *Hachshara* in Shropshire during July 1940 to accept paid work as a domestic servant, and also a seventeen-year-old Polish boy, an engineering student prior to Kindertransport, left in August 1940 to work at Sunan Ford Farm, in Middleton, Lancashire.

403 Friedenfeld, Gerard, Kindertransport Association Oral History Project Interview, November 13, 1993.

404 This may be the reason, but there is some debate. An alternative is that the children were removed when a nearby Canadian airbase raised concerns about potential spies within the community. I am grateful to Laura Henley for researching the Llandough centre and for offering this suggestion.

405 Friedenfeld, Gerard, Kindertransport Association Oral History Project Interview, November 13, 1993.

406 Friedenfeld, Gerard, Kindertransport Association Oral History Project Interview, November 13, 1993.

407 Friedenfeld, Gerard, Kindertransport Association Oral History Project Interview, November 13, 1993.

408 Friedenfeld, Gerard, Kindertransport Association Oral History Project Interview, November 13, 1993.

409 Friedenfeld, Gerard, Kindertransport Association Oral History Project Interview, November 13, 1993. Although not aware at the time, Friedenfeld was one of 669 Czech children saved by Kindertransports arranged by Sir Nicholas Winton. When Winton was the first person to be inducted into the new Rotarian Peace Hall of Fame at the Illinois Holocaust Museum, but unable to attend in person, Friedenfeld and another of 'Winton's Children' were chosen to represent him.

410 Friedenfeld, Gerard, Kindertransport Association Oral History Project Interview, November 13, 1993.

411 Friedenfeld, Gerard, Kindertransport Association Oral History Project Interview, November 13, 1993.

412 Ormond, Mimi, United States Holocaust Memorial Museum Collection, Gift of the National Council of Jewish Women, Cleveland Section, interview with Minda Jaffe, 1985, Accession Number: 1993.A.0087.37.

413 Ormond, Mimi, United States Holocaust Memorial Museum Collection, Gift of the National Council of Jewish Women, Cleveland Section, interview with Minda Jaffe, 1985, Accession Number: 1993.A.0087.37.

414 Various authors, *Sefer ha-shanah, Gwrych Castle Yearbook*, Jewish Agency for Israel, Youth *Aliyah* Department, 1940.

415 Sperber, Miriam, *Grandmother's Tales: An Autobiography*, Imrei Shefer Publications, 1990.

416 Ormond, Mimi, United States Holocaust Memorial Museum Collection, Gift of the National Council of Jewish Women, Cleveland Section, interview with Minda Jaffe, 1985, Accession Number: 1993.A.0087.37.

417 *Liverpool Echo*, 8 August 1940, and a claim repeated by *historypoints.org* on its page about Gwrych Castle.

418 *Liverpool Echo*, 8 August 1940.

419 *North Wales Weekly News*, 15 August 1940.

420 Seligmann, Erwin, letter, Wiener Library, document 1372/1/53.

421 It is interesting to note that Seligmann rarely features in sources from after the summer of 1940, following Burke's arrival.

422 Almost certainly written by Rabbi Sperber, within Various authors, *Sefer ha-shanah, Gwrych Castle Yearbook*, Jewish Agency for Israel, Youth *Aliyah* Department, 1940.

423 Sperber, Miriam, *Grandmother's Tales: An Autobiography*, Imrei Shefer Publications, 1990.

424 Rothman, Herman, Imperial War Museum oral history sound file, interview recorded with Peter Hart, February 2008, catalogue number 30627.

425 Steinberg, Henry, Shoah Project, interview, August 1996.

426 Spergel, Baruch, Voice/Vision Holocaust Survivor Oral History

Archive, University of Michigan, interview with Zivla Fischler and Baruch Spergel, February 2008.

427 Kessel, Ruth, in Kon, Helen, *The Book of Ruth: The Journey of a Kindertransport Teenager*, Helemy, 2014.

428 Ormond, Mimi, United States Holocaust Memorial Museum Collection, Gift of the National Council of Jewish Women, Cleveland Section, interview with Minda Jaffe, 1985, Accession Number: 1993.A.0087.37.

429 Lovenheim, Barbara, *Perilous Journeys: Personal Stories of German and Austrian Jews Who Escaped the Nazis*, Center for Holocaust Awareness and Information, 2001.

430 Rothman, Herman, Imperial War Museum oral history sound file, interview recorded with Peter Hart, February 2008, catalogue number 30627.

431 Glanz, Henry, interview with the author, December 2020.

432 Roper, Erich, in Various authors, *Sefer ha-shanah, Gwrych Castle Yearbook*, Jewish Agency for Israel, Youth *Aliyah* Department, 1940.

433 *Jewish Chronicle*, 27 September 1940.

434 Roper, Erich, in Various authors, *Sefer ha-shanah, Gwrych Castle Yearbook*, Jewish Agency for Israel, Youth *Aliyah* Department, 1940.

435 Roper, Erich, in Various authors, *Sefer ha-shanah, Gwrych Castle Yearbook*, Jewish Agency for Israel, Youth *Aliyah* Department, 1940.

436 Roper, Erich, in Various authors, *Sefer ha-shanah, Gwrych Castle Yearbook*, Jewish Agency for Israel, Youth *Aliyah* Department, 1940.

437 Roper, Erich, in Various authors, *Sefer ha-shanah, Gwrych Castle Yearbook*, Jewish Agency for Israel, Youth *Aliyah* Department, 1940.

438 Roper, Erich, in Various authors, *Sefer ha-shanah, Gwrych Castle Yearbook*, Jewish Agency for Israel, Youth *Aliyah* Department, 1940.

439 Steinberg, Henry, unpublished autobiography.

440 *Abergele Visitor*, 12 October 1940.

441 The sisters are memorialised within Singlehurst, Peter, Common-

wealth War Graves Commission, *Civilian War Dead in the United Kingdom, 1939–1945*.

442   Dr Bryan Jones, 'Abergele in Shorts', *www.aberth.com/aish*, 2005.

443   Griffiths, Robert J., *The War Years, Personal Memories of Pensarn and the Abergele Area, 1939–45*, self-published, year unknown.

444   *North Wales Weekly News*, 17 October 1940.

445   *Abergele Visitor*, 19 October 1940.

446   *Liverpool Echo*, 9 December 1940.

447   Barton, Brian, *The Blitz: Belfast in the War Years*, Blackstaff Press, 1990.

448   Phyllis Kaye, later Phyllis Thomas, was the author's mother-in-law. Determined on the spot to do more for the war effort, she joined the Women's Land Army and served for the remainder of the war on Anglesey.

449   Presumably Slater and Wheeler's garage, which took some of the refugees as occasional workers.

450   Moloney, Alison, quoting Henry Glanz, 'How *I'm a Celeb*'s Grwych[sic] Castle saved life of terrified Jewish refugee who fled as family was murdered in the Holocaust', *The Sun*, 3 September 2020.

451   Griffiths, Robert J., *The War Years, Personal Memories of Pensarn and the Abergele Area, 1939–45*, self-published, year unknown.

452   Thompson, Kate, quoting Henry Glanz, '*I'm a Celeb*'s Gwrych Castle was safe haven for Jewish children fleeing Nazi regime', *Daily Mirror*, 27 November 2020.

453   *Abergele Visitor*, 4 January 1941.

454   *Jewish Chronicle*, 'Tributes to Arieh Handler', 23 May 2011.

455   Friedenfeld, Gerard, Kindertransport Association Oral History Project Interview, November 13, 1993.

456   Rothman, Herman, Imperial War Museum oral history sound file, interview recorded with Peter Hart, February 2008, catalogue number 30627.

457   Rose, Aubrey, *Arieh Handler: Modest Jewish Hero*, Harpenden: Lennard, 2010.

458   Katz, Deborah, 'Little-Known Holocaust History: Fleeing Germany, Then Living In a British Castle', *jewishpress.com*, May 2019.

459   *Bnei Akiva* website: *www.bauk.org/a-brief-history*.

460 *Bnei Akiva* website: *www.bauk.org/a-brief-history*.

461 Interestingly, the 13ᵗʰ Earl's younger brother had fallen on very hard times and was not helped out by his brother for one reason or another. The Honourable Douglas Robert Hesketh Roger Cochrane, known as Robin, had been gazetted into the 3rd Royal Welsh Fusiliers as a 2nd Lieutenant in October 1914 and was then transferred to his father's regiment, the 2nd Life Guards. He underwent a major operation June 1916 and did not serve overseas. He got engaged to Enid Marion Davis of Llanrhaiadr Hall, working as a VAD nurse in London, in October 1917 and they married 16 January 1918 in Romford, Essex. He and his wife separated in 1929 and he spent the next few years living between London, Madeira and Mauritius. He appeared in front of the London Bankruptcy Court in June 1940 having squandered just about all he owned. When asked if he had lived a life of idleness he replied that was incorrect: it had been a life of ill-health and idleness. He came 'home' to Gwrych but lived in one of the lodges on the estate. He died 19 May 1942 at West Denbighshire Hospital, Colwyn Bay, aged forty-eight, and was buried in the family plot in Llanddulas.

462 *Chayenu*, Organ of the *Torah Va'Avodah* Movement and *Brit Chalutzim Dati'im* of Western Europe, Vol. I, No. 2, November–December 1939.

463 Baumel-Schwartz, J. T., *Never Look Back: The Jewish Refugee Children in Great Britain, 1938–1945*, Shofar Supplements in Jewish Studies, Purdue University Press, 2012.

464 *Abergele Visitor*, 4 May 1940.

465 *Liverpool Echo*, 19 August 1941.

466 *Chayenu*, Organ of the *Torah Va'Avodah* Movement and *Brit Chalutzim Dati'im* of Western Europe, Vol. I, No. 2, November–December 1939. This would be the modern equivalent of around a half a million pounds at the time of writing according to the Bank of England Inflation Calculator.

467 *www.eastlothianatwar.co.uk*. The site includes a superbly detailed account of Whittingehame Farm.

468 The equivalent of over £2 million at the time of writing, according to the Bank of England Inflation Calculator. It is also of note that

Whittingehame Farm was also closed in September 1941, having grown to a similar size as Gwrych.

469   *Chayenu*, Organ of the *Torah Va'Avodah* Movement and *Brit Chalutzim Dati'im* of Western Europe, Vol. II, No. 2, February–March 1940.

470   *Chayenu*, Organ of the *Torah Va'Avodah* Movement and *Brit Chalutzim Dati'im* of Western Europe, Vol. I, No. 2, November–December 1939.

471   Roper, Erich, in Various authors, *Sefer ha-shanah, Gwrych Castle Yearbook*, Jewish Agency for Israel, Youth *Aliyah* Department, 1940.

472   *Chayenu*, Organ of the *Torah Va'Avodah* Movement and *Brit Chalutzim Dati'im* of Western Europe, Vol. IV, No. 6, September 1941.

473   *Chayenu*, Organ of the *Torah Va'Avodah* Movement and *Brit Chalutzim Dati'im* of Western Europe, Vol. IV, No. 6, September 1941.

474   *Chayenu*, Organ of the *Torah Va'Avodah* Movement and *Brit Chalutzim Dati'im* of Western Europe, Vol. IV, No. 6, September 1941.

475   Marder (née Better), Sonia, USC Shoah Project, interview, August 1996.

476   *North Wales Weekly News*, 10 April 1941.

477   Glanz, Henry, interview with the author, January 2021.

478   *Chayenu*, Organ of the *Torah Va'Avodah* Movement and *Brit Chalutzim Dati'im* of Western Europe, Vol. IV, Nos. 1 & 2, May 1941.

479   Wynne Williams, E., 'Jewish Refugees at Gwrych Castle', *Abergele Field Club and Historical Society Review* No. 1, 1982.

480   Glanz, Henry, interview with the author, December 2020.

481   Roughly the equivalent of half a million pounds at the time of writing.

482   Williams, Bill, *Jews and Other Foreigners: Manchester and the Rescue of the Victims of European Fascism, 1933–40*, Manchester University Press, 2013.

483   Edelnand, John, 'There's a Welcome in the Hillside', *Abergele Field Club and Historical Society Review* No. 6, 1987.

484 Arieh Handler's speech at the Castle on their first anniversary, in Various authors, *Sefer ha-shanah, Gwrych Castle Yearbook*, Jewish Agency for Israel, Youth *Aliyah* Department, 1940.

485 Handler, Julius, letter to Mrs Williams, 16 January 1981, author's collection.

486 Letter to the author by John Edelnand.

487 Friedenfeld, Gerard, Kindertransport Association Oral History Project Interview, November 13, 1993. His return 'home' was traumatic. 'I went to my home town and I saw our house in shambles. The whole place was in shambles. There was a bridge about a block away, and the bridge and the houses changed hands between the Germans and the Russians, several times. And then as the Germans retreated, they dynamited the bridge. And when they blew up the bridge, all the houses in the neighbourhood sort of jumped up and cracked. What a mess. I went up into my parents' bedroom. Awful mess. The Russians lived in there. There was dirt, filth, and would you believe, a copy of Hitler's *Mein Kampf* lay there.' As the Iron Curtain descended on Czechoslovakia in 1948 he hastily left for Vienna, where he met his future wife, and in 1950 the pair emigrated to the USA. He died in Milwaukee in 2015.

488 Lovenheim, Barbara, *Perilous Journeys: Personal Stories of German and Austrian Jews Who Escaped the Nazis*, Center for Holocaust Awareness and Information, 2001.

489 Bingham, Walter, *www.bauk.org/1936-1939/*.

490 'Walter Bingham at 91', *The Jerusalem Post*, 22 January 2015.

491 'Walter Bingham at 91', *The Jerusalem Post*, 22 January 2015.

492 'Walter Bingham at 91', *The Jerusalem Post*, 22 January 2015.

493 'Walter Bingham at 91', *The Jerusalem Post*, 22 January 2015.

494 'Walter Bingham at 91', *The Jerusalem Post*, 22 January 2015.

495 Bingham, Walter, *www.bauk.org/1936-1939/*.

SOURCES AND BIBLIOGRAPHY

Personal accounts provided to the author

John (Salli) Edelnand, member of the Gwrych *Hachshara*.

Henry Glanz, member of the Gwrych *Hachshara*.

Heidi Goldsmith, child evacuee in Abergele 1940–41 and relation of Leo Silbermann, member of the Gwrych *Hachshara*.

Freema Gottlieb, on behalf of her father, Wolf Gottlieb.

Danny Handler and Aviv Handler, on behalf of their father and grandfather, Arieh Handler, and their mother and grandmother, Henny Prilutsky.

Helen Levy, on behalf of her father, Josef Altberg, member of the Gwrych *Hachshara*.

Debbie Nead and Jacqui Press, on behalf of their father and grandfather, Dr Julius Handler.

Ariel and Daniel Roper, on behalf of their father, Erich Roper, member of the Gwrych *Hachshara*.

Hanna Seligmann-Prokocimer, written biography of her father, Erwin Eliezer Seligmann, translated by Verity Steele.

Professor Daniel Sperber, on behalf of his parents, Rabbi Shmuel and Miriam Sperber.

Alan Steinberg, on behalf of his father, Henry (Heinrich) Steinberg, member of the Gwrych *Hachshara*.

Oral sources from Gwrych refugees

Ascher (née Katz), Hanni, USC Shoah Project, interview, March 1996.

Bendror (Peterseil), Itzchak (Isaak), USC Shoah Project, interview, November 1997.

Better, Eddie (Avraham), USC Shoah Project, interview, August 1996.

Better (née Marder), Sonia, USC Shoah Project, interview, August 1996.

Bingham (Billig), Walter (Wolfgang), interview with Cross Rhythms Radio, July 2018.

Braun, Wilhelm, Oral History Project, Jewish Community of Rochester, New York, January 1977, interview with Dennis Klein (transcript).

Braun, Wilhelm, USC Shoah Project, interview, December 1996.

Drellich (née Heisler-Lieberman), Erika, USC Shoah Project, interview, August 2000.

Duchinsky, Erich, British Library, interview with Mark Burman, February 1988.

Dux (née Weissmann), Inge, USC Shoah Project, interview, May 1995.

Findling, Osias, Holocaust Survivors Centre Interviews, Jewish survivors of the Holocaust, British Library, interview recorded with Gillian van Gelder, July 2000.

Friedenfeld, Gerard, Kindertransport Association Oral History Project Interview, United States Holocaust Memorial Museum Collection, Gift of Melissa Hacker on behalf of the Kindertransport Association, Inc., November 1993.

Friedenfeld, Gerard, USC Shoah Project, interview, 1997.

Friedenfeld, Gerard, Wisconsin's Wartime Oral Histories, interview with Doris Chortek, 2007.

Geller, Samuel, USC Shoah Project, interview, December 1998.

Glanz, Henry, interviewed by the author, December 2020 and January 2021.

Glanz, Henry, 'The Kindertransport with Herman Rothman and Henry Glanz' *Dan Snow's History Hit* podcast, BBC, January 2019.

Goodman (née Zollmann), Anni, USC Shoah Project, interview, September 1996.

Handler, Arieh, Imperial War Museum oral history sound files, interview with Lyn E. Smith, September 2002, catalogue number 23830.

Hochberg (née Auskerin), Mary, USC Shoah Project, interview, May 1997.

Kanner (née Blum), Rachel, USC Shoah Project, interview, February 1988.

Kempler (née Sussmann), Tosca, USC Shoah Project, interview, August 1996.

Ormond (née Schleissner), Mimi, interview with Minda Jaffe, 1985, United States Holocaust Memorial Museum Collection, Gift of the National Council of Jewish Women, Cleveland Section, Accession Number: 1993.A.0087.37.

Ormond (née Schleissner), Mimi, *Mimi Ormond remembers her Kindertransport rescue, www.youtube.com.*

Ormond (née Schleissner), Mimi, United States Holocaust Memorial Museum Collection, Gift of Congregation Shaarey Tikvah, Beachwood, Ohio, 2006, Accession Number: 2014.37.18.

Rothman, Herman, Imperial War Museum oral history sound files, interview with Peter Hart, February 2008, catalogue number 30627.

Rothman, Herman, 'The Kindertransport with Herman Rothman and Henry Glanz', *Dan Snow's History Hit* podcast, BBC, January 2019.

Schnitzer, Edmund, USC Shoah Project, interview, 1997.

Seligmann, Eliezer (Erwin), Oral History Division, Faculty of Humanities, The Hebrew University of Jerusalem, interview with Rivka Banitt, 1967.

Spergel, Baruch, Voice/Vision Holocaust Survivor Oral History Archive, University of Michigan, interview with Zivla Fischler and Baruch Spergel, February 2008.

Steinberg, Henry, USC Shoah Project, interview, August 1996.

Steinberg, Judith, British Library, interview with Estelle Hakim, November 1991.

Steinberger, Martin, Jewish survivors of the Holocaust, British Library, interview with Hermione Sacks, date unknown.

Winczelberg, Morris (Mondek), USC Shoah Project, interview, October 1999.

Winczelburg (née Kreisel), Celia, USC Shoah Project, interview, October 1999.

Various, including Osias Findling, Arieh Handler, Ruth Kon and Herman Rothman, *Time May Change Me*, BBC, 2008.

Personal accounts by Gwrych refugees

Alweiss, Manfred, *Kindertransport Newsletter*, April 2006.

Benjamin, Alfred, *Journey to Self: A True Story*, XLibris Corporation, 2005.

Bingham, Walter (Wolfgang Billig), *www.bauk.org/1936-1939/*.

Edelnand, John (Salli), correspondence with the author, 2018–19.

Edelnand, John (Salli), 'There's a Welcome in the Hillside', *Abergele Field Club and Historical Society Review* No. 6, 1987.

Glanz, Henry, in Brackman, Eli, 'Holocaust Survivor Henry Glanz at the Oxford Chabad Society', *Oxford Jewish Thought – Essays by Rabbi Eli Brackman*, January 2019, *www.oxfordchabad.org*.

Glanz, Henry, in Emde, Constanze, *Ein Kieler Jude erinnert sich*, shz. de 27 January 2014.

Glanz, Henry, in Goldberg, Bettina, *With a Children's Transport to the UK*, *www.akens.org*.

Glanz, Henry, in Katz, Deborah, *Little-Known Holocaust History: Fleeing Germany, Then Living in a British Castle*, *jewishpress.com*, May 2019.

Handler, Julius, letter to Mrs Williams, 16 January 1981, provided by Jacqui Press. Extracts from the same letter are also contained within: Wynne Williams, E., 'Jewish Refugees at Gwrych Castle', *Abergele Field Club and Historical Society Review* No. 1, 1982.

Kempler, Tosca (née Sussmann), within Leverton, Bertha and Lowensohn, Shmuel, *I Came Alone: The Stories of the Kindertransports*, The Book Guild Ltd, 1990.

Kessel, Ruth, in Kon, Helen, *The Book of Ruth: The Journey of a Kindertransport Teenager*, Helemy, 2014.

Ormond, Mimi (née Schleissner), *Kindertransport: A Rescued Child*, self-published book, 2016.

Rothman, Herman, *Hitler's Will*, edited by Helen Fry, History Press, 2011.

Sperber, Miriam, *Grandmother's Tales: An Autobiography*, Imrei Shefer Publications, 1990.

Steinberg, Henry, unpublished autobiography.

Zierler, Jesse, within Leverton, Bertha and Lowensohn, Shmuel, *I Came Alone: The Stories of the Kindertransports*, The Book Guild Ltd, 1990.

Primary sources

Chayenu (Hamizrachi/Chajenu), *Brit Chalutzim Dati'im*, *Torah Va'Avodah* Organisation, London; Vol. I, No. 2 Nov–Dec 1939; Vol. II, No. 2 Feb–Mar 1940; Vol. IV, Nos. 1 & 2 May 1941; Vol. IV, No. 5 Aug 1941; Vol. IV, No. 6 Sep 1941; Vol. IV, No. 7 Oct–Nov 1941; British Library, General Reference Collection P.P.3554.ehu.

Da'at ha-hevrah, Erich Roper (Yis'akhar Roper), Willy Braun (Ze'ev Hayim Broyn), Bernhard Liwerant (Binyamin Liverant), editors, 2 February 1940. In Hebrew, German and English.

Da'at ha-hevrah, Erich Roper, Carl Schäfler, Eli Freier, Mary Auskerin, editors, 26 May 1940. In Hebrew, German and English.

Dunstan, Fred, papers re Youth *Aliyah*, Wiener Library, 1372/1/8.

Edelnand, John (Salli), letter, Wiener Library 1368/2/2/32.

Freier, Eli (Eli Dror), letter, Wiener Library 1368/2/2/29.

Handler, Dr Julius, letter to Mrs Williams, 16 January 1981, provided by Jacqui Press.

Natawovicz, Gitta (née Bluman), letter, Wiener Library 1368/2/2/14.
Perlmutter, Edith, letter, Wiener Library 1368/2/2/117.
Sefer ha-shanah, Gwrych Castle Yearbook. Various authors, for the
    Jewish Agency for Israel, Youth *Aliyah* Department, September
    1940. In Hebrew, German and English.
Seligmann, Erwin, letter, Wiener Library 1372/1/53.

Contemporary newspapers (various dates 1939–41)

Abergele Visitor
Birmingham Daily Gazette
Birmingham Daily Post
Daily Mirror
Flintshire County Herald
Jewish Chronicle
Liverpool Daily Post
Liverpool Echo
Liverpool Evening Express
Manchester Evening News
North Wales Weekly News
Rhyl Journal
Western Mail

Archival sources

1939 National Register.
Home Office Aliens Department, Internees Index, 1939–1947.
    National Archives HO/396.
Kindertransport Survey 2007, Association of Jewish Refugees.
Ministry of Health: Health Divisions: Public Health Services,
    Registered Files. National Archives MH55/704.
Prisoner of War/Internee Files, MP1103, Certificates of Identity
    SP11, National Archives of Australia.
Salford Police Register of Aliens 1916–1965, Manchester Police
    Museum.

Various additional records searched via genealogical research websites *ancestry.co.uk, findmypast.co.uk* and *jewishgen.org.*

Select bibliography

Association of Jewish Refugees, *AJR Journal*, and *Kindertransport Newsletter*, various issues.

Baker, Mark, *Gwrych Castle: An Official Guide*, Gwrych Castle Preservation Trust, 2018.

Baumel-Schwartz, J. T., *Never Look Back: The Jewish Refugee Children in Great Britain, 1938–1945*, Shofar Supplements in Jewish Studies, Purdue University Press, 2012.

Byers, Ann, *Saving Children from the Holocaust: The Kindertransport*, Enslow, 2011.

Fast, Vera K., *Children's Exodus*, I. B. Tauris, 2011.

Gillis-Carlebach, Miriam, *Jewish Everyday Life as Human Resistance 1939–1941: Chief Rabbi Dr Joseph Zvi Carlebach and the Hamburg-Altona Jewish Communities*, Peter Lang AG, new edition, 2008.

Griffiths, Robert J., *The War Years, Personal Memories of Pensarn and the Abergele Area, 1939–45*, self-published, year unknown.

Jones, Richard Wyn, *The Fascist Party in Wales? Plaid Cymru, Welsh Nationalism and the Accusation of Fascism*, University of Wales Press, 2014.

Leverton, Bertha and Lowensohn, Shmuel, *I Came Alone: The Stories of the Kindertransports*, The Book Guild Ltd, 1990.

Parry-Jones, Cai, *A History of Welsh Jewry*, unpublished thesis, Bangor University, 2014.

Parry-Jones, Cai, *The History of the Jewish Diaspora in Wales*, unpublished thesis, Bangor University, 2014.

Parry-Jones, Cai, *The Jews of Wales: A History*, University of Wales Press, 2017.

Reupke, Beate, *Jüdisches Schulwesen zwischen Tradition und Moderne: Die Hascharath Zwi Schule in Halberstadt (1796–1942)*, De Gruyter

Oldenbourg, 2017.

Rose, Aubrey, *Arieh Handler: Modest Jewish Hero*, Harpenden: Lennard, 2010.

Sadan, I. (ed.), *No Longer a Stranger in a Strange Land*, University of Michigan, 1999.

Turner, Barry, … *And the Policeman Smiled: 10,000 Children Escape from Nazi Europe*, Bloomsbury Publishing plc, new edition, 1991.

Williams, Bill, *Jews and Other Foreigners: Manchester and the Rescue of the Victims of European Fascism, 1933–40*, Manchester University Press, 2013.

Wynne Williams, E., 'Jewish Refugees at Gwrych Castle', *Abergele Field Club and Historical Society Review* No. 1, 1982.

INDEX